Fostering Adolescents

Elaine Farmer, Sue Moyers and Jo Lipscombe

Jessica Kingsley Publishers
London and Philadelphia

Table 2.1 from *Joining of New Families: A study of adoption and fostering in middle childhood* by David Quinton, Alan Rushton, Cherilyn Dance and Deborah Mayes (p.37) Copyright © John Wiley and Sons Ltd 1998. Reprinted with permission of John Wiley and Sons Ltd.

First published in the United Kingdom in 2004
by Jessica Kingsley Publishers
116 Pentonville Road
London N1 9JB, England
and
400 Market Street, Suite 400
Philadelphia, PA 19106, USA

www.jkp.com

Copyright © Elaine Farmer, Sue Moyers and Jo Lipscombe 2004

Library of Congress Cataloging-in-Publication Data

Farmer, Elaine.
    Fostering adolescents / Elaine Farmer, Sue Moyers, and Jo Lipscombe.
        p. cm.
    Includes bibliographical references and index.
    ISBN 1-84310-227-7
    1. Foster home care--Great Britain--Case studies. 2. Teenagers--Great Britain--Interviews. I. Moyers, Sue, 1948- II. Lipscombe, Jo. III. Title.
    HV887.G5F37 2004
    362.73'3'0941--dc22

                                        2004001078

British Library Cataloguing in Publication Data

A CIP catalogue record for this book is available from the British Library

ISBN 1 84310 227 7

Printed and Bound in Great Britain by
Athenaeum Press, Gateshead, Tyne and Wear

Fostering Adolescents

Supporting Parents

This important series is the result of an extensive government-funded research initiative into how we can best support parents and carers as part of an integrated service for children. Underpinning current policy directives including the Children's National Service Framework, the titles in the series are essential reading for practitioners, policy makers and academics working in child care.

Other titles in the series

Supporting Parents
Messages from Research
David Quinton
ISBN 1 84310 210 2

Foster Carers
Why They Stay and Why They Leave
Ian Sinclair, Ian Gibbs and Kate Wilson
ISBN 1 84310 172

Foster Placements: Why They Succeed and Why They Fail
Ian Sinclair, Kate Wilson and Ian Gibbs
ISBN 1 84310 173 4

Foster Children
Where they go and how they get on
Ian Sinclair, Claire Baker, Kate Wilson and Ian Gibbs
ISBN 1 84310 172 6

Parenting in Poor Environments
Stress, Support and Coping
Deborah Ghate and Neal Hazel
ISBN 1 84310 069 X

Supporting South Asian Families with a Child with Severe Disabilities
Chris Hatton, Yasmeen Akram, Robina Shah, Janet Robertson and Eric Emerson
ISBN 1 84310 161 0

of related interest

Imprisoned Fathers and their Children
Gwyneth Boswell and Peter Wedge
ISBN 1 85302 972 6

Contents

List of Tables

Figure

Acknowledgements

This research was funded by the Department of Health as part of the research initiative on Supporting Parenting. We are very grateful for this assistance and for the help of our research liaison officers, Dr Carolyn Davies and Dr Caroline Thomas.

We are indebted to the fourteen local authorities and two independent fostering agencies and their staff who made it possible for us to undertake the research. They gave their valuable time to refer young people to the study, to facilitate our case file scrutiny and to talk to us about their policies and practice. We are particularly grateful to the young people, their foster carers and their social workers who agreed to talk to us at length on two separate occasions to enable us to learn about the issues involved in fostering adolescents.

Regular meetings with our Research Advisory Group kept us on track and helped us to solve some of the difficulties along the way. We are very grateful for the help, advice and support from Helen Jones, Jane Alberry and Caroline Thomas from the Department of Health, Professor David Berridge, Professor David Quinton, Professor Ian Sinclair, Professor Kate Wilson, Dr Ian Gibbs and Dr Jean Packman, for academic and practical advice and to Ena Fry from the Fostering Network for her knowledge of the issues.

Annual meetings with researchers working on other projects within the Department of Health Initiative were also timely and invaluable in temporarily removing us from the day-to-day work of conducting the research and in helping us to clarify our thinking and look at the wider issues.

We are particularly indebted to Professor David Quinton who gave us valuable advice and assistance throughout the project.

Lastly, but most importantly, we are extremely grateful to Patricia Lees, our research support officer, who set up the database and entered the coded material from the case file study and the interviews and coded the standardised questionnaires. In particular we thank her for her meticulous and accurate work in preparing the report and this book.

Chapter One

Introduction

Background to the study

Foster care for adolescents is widely used yet surprisingly little is known about what makes it work well (Berridge 1997). This is particularly important given the consistent evidence that it is more problematic to provide foster care for adolescents than for younger children. For example, Rowe and her colleagues showed that twice as many placements for teenagers as for younger children did not last as long as planned. Their study also showed that age at placement reduced the 'success rate' for all types of placement from 70% for under fives to 43% of those who were over eleven when the placement ended (Rowe, Hundleby and Garnett 1989).

The disruption rate for the placements of adolescents is very high (see for example Baxter 1989; Berridge and Cleaver 1987; Scottish Office 1991; Triseliotis *et al.* 1995). We do know that most studies confirm that children's behaviour problems play a major part in the breakdown of foster placements (see for example Aldgate and Hawley 1986a; Baxter 1989; Fenyo, Knapp and Baines 1989; Fratter *et al.* 1991; Scottish Office 1991; Triseliotis 1989) and behavioural difficulties are particularly likely to be an issue with adolescents. However, we have much less idea about what would help to sustain the placements of young people with these behaviour difficulties.

The research

The study described in this book was undertaken in order to provide information about what helps to make adolescent foster placements succeed. The main aim was to discover how far foster carers' parenting strategies and the supports they receive relate to the outcomes of placements for adolescents and what other factors within the placed child or the foster family relate to the stability and effectiveness of placements. We wanted the study to provide information that would be of immediate use to practitioners and policy makers who have responsibility for these foster placements.

Structure of the book

This chapter gives the background to the study, describes the structure of the book and looks ahead at some of the findings of the research. Chapter 2 sets the scene in terms of the policy and legislative context of the study and the research literature that informs it. The third chapter gives the aims of the research, the methods used to draw the sample and collect and analyse the data and our approach to the outcomes of the placements. Chapter 4 outlines the key demographic characteristics of the young people and foster carers in the sample. Chapter 5 describes the social workers in the study and the planning and preparation for the young people's placements. In particular, it looks at whether the information given to the foster carers was sufficient and how far the young people and their parents had been involved in placement decisions.

In the sixth chapter the young people's behaviour in the placement, their friendships, leisure activities and their impact on other children in the family are discussed, as well as the educational provision made for them. Changes in their behaviour by the time of follow-up are considered as well as the impact of their behaviour on placement outcomes. Chapter 7 examines the strains on the foster carers in the study, the impact of such strain on their parenting approaches, what intensified or alleviated stress and its overall impact on placement outcome. In Chapter 8 the supports that foster carers received from formal and informal sources are explored along with the changes made to the services provided over the one year follow-up. This chapter also addresses the important question of how far good support leads to better placement outcomes.

Chapter 9 describes the parenting strategies and approaches used by the foster carers at the start of the placements and how far these appeared to influence the outcomes of the placements. It also charts the changes in parenting that occurred over the one year follow-up and looks at the factors that were connected to such changes. Chapter 10 focuses on the contact that the young people had with family members, how far it changed over time and its impact on the foster families, the young people and on the placements themselves.

The factors that were significantly related on statistical tests to placement outcomes are drawn together in Chapter 11. The final chapter concludes the book with a discussion of the implications and messages for policy and practice that arose from the study.

We end this chapter by looking ahead to some of the key findings from this study.

Key findings of our study

Before the placement is made

There are a number of ways in which the chances of placement success can be increased. Some of these involve decisions that are taken before a placement is made. The research showed that practitioners should avoid making placements when the foster carers are reluctant to take a young person or have expressed a general preference for an adolescent of the opposite sex. Careful consideration should also be given to whether carers are already under strain before the placement starts and to the age of the children already in the foster family.

Much more attention is then needed to giving the foster carers full and honest information about the young person who is to be placed. Placements disrupted much more often when social workers had not been open with carers about the extent of the young people's difficulties and the plans that had been made for them. Foster carers were able to deal with some very difficult behaviour, provided that they knew what they were taking on, that the child's problems had not been downplayed and that social workers responded to their requests for assistance. The young people too wanted more information about the foster families before they moved. Most had not felt sufficiently involved in pre-placement decisions.

There were certain young people who were particularly difficult to manage and whose placements were highly likely to break down if additional help had not been organised in advance for their placements. These were young people with histories of aggressive behaviour or with no attachment to an adult before the placement (for example because of a failed adoption or long-term care) and those who were hyperactive or who showed conduct problems in the placement. Local authorities need to consider organising more extensive packages of support for such placements if they are to survive. Such approaches might include for example, shared care between two foster families, dedicated respite care, buying in the services of specialist helpers for these young people or purchasing therapeutic counselling.

During the placement

EARLY WARNING SIGNS

The study showed that a number of key factors are related to poor placement outcomes. Catching these at an early stage might avert placement breakdown. They need to be regularly checked during visits and at reviews. The initial reactions of the foster carers towards the young people, for example, whether or not they liked them, often continued and affected the course of the placement, and initial dissatisfaction on the part of either the foster carer or the young person with the placement was linked to later unsuccessful placements. Such early difficulties therefore warrant vigorous action.

A very strong finding in the study was that when the fostered young person had a negative impact on the other children in the foster family, the placement was more likely to disrupt. Ultimately, foster carers will end placements that threaten the well-being of other children in their family. When signs of these difficulties occur, social workers need to take action to try to improve relationships and lessen the impact of the placed young person.

THE FOSTER CARERS' PARENTING SKILLS

Very little research has been done into how foster carers parent the children they look after or which parenting skills are most important in caring for adolescents. We found that, at the start of the placements, four parenting approaches used by the foster carers predicted placement outcomes. It is therefore important that these key parenting skills are included in training and support and considered during recruitment.

Factors associated with *fewer disruptions*:

- The foster carers' ability to respond to the young person's 'emotional age' when it was considerably younger than their chronological age. Such responsiveness indicates sensitivity and understanding that many looked-after young people function emotionally at an immature level well below their chronological age and need regular opportunities for play and nurture appropriate to a much younger child to meet these earlier unmet needs.

- The young people had been able to talk about their past histories with their carers. Such sharing of sensitive information implies time made for the teenagers to share difficult issues and probably the capacity on the part of carers to bear to hear painful past events. We also found that disruption occurred less frequently when young people had access to other people in whom they could confide.

Factors associated with *more successful* placements:

- The foster carers had given a moderate level of encouragement to young people to learn life skills that would prepare them for leaving care and for later life, such as budgeting, helping with cooking meals and completing forms.

- The carers monitored the activities of the young people when they were outside the house. This required skill and an extended view of the foster carer role and was important for those young people who were unable to keep themselves safe or out of trouble when away from the foster family.

STRAIN AND PARENTING SKILLS

We found that strain had a major impact on carers' capacity to parent well. In particular, strained carers responded less sensitively to the young people, disliked them more often and showed them less warmth. Many of the foster carers faced the arrival of a newly placed young person at a time when they were already under significant pressure from stressful life events, such as bereavements, relationship difficulties, accidents, illness, financial worries and people joining and leaving the family, including recent foster placement breakdowns. Two-fifths (41%) had experienced four or more of these stresses in the six months prior to the adolescent's placement. The presence of the fostered adolescent, not surprisingly, was often itself very stressful. The extent of strain on carers, not only during but also *before* the placement began, had a statistically significant effect on outcomes: the more strain on the carers, the more often placements disrupted.

These findings suggest that family placement workers should review the stresses on carers *before* each placement is made, as well as during its course, in order to match those who are under a great deal of strain with less demanding adolescents and/or to offer them enhanced levels of support or a paid break.

GAPS IN THE PARENTING OF THE FOSTER CARERS

Although the experienced foster carers in this study generally parented the young people very well, there were some important gaps in their practice that were likely to have an impact on the young people's future life chances. It seems likely that there has been a lack of clarity with foster carers about how far these tasks are part of their remit. Greater clarification of who is responsible for these tasks is therefore important and they need to be highlighted during foster carer training.

- Two-fifths of the carers did not discuss sexual health or sexuality with the young people, even though many looked-after young people are poorly informed about normal sexual development, sexual health and contraception.

- Half of the foster carers had little involvement with schools, including 20 who reported having no contact with the young people's school teachers.

- Two-fifths of the carers gave little encouragement to the young people to develop age-appropriate life skills that would prepare them for leaving care and later life, such as budgeting, helping with cooking meals and completing forms.

- Foster carers were significantly less sensitive to the needs and anxieties of girls than boys. The interviews revealed a small number of girls whose worries and real unhappiness about their placements were not apparent to their foster carers.

EDUCATION

We thought that whether or not the young person attended school would predict outcome, but this was not the case. Two related factors were, however, important. Low confidence in schoolwork was significantly related to disruption, and low confidence in social relationships at school was linked to low success rates in placements. On the other hand, young people with particular skills and interests (which may have been developed at school or at home) had an increased chance of having a successful placement. Action to assist young people with their education and relationships with other children is important not only to enhance their life chances but may also help to maintain placements.

SUPPORT FOR THE PLACEMENTS

The provision of appropriate counselling for the fostered teenagers proved to be very important in maintaining placements. Over a third of the young people were seeing a specialist for counselling and carers felt better supported when this was the case. Over and above this, there were more successful placements when young people reported that they were receiving such assistance. Foster carers' requests for such help should therefore always be taken seriously.

Carers who received a lot of support from their own children also had fewer disruptions. This included adult children who lived in the family or nearby. These children wanted their views to be listened to and their difficulties acknowledged, including sharing their parents, feelings of jealousy and lack of attention. More recognition is needed of the important role played by the carers' children in supporting placements.

In addition, there were significantly more successful placements when the carers were receiving substantial support from family members or from their social networks and local professionals, such as doctors and teachers.

Higher levels of successful placements were also related to situations when social work support was good. Unfortunately, at present children's social workers provide a very variable service ranging from excellent to poor. The considerable difficulties in contacting the young people's social workers (experienced by 70% of carers) and low levels of visiting by some (21% saw the child and 37% the carers less often than monthly) were significantly related to carers feeling under strain and poorly supported. On the other hand, foster carer strain was reduced when the young person's social worker was regularly and reliably available, by continuity of social work help and when the carers' views were taken seriously. Given the intense pressures on children's social workers, improvements to the service they provide are likely to require organisational change that allows specialisation or major task reallocation or both.

More than half the foster carers did not feel that they were an important part of the professional team and just under half did not usually find that their views were taken seriously. Moreover, foster carers were more likely to feel under strain when they felt that their views were not taken seriously. Whilst foster carers were full of praise for social workers who involved them and valued their views, this suggests that there is some way to go before partnership with foster carers is achieved.

Local authority support did not always match the needs of carers – for example, young people's social workers visited the foster carers with good social and local professional support more often than those with poorer support networks. If services are to match individual needs better, family placement workers and social workers may need to find out more about foster carers' overall support systems (support from friends, relatives and local professionals) to identify those who lack adequate support and consider how to reach those who do not readily request or use help.

Foster carers experienced local authority support rather like a net: it was only as strong as its weakest point. All four basic elements of the formal support system for foster carers (the family placement worker, foster carer groups, the child's social worker and the out of hours service) need to be in place and working well if foster carers are to feel adequately supported. Out of hours services run by the family placement service were experienced as much more useful than those provided by emergency duty teams.

CONTACT

Almost two-thirds of the young people had contact with someone in their network that was detrimental to them and difficulties with contact were significantly related to higher disruption rates. The main problems with contact were repeated rejection by parents, unreliable visiting and young people being at risk during visits. As a result, the young people often returned from contact extremely upset and acted out their distress in regressive, disturbed or violent behaviour. Over the one year follow-up there was little change in the quality of the young people's contact. For most (57%) poor quality contact was still poor one year after placement. In a few cases proactive social workers had taken action to improve contact, usually by arranging for less frequent contact but of a higher quality or by involving another family member in contact, like a grandparent or aunt, who could provide attention and nurture. This had been very beneficial for the young people and their placements.

The young people who had contact with their maternal grandparents had more successful placements partly because grandparents often ensured that contact with other family members occurred and because they themselves provided enriching relationships for the young people.

A third of the young people, whilst having some contact, had none that was rated as beneficial to them. In addition, a small number (13%) had no contact with any family member, generally because of an adoption breakdown, because their parents had died or in the aftermath of an allegation of sexual abuse. In such cases the appointment of an Independent Visitor under the Children Act needs to be considered, but this had occurred in only one case.

The widespread idea that adolescents can manage their own contact was not borne out in the study. More work with parents might be useful to help them to negotiate meaningful contact with their children whilst the involvement of other family members, such as grandparents, who can offer a positive relationship is to be encouraged. There is also a real need for work with young people to help them to integrate the reality of their parents' actions in ways that allow them to move on and make use of other more sustaining relationships.

THE PARTICULAR DIFFICULTIES OF SINGLE CARERS

One-third of the foster carers were looking after the adolescents alone and they were more disadvantaged than couple carers in a variety of ways. These single carers received less training, lower levels of local authority services and less support from local professionals than the foster carer couples even though they had weaker social support networks. For single carers support from their friends was therefore particularly important. In addition, significantly fewer of the single carers took active steps to facilitate the young people's education or attended the foster carer groups – principally because of pressure on their time if they worked and the lack of childminding. Increased understanding of the needs of single carers and some supplementary services might well benefit lone foster carers and the young people they look after.

TRAINING

Placement outcomes are likely to be improved if training includes:

- helping foster carers to respond to young people's emotional and developmental age
- dealing with contact issues
- talking to young people about the past and about difficulties in their relationships with their families
- monitoring adolescents' activities outside the home.

In addition, training gaps identified by the carers included working with withdrawn, depressed and suicidal young people, the management of deliberate self-harm, dealing with young people who sexually abuse others and managing violent behaviour.

Overall, our evidence clearly shows that improved support is related to less strain for foster carers and to better parenting skills and so to better placement outcomes. Thus, if support services to foster carers and young people are improved, disruption rates are likely to fall. This is the vital positive message of the research.

Now that some of the key findings of the study have been highlighted we turn to look at the policy and legislative context of the study and the research literature that informs it.

Chapter Two

Background and Research Literature

Background to the study

Perspectives on the foster care task with adolescents

Given the central position of foster care as a preferred alternative for adolescents who cannot live with their parents, it is remarkable how little is known about what fostering actually entails. A preference for foster care over other forms of provision reflects a view that a close approximation to good quality family care is the most satisfactory kind of placement. Prior to the implementation of the Children Act 1989, foster carers were asked 'to care for the child as if he were a member of [the foster parents'] family...' (Department of Health 1988, p.7). More recently, the Looking After Children Initiative has defined the acceptable level of care provided by public services in terms of what would be expected from conscientious birth parents (Ward 1995).

As general statements both of these formulations are uncontroversial. On the other hand, it does not follow that optimum outcomes for the children will be achieved by foster parents approaching the parenting task in a way that parallels that of birth parents as closely as possible (Shaw and Hipgrave 1983). The situation has been made more complex by the shift in emphasis in the Children Act 1989 towards partnership between foster carers and birth parents. The issue of the foster carers' role in supporting parents and the importance of the children's continuing contact with their families is not, itself, new. A number of writers followed Holman (1975) and suggested that more use should be made of 'inclusive' foster placements to facilitate the reunification of children and their families (Aldgate 1977; Sinanoglu and Maluccio 1981; Thorpe 1974). It is clear that foster carers can play an important part in assisting and sustaining parents as they work towards family reunification but this work is rarely acknowledged (Farmer and Parker 1991).

The change in emphasis occasioned by the implementation of the Children Act 1989 has implications for the fostering task that highlight the need for a closer look at what successful foster carers do and how they see their role. The task cannot simply be to reproduce the quality of parenting seen in stable birth families. To what extent should foster carers encourage attachments between themselves and the young people? What are their responsibilities for setting boundaries, for educational progress or for facilitating peer relationships? How are they to handle issues of discipline? Is their task a restricted and specialist one, involving the provision of a safe environment and managing the young person's relationship with the birth family, but leaving as much parenting responsibility as possible with the birth parents? Given the existence of two sets of parenting figures, it is important that there is clarity about the boundaries of the roles taken by each. For example, Farmer and Pollock's study (1998) and those of others (see for example Cliffe with Berridge 1991) has shown that foster carers take varying views about whether and how far it is their responsibility to be involved with the child's school.

Issues in fostering adolescents

Apart from the complications arising through 'partnership' with birth parents, the fostering of adolescents raises a number of other issues. First, the young people enter placements with a range of unresolved issues from the past that foster carers are likely to have to deal with. Two recent studies have shown that a key issue for many young people is their relationship with their own families and how accepting of this the foster carers are able to be (Triseliotis *et al.* 1995; Ward 1995):

> while those in the community are planning future occupations and qualifications, those looked after may be devoting their energies to worrying about their relationships with family members or their ability to cope with early independence. (Ward 1995, p.78)

Second, foster care differs from ordinary parenting in that the young people need to make a secure base in the foster family at the same time as they are striving to establish their autonomy. Similarly, they need to form their own identity whilst separated from their birth families (Aldgate, Maluccio and Reeves 1989). However, some adolescents in the care system are not yet ready for these developmental tasks as a result of previous experiences and the number of adversities in their background histories. Conflicting loyalties and ambivalent feelings towards members of their birth families may further complicate this stage for some teenagers in the care system.

Third, many placed adolescents are impaired in their capacity for attachment (see for example Howe *et al.* 1999; Rushton, Treseder and Quinton 1988; Thoburn 1990; Thoburn, Murdoch and O'Brien 1986). The optimum environment for the amelioration of these problems is not known. It has been suggested that detached and hostile adolescents may fit more comfortably into a more distanced family and the anxiously attached into a close-knit family (Downes 1982 and 1988). Finally, it is clear that given the early age at which looked-after children leave substitute care (see for example Biehal *et al.* 1995) there will be a heightened need for these children to attain tangible life skills whilst in placement to enable them to deal with this premature transition to adulthood.

Supporting foster placements

Research has suggested that an important element in successful placements may be the degree of support that social workers offer (see for example Berridge and Cleaver 1987; Lowe 1990) but other studies, as we shall see, have not found this effect. Although researchers have described different aspects of support, little is known about those supports that make a difference to foster carers' ability to cope, nor even whether these are from family, friends, work colleagues, social institutions such as doctors, police, schools or religious organisations, other foster carers, or from the professional network. Nonetheless, research by Jane Gibbons and colleagues (1995) suggests that adequate support for substitute carers may be crucial to good outcomes for children. This research examined the effects of both formal and informal supports on placement outcomes.

However, before we move on to look at our study in more detail, the remainder of this chapter will provide an overview of developments and research on fostering that are relevant to our research.

Changes in foster care

Foster care has become the preferred option for looking after children who cannot live with their parents, so that, for example, in 2002 66% of children in the care system were living in foster families (Department of Health 2003). The percentage of looked-after children who are in foster care has more than doubled from 32% 20 years ago (Prosser 1978), although this has occurred because of a fall in the overall number of children looked after and is not due to an expansion in foster care (Berridge 1997). At the same time a number of changes have occurred in foster care that require consideration.

First, the children now in foster care are rather different from those in such placements 20 years ago (Bebbington and Miles 1989; Sinclair, Garnett and Berridge 1995; Triseliotis *et al.* 1995). Many of those in foster homes today would in the past have been placed in residential care and those who would have been in foster care then may now be maintained with support in their own homes. The implementation of the Children Act 1989 has raised the threshold for compulsory care for children, so that those who enter by this route present a greater concentration of serious problems than formerly (Hunt, Macleod and Thomas 1999). At the same time research on the Children Act shows that many of the children who were previously removed from home on a court order are now being voluntarily accommodated and that teenagers are prominent amongst those admitted in this way (Packman and Hall 1998). Packman and Hall (1998) also show a steep rise in repeat admissions compared to the position 20 years earlier. This may not have been fully antici- pated since there is little discussion of disruptive adolescents as candidates for Section 20 admission in the volume of Department of Health guidance on family support (Department of Health 1991a).

Second, it is generally assumed that the fostering task has become more complex as carers are encouraged to maintain links between children and their birth families and to work in partnership with birth parents. Foster carers are expected to supplement the parents' role and to encourage links between children and birth parents, including visits by parents and relatives to the foster home. The Children Act Guidance emphasises that potential foster carers should be assessed in relation to their ability to work 'with parents in pursuance of the aims of the placement and the plan for the child' with the aim of achieving 'the required partnership with parents' (Department of Health 1991b, p.26).

A third issue is increasing concern about the insufficient supply of foster carers. Such shortages apply in particular to placements for adolescents, ethnic minorities and sibling groups (Association of Directors of Social Services (ADSS) 1997; Cliffe with Berridge 1991; Department of Health 1996; Greef 1999; Lowe 1990; National Foster Care Association (NFCA) 1997 and 1998; Triseliotis, Borland and Hill 2000; Triseliotis *et al.* 1995; Waterhouse 1997). One crucial factor is the retention of foster carers already undertaking the task. Some studies have reported high levels of carers ceasing to foster (for example Baxter 1989; Bebbington and Miles 1990; Caesar, Parchment and Berridge 1994; Cliffe with Berridge 1991) and others have linked recruitment and retention with levels of pay (Campbell and Whitelaw-Downs 1987; Chamberlain, Moreland and Reid 1992). Recent research by Triseliotis and his colleagues (2000) has provided a more positive picture. In 1996–7 new carer recruitment in their study exceeded losses by 46% and it was found that most carers start to foster when it suits their personal and family circumstances and leave when these change. Sinclair and his colleagues (2000) have similar findings. In the light of this, Triseliotis and his colleagues recommended that authorities should make fostering attractive enough for carers to see it as a career, since they had found that some authorities were able to hold onto their carers for considerably longer than others. However, over half of those who left did so because of dissatisfaction with fostering, including with the children's behaviours.

Denby and his colleagues (1999) found that foster carers' intention to continue fostering was correlated not only with children's difficult behaviour and carer satisfaction with fostering but also with readiness to telephone the social worker whenever necessary; not being treated as if they themselves were in need of help and more frequent opportunities to share experiences with other carers. Sinclair and his colleagues (2000) found that carers considered leaving foster care at the time of placement breakdown if they had no obligations to other foster children and that the experience of stressful events was connected with the intention to leave fostering. On the other hand, support from other foster carers, above average levels of training and income from fostering, and good support from family placement workers and other professionals were all related to continuing fostering.

Difficulties in the recruitment or retention of foster carers have led to the common situation where there is no choice of placement for a child and matching therefore becomes impossible (Berridge and Cleaver 1987; Shaw and Hipgrave 1989a, b; Sinclair *et al.* 1995; Triseliotis *et al.* 1995). The House of Commons Health Committee Report (1998) referred to a Social Services Inspectorate survey in England which found that for 75% of children there was no choice of placement. The result can be that children are placed with carers who are far away from the children's families or whose skills do not match the children's needs, especially in the case of adolescents (Triseliotis *et al.* 1995).

As difficulties in recruiting and retaining foster carers continue and the cost of independent agency placements rise, it is likely that local authorities in the UK will increasingly seek to place children with family or friends. Certainly, in the USA and Canada since the mid 1980s, pressures on child care agencies have led to increasing numbers of children being placed with the extended family (McFadden 1998). The proportion of children fostered with relatives or friends in the UK has been rising in recent years from 6% of looked-after children in 1989 (3984) to 12% in 2002 (6900) (Department of Health 1991c, 2003). It is also clear that relatives and friends are increasingly looking after young people between the ages of 10 and 15, the age group for which it is the hardest to find a suitable placement.

A fourth area of change has been concern about the ability of foster care to deliver stability for children (see for example Aldgate and Hawley 1986a; Baxter 1989; Berridge and Cleaver 1987; Millham *et al.* 1986; Triseliotis *et al.* 1995) or to give adequate attention to the health care (Butler and Payne 1999; Sinclair *et al.* 1995) and educational needs of looked-after children (Blyth and Milner 1993; Department of Health, Social Services Inspectorate and Office for Standards in Education 1995; Fletcher Campbell and Hall 1991; Heath, Colton and Aldgate 1989, 1994; Jackson 1987; Scottish Office 1991). Research by Wade and his colleagues (1998) has further shown that children who have experienced high levels of placement movement are more likely than other children to go missing from care. The disadvantages of children after they leave care speak to the deficiencies of the care system and the lack of after-care provided (see for example Biehal *et al.* 1992, 1995; Fry 1992; Garnett 1992; Lowe 1990; Stein and Carey 1986).

A fifth recent change is the growth of the independent foster care sector. Shortages of foster carers are likely to become more acute as foster carers leave local authorities to join independent fostering agencies which offer higher levels of support and remuneration and better services for the children. According to the Association of Directors of Social Services (ADSS 1997), in 1997 nearly one-third of local authorities were affected by this process. Concern has also been expressed about the impact of this sector on local authority costs (Sellick 1992).

One other change deserves a mention. This is the increasing awareness of the possibility of abuse of children in care either by their adult caregivers or by other children (see for example Farmer and Pollock 1998; Lowe and Verity 1989; National Children's Home 1992; NFCA 1988; Nixon and Hicks 1989; Sinclair and Gibbs 1998; Utting 1991, 1997). The National Foster

Care Association (now the Fostering Network) has suggested that about one in six foster carers will experience a complaint or allegation against them in the course of fostering (Wheal 1995) and the incidence of complaints is increasing (Coffin 1993). There is continuing disquiet about how such allegations by children against their carers are managed and the impact on the carers (Farmer and Pollock 1998; Hicks and Nixon 1989; Wilson, Sinclair and Gibbs 2000). Sinclair and his colleagues (2000) found that the experience of an allegation of abuse, as with other stressful events, was associated with the frequency with which carers considered giving up fostering and Baxter (1989) reported allegations as a contributory factor in placement breakdown.

Recognition of the risks to children by other looked-after children has been yet more recent. Farmer and Pollock (1998) found that one in five of the sexually abused and/or abusing children aged ten or over in their research sexually abused another child in the placement. Furthermore, when the histories of the sexually abused adolescents in the study were examined it was found that half of them had sexually abused another child at some stage. Since as many as 38% of children who enter substitute care are likely to have been sexually abused or to have abused another child (Farmer and Pollock 1998) there are clear implications about the need for careful supervision and monitoring of children by their carers.

In the late 1990s this set of changes led a number of commentators to consider that foster care had reached a crisis and that research in the area was needed (ADSS 1997; NFCA 1997, 1998; Waterhouse 1997). Concerns about serious deficits in the system for looked-after children expressed in the Second House of Commons Report on Children Looked After by Local Authorities (House of Commons Health Committee 1998) led to the Quality Protects programme to try to raise standards (Department of Health 1998b) and subsequently to the Choice Protects initiative. By setting specific targets for local authorities the government hoped that the stability of placements would improve along with the education, health and after-care of children in the care system. In addition, national standards have now been set for foster care (NFCA 1999) and a major recruitment campaign run. At the same time, whilst some local authorities have moved to pay a system of allowances based on the carers' competencies rather than on the difficulty of the child, the debates about whether foster care should become a professional, salaried service continue (Lowe 1989, 1990; Pithouse and Parry 1999; Triseliotis 1990; Triseliotis *et al.* 2000).

These changes are likely to have had a considerable effect on foster care in general and some have particular relevance for the fostering of adolescents.

Foster care for adolescents

The legislative context

The Children Act 1989 introduced the idea of voluntary accommodation for children as a service to families. Whilst this may not be quite the way it is used in practice, research has shown that many teenagers are now accommodated and entrants to foster care by any route now include a higher proportion than previously of teenagers, a good proportion of whom will have experienced a number of failed attempts to live at home (Packman and Hall 1998).

The Act also made it easier for young people over the age of 16 to make their own requests for accommodation and strengthened the requirement for social workers to consult young people about plans being made and reviewed. In addition, the rights of young people to complain if they feel aggrieved were addressed through a new 'representations' procedure. The arrangements for providing 'advice, guidance and assistance' to care leavers were overhauled and have been subsequently developed further. Some of these changes have been given added impetus through the ratification of the United Nations Convention on the Rights of the Child. Although a number of these changes were targeted at the difficulties facing older adolescents and particularly care leavers, teenagers as a whole were not singled out in the Children Act for special attention to their particular needs (Triseliotis et al. 1995).

Entry to and exit from care

National statistics for children in care during the 1980s (Rowe et al. 1989) confirmed the findings of Bebbington and Miles (1989) that 14–15-year-olds were especially vulnerable to admission. When Packman and Hall (1998) returned in the late 1990s to the same authorities in which they had conducted research nearly 20 years earlier, they found that the proportion of teenagers accommodated had more than doubled and that 38% were aged between 13 and 16. Forty per cent of the accommodated children had been in care before and troublesome behaviour was associated disproportionately with adolescents.

Children who grow up in foster care and become teenagers within this setting need to be distinguished from those who enter care as adolescents or 'teenage entrants' or 'teenage erupters' as they have been called (Bullock,

Little and Millham 1998; Garnett 1992). The first group has always been common, the second less so (Berridge 1994). Two trends will have affected these groups. The permanence planning movement, assisted by legal and practical changes such as adoption and residence order allowances, is likely to mean that many young children in stable foster homes are now adopted (Hill, Lambert and Triseliotis 1989), whilst others are placed on residence orders, although predictions about the demise of long-term fostering have always been over-estimated (Kelly 2000; Rowe *et al.* 1989; Schofield *et al.* 2000). Conversely, the development of specialist foster schemes has enabled more adolescents to be fostered, although this development has not been uniform. In addition, some authorities now make little or no use of residential care so all children are placed in foster care (Cliffe with Berridge 1991), and this change is likely to have been speeded up by the creation of small unitary authorities.

Specialist schemes for adolescents

Specialist or 'professional' schemes generally provide better support (and possibly training) and enhanced financial rewards to carers who look after more challenging children. Over half of the agencies that responded to the National Foster Care Association survey of teenage foster care (NFCA 1998) reported that they operated a specialist scheme for adolescents. Where agencies did not have a specialist scheme, two-thirds used specialist carers for teenagers. The pioneering specialist scheme in the UK was the Kent Family Placement Project, established in the 1970s to show that teenagers with major difficulties could be placed in family settings. Intensive preparation and support was provided, enhanced payments were made and detailed time-limited plans were specified in written agreements (Hazel 1981; Hazel and Fenyo 1993). The scheme was evaluated both independently and by project staff at different points (Hazel 1990). An initial external evaluation showed that 64% of placements were completed as planned and 76% bene-fited the young person (Yelloly 1979). Later results from the project showed that similar levels of success had been maintained (Kent Social Services 1986; Smith 1986). The combination of truancy and behaviour problems was a par-ticularly high risk factor for breakdown, whilst experienced foster carers had a lower probability of breakdown (Fenyo *et al.* 1989). In the US, studies using matched comparison groups of children have shown that specialist or 'treat-ment' foster care placements are more successful than alternative arrange-ments in terms of personal development and subsequent avoidance of institu-tional care (Almeida *et al.* 1989; Bogart 1988; Chamberlain 1990).

Reports on specialist schemes from both statutory and voluntary agencies showing low breakdown rates have confirmed the positive findings from Kent and North America (King 1991; O'Brien 1990). However, a survey of all child care placements made in six local authorities in the UK (Rowe *et al.* 1989) suggested that the success rates of specialist placements were mixed. Just over half had ended sooner than planned, whilst slightly under half lasted as long as needed, according to social work judgements. However, one-third were thought to have been 'very helpful' and a further 40% 'fairly helpful'. The teenagers placed in these specialist schemes tended to have more behaviour difficulties than those in other kinds of foster placements.

Two surveys of specialist fostering schemes were conducted in the 1980s by Shaw and Hipgrave (1983, 1989a). The first showed that specialist schemes had become widespread and mostly focused on difficult or delinquent adolescents. The second demonstrated that the number of schemes had continued to expand and had also diversified to embrace a wider variety of children. A survey by the NFCA (1998) also showed that schemes now take a much wider age range of children and young people than previously, reflecting the more complex needs of younger children. More recent developments include the development of fostering as an alternative to secure accommodation (Walker, Hill and Triseliotis 2002) and remand foster care (Lipscombe 2003a). However, one study showed that, when an authority tried to rely on placing nearly all teenagers in their specialist foster care scheme without using any residential care, it was hard to find enough suitable families and there was rarely a choice at the point of placement (Cliffe with Berridge 1991).

By the late 1980s, concerns were being expressed about the potential for unfairness with a two-tier system of mainstream and specialist fostering (Shaw and Hipgrave 1989b). Some agencies responded by paying fees and increasing support to all or most of their foster families (Hill *et al.* 1993; Lowe 1990; Maclean 1989).

Preparation for placement

Research has shown that placement instability is connected with carers who lacked preparation and training (Berridge and Cleaver 1987; Lowe 1990; Triseliotis *et al.* 1995). A number of studies have shown that carers often receive insufficient pre-placement preparation from social workers (Berridge 1997; Farmer and Pollock 1998). Quinton and his colleagues (1998) recommend that preparation for foster carers needs to be informed by research findings on the factors likely to destabilise placements. They found that foster carers needed to be prepared for the kinds of difficulties often shown by rejected children, such as problems with self-esteem, trust and relationships, and they recommended that preparation include anticipation of the possible relationship conflicts when other children are present in the home. Research has shown the difficulties that can occur when the carers have their own or other children in the household (Berridge and Cleaver 1987; George 1970; Parker 1966; Quinton *et al.* 1998; Trasler 1960; Triseliotis 1989) and the views of the children of foster carers highlight that they can feel pushed aside because of the demands of the fostered child (Martin 1993; Part 1993). Adequate preparation will therefore also involve the children living in the foster home (Quinton *et al.* 1998).

In addition, the importance of giving good quality information concerning the children about to be placed was confirmed in the studies by Triseliotis and his colleagues (2000) and by Quinton and his team (1998). Triseliotis and colleagues (2000) showed that lack of information handicapped carers in looking after children. Quinton and his colleagues (1998) showed that good information was of great assistance in helping the carers to understand the history of the placed child and to take account of any medical, educational and behavioural problems. Ideally it was needed in verbal and written form. Information given to the new parents was poor for a third of the families. Farmer and Pollock (1998) emphasised this point in their study of sexually abused and/or abusing adolescents. They found that information about the sexual abuse in the background of 42% of the abused teenagers had not been passed on to the caregivers and in over half of the cases where children had sexually abused others this was not shared with the residential or foster carers with whom they were placed.

Training and support for foster carers

Adequate training and support for foster carers is important and this has been highlighted in the literature (see for example Berridge 1997; Farmer and Pollock 1998; Quinton *et al.* 1998; Schofield *et al.* 2000; Triseliotis *et al.* 2000). One study discovered fewer placement breakdowns for carers who had experienced even rudimentary induction training as compared with those who had experienced none (Berridge and Cleaver 1987). A recent study (Triseliotis *et al.* 1995) found that half of the carers in the sample had had no training at all.

Ongoing support from social workers has been found to vary greatly. Its value was shown by a Scottish Office study (1988, 1991) which revealed a higher rate of premature endings for placements where social workers did not keep in regular contact with the foster carers. Research in Northern Ireland concluded that social work support to placements was felt to be adequate (Baxter 1989) and feedback from carers in one special project was positive about the social work support provided (Caesar *et al.* 1994). The link worker system in one authority was also well regarded (Cliffe with Berridge 1991) although a survey by the NFCA (1998) showed that only a third of agencies had a specific link worker or family placement worker for support.

However, other findings have been more mixed. Rowe *et al.* (1984) reported large variations in the frequency of visits by social workers whilst, in another study, advice for carers on dealing with specific problems such as enuresis was not forthcoming (Rushton, Treseder and Quinton 1988, 1993). Assistance in providing specific items, such as equipment, has not always been efficient (Ames 1993). Research into placement disruption showed that foster carers had often been left to struggle on until they reached a point of desperation (Aldgate and Hawley 1986b). Another study of placement breakdowns found that carers were often isolated from social work support and some social workers felt uneasy about their role and chose to restrict their involvement (Berridge and Cleaver 1997). Indeed, foster carers have sometimes been ambivalent about social work visits (Rowe *et al.* 1984).

In a survey of provision for adolescents, 40% of local authorities reported that they offered an informal out of hours emergency service (Lowe 1990). Moreover, carers of children with severe learning disabilities have found opportunities for respite care invaluable (Ames 1993). However, this service was not always forthcoming and it was recommended that its availability should be made explicit at the point of placement.

Triseliotis and his colleagues (2000) report that three-fifths of all carers agreed that the agency could do more in a number of areas of support. Leaving aside pay and conditions of service, the package that carers wanted comprised: more frequent social work visits mainly for direct work with the child; greater social work availability and reliability, including 24-hour cover; being listened to, valued and appreciated; working as a team and in partnership, including receiving full information about the children and their families; continued training, including more training and support over contact; more support for the whole family when children leave; support through false allegations and more respite care. For some carers levels of pay and the efficiency of the agency in relation to payments were seen as a crucial component of support. Higher rates of payment for fostering have been found to be associated with placement stability (Thomas and Beckett 1994).

Sinclair and his colleagues (2000) found that foster carers wanted social workers who: were 'there for them', that is, available when needed; reliable and prompt; respectful of carers' views; kept them informed and involved in plans for the child; were considerate and aware of the carers' other commitments, and were supportive, warm and approving of the carers. They wanted to find these qualities in evidence in all aspects of the social work role including sorting out financial and transport arrangements, arranging professional services, working with the birth family and the child, enabling the carer to work well with the child and in the support they provided.

However, Sinclair and his colleagues (2000) found no relationship between any measure of support from the family placement worker or the children's social worker and disruption. They did find an association between their overall measure of support from the social worker and their success rating but this may have been because social workers gave favourable ratings to the placement when they and the carers got on well. The authors suggest that a package of professionally delivered help associated with a careful assessment of the child's needs could be effective. The study showed a significant association between the involvement of educational psychologists and both the avoidance of disruption and the success of placements.

The National Foster Care Association also identified the need for carers to have access to specialist support on those occasions 'when the needs or demands of a particular child will confound the team of people working immediately with him/her' (NFCA 1994, p.5) and that carers should have access to a foster carer support group. The report states that 'Ensuring that carers are able to use a variety of support empowers the carer' and 'facilitates the provision of support for minority groups' (NFCA 1994, p.2).

In their study of late-placed adoptions (which differ from foster placements in their expectations and assumptions), Quinton and his colleagues (1998) found little evidence that even well-targeted social work support had much effect on either placement stability, parental stress or on the level of children's problems during the first year of placement. They do suggest, however, that there 'did seem to be some evidence that social work intervention may have helped [adoptive] parents deal with crises that might otherwise have threatened the placement' (Quinton *et al.* 1998, p.188). Half of the new parents in this study found the children's social workers supportive and they recommended that more should be done by them to enhance parenting skills and to work on sibling disputes. Lowe (1990) listed the support of social workers as one of her three most important factors in relation to outcomes; and one study found that intensive social work support during the early stages of placement was associated with stability (Berridge and Cleaver 1987).

Of course, much important support comes from outside the professional system. Other foster carers play an important part in giving advice and encouragement (Berridge and Cleaver 1987). Sellick's study (1992) of support to short-term carers found that the local authorities involved were often of limited assistance. Foster carers themselves developed mutual forms of support when faced with a lack of attention from social workers. Elsewhere it has been shown that foster carers' groups are not always easy to maintain and attendance can be low (Shaw and Hipgrave 1989a).

An important focus of this study is an investigation of the relationship between support and placement outcome. One advantage of our research methods was that we were in a good position to tease out these associations more precisely than has been possible in previous studies.

The impact of fostering on other children

There has been an increasing interest in the impact of fostering on carers' own children. In a study in Scotland, 80% of the children of foster carers who responded to a postal questionnaire stated that they liked fostering but the views of the remainder were more mixed (Part 1993). Some, although feeling positive about the experience, commented that it could often be difficult and upsetting. A number of children disliked sharing bedrooms or giving up privacy. Work done by Martin (1993) with a group of foster carers' children revealed that they had all had to manage disclosures of sexual abuse from foster children. They were then faced with the dilemma of whether to tell an adult even when they had been asked not to do so. Cautley (1980) found that difficulties between the foster children and the foster carers' children were given as a reason for ending the placement in 75% of foster placement terminations in the first three months of placement.

Similar issues were explored in an in-depth study in England, focusing on placements for children with severe learning disabilities (Ames 1993). It emerged that the carers' own children were profoundly affected by living with children with severe disabilities. The views were again mostly positive but children were often much involved in caring tasks and those with negative views were almost all girls, particularly where the foster child was of a similar age. A main conclusion was that children's feelings had not been taken seriously enough by social workers and parents when the placements were being negotiated. The findings of this study show the important part that the foster carers' own children play, both in providing support to the carers and in terms of the impact of the fostered child on them.

Contact

Prior to the Children Act 1989 contact with family members was given little consideration by social workers and little practical help was offered to encourage parents' visits (Packman, Randall and Jacques 1986; Vernon and Fruin 1986). However, a number of studies showed the range of obstacles facing parents who wanted to see their children and the 'no win' situation in which they were placed, first when visits were discouraged to let children settle and then when visiting after this initial gap, was viewed as unsettling (Millham *et al.* 1986; Rowe *et al.* 1984). Other research emphasised the importance of contact in providing continuity and later refuge with parents or the extended family for children whose care careers were unstable (Biehal *et al.* 1992; Farmer and Parker 1991; Marsh and Peel 1999; Millham *et al.* 1986; Stein and Carey 1986). It was also argued that children need knowledge of their origins, particularly after adoption, but also when looked after by local authorities (Haimes and Timms 1985; Howe and Hinings 1989).

These research findings were influential in the development of the Children Act 1989 and its emphasis on the importance of contact to promote continuity for children and assist in reunification with their families. The result has been a major change in attitudes to contact: the proportion of children who now see a parent on a weekly basis has increased fourfold from the position identified in earlier studies, although the proportion of fostered children who have no parental visits has remained stable (Cleaver 2000). Several studies have demonstrated the importance of contact with siblings (see for example Caesar *et al.* 1994; Dance and Rushton 1999; Harrison 1999; McAuley 1996) and the part that other adults, relatives and former foster carers can play when relationships with parents are poor (Berridge 1997; Cleaver 2000; McAuley 1996; Rowe *et al.* 1984; Sinclair *et al.* 2003).

Into this tranquil picture of increased contact levels underpinned by the widespread assumption that contact with family members for separated children is beneficial, a more sceptical note was introduced by Quinton and his colleagues (1997). After evaluating the research evidence to date, they concluded:

> In our present state of knowledge it is seriously misleading to think that what we know about contact is at a level of sophistication to allow us to make confident assertions about the benefits to be gained from it regardless of family circumstances and relationships. At least in the case of permanent placements the social experiment that is currently underway needs to be recognised as an experiment, not as an example of evidence-based practice. (Quinton *et al.* 1997, p.393)

Post-Children Act research has raised questions about practice in relation to contact. Cleaver's study of this issue found that contact was often not associated with a specific objective – 'for contact to occur was sufficient in itself' (Cleaver 2000, p.273). The findings also showed that contact alone was often insufficient to promote a child's return home. Direct work on existing attachments was often also needed. Similarly, Packman and Hall (1998) found that it was not clear how contact was linked with restoration plans. By the mid 1990s a study by the Social Services Inspectorate, that focused on public law applications under the Children Act 1989 involving issues of contact between looked-after children and their families, suggested that 'the pendulum might now have swung too far' (Department of Health, Social Services Inspectorate 1994, p.24), with courts bending over backwards to allow parents opportunities to prove their suitability. The report showed the complexity of many contact arrangements, the importance attached to them by courts and local authorities, and concerns about delays. In some cases, where parental abuse was established and there was little likelihood that parents would ever be able to offer adequate care, contact was found to have worked against the interests of the child.

At the same time, researchers and practitioners, in the areas of domestic violence and sexual abuse in particular, have drawn attention to particular situations in which contact may be contra-indicated or problematic. Hester and her colleagues (Hester and Radford 1992; Hester *et al.* 1994) have shown the risks to children when contact occurs with violent fathers. Jones and Parkinson (1995) and Smith (1995) argue that contact with a sexually abusing parent figure after placement can impede the child's recovery by keeping the traumatic material alive. They believe that a period without contact with the abuser ensures that the child is not pressured to retract. Continued contact can mean that the abuser reinforces his power over the child and some children are re-abused during contact. Jones and Parkinson (1995) suggest that pressure may be put on a child to retract through the siblings who see the perpetrator or, alternatively, that the parents of sexually abused adolescents may forbid contact with their siblings in order to maintain the fiction that the abuse did not take place (Elgar and Head 1997; Farmer and Pollock 1999a). In addition, in a study of looked-after sexually abused and abusing children, Farmer and Pollock (1998) found that some contacts with relatives or friends placed children at risk of abuse or could lead children back into high risk sexual behaviours, since these relatives or friends had sometimes initiated the children into sexually high risk practices in the first place.

A small number of studies are now beginning to suggest that contact for separated children is a complex phenomenon and needs to be re-appraised so that it can be better managed. A few studies have shown that whilst children might want more contact with one set of relatives, they may also want less with others. A quarter of the children in Sinclair and Gibbs' study of residential care (1998) mentioned someone with whom they would have liked less contact and over half (56%) of the sexually abused and/or abusing adolescents in care in Farmer and Pollock's study (1998) found that either some or most of their contacts were unhelpful to them. Still more recently, Sinclair and his colleagues in a large study of fostered children of all ages have shown that at the one and three year follow-up stage, in cases of previous abuse, unrestricted access to family members was associated with placement breakdown and further abuse (Sinclair *et al.* 2000; Sinclair *et al.* 2003). The authors concluded that the impact of contact depends on the degree of unresolved yearning of children for their relatives and the effect of this on the child's desire to be in the placement and attach to the carers.

This study also shows that a more differentiated approach to contact is needed with children able to select which family members they wish to see and by which means (telephone or visits for example) with as few conflicts of loyalty as possible between carers and family. Schofield and her colleagues (2000) too found most contacts problematic to at least some degree. Macaskill (2002) in a study of contact in adoptive and a small number of permanent foster placements found that contact often provoked immensely painful dormant feelings and had an impact on the child, parents and new family members. In one in seven cases contact had led to placement disruption or seriously undermined the stability of the placement.

Most of the information about contact does not distinguish between the issues for adolescents and those for younger children and it is clear that patterns have changed a great deal with the implementation of the Children Act. We need to know more about the effects of contact on young people and on their foster placements. Little is known about how far foster carers do get involved in sustaining contact arrangements for adolescents and the impact that this has on them. These are issues that the current study investigates in some depth.

Theories of parenting

Clearly a key factor in the development of placements and children's relationships with their carers will be the parenting skills of the carers. Belsky (1984) has drawn attention to the many determinants of parenting. These include: the characteristics of the child; the developmental histories of the parents; their personalities and psychological resources; the quality of the relationship if the parent is in a partnership and sources of stress and support. It is known that the father affects the mother's style of handling a child and that a stable, supportive relationship acts as a strong protective factor in the case of mothers who have had extremely adverse backgrounds (Quinton and Rutter 1988; Rutter, Quinton and Liddle 1983). Abidin (1992) has argued for the inclusion of social and environmental factors in considering the determinants of parenting behaviour.

Parenting covers a wide range of activities apart from basic physical care and nurture, including management and control strategies, warmth and responsiveness and the fostering of relationships, inputs to cognitive and intellectual development and the provision of security and stability. The optimum approach involves, first, sensitive and responsive interactions that foster emotional security, attachment and exploration (Baumrind 1971; Parker, Tupling and Brown 1979) and, second, consistent, non-aggressive but firm control that sets boundaries but also fosters mastery and a sense of control (Patterson 1982). The more parenting departs from this, the more it is insensitive, inconsistent, confrontational and aggressive, the more problematic children's emotional, behavioural and intellectual development tends to be.

These characteristics were highlighted in Maccoby and Martin's (1983) classification of parenting patterns which is summarised in the study by Quinton and his colleagues (1998) (see Table 2.1). Maccoby and Martin produced a model with two dimensions: an accepting/rejecting axis and a demanding/undemanding axis. The intersection of these axes gives four patterns of parenting. In this scheme the authoritative/reciprocal pattern has been associated with greater competence, social responsibility and independence in children.

Table 2.1 Maccoby and Martin's classification of parenting

	Responsive	*Unresponsive*
	Child-centred	*Parent-centred*
Demanding, controlling	Authoritative/reciprocal	Authoritarian/ power assertive
Undemanding, low in control attempts	Indulgent/permissive	Indifferent/uninvolved, neglecting, ignoring

Reproduced from Quinton *et al.* 1998, p.21

Foster carers are likely to fall into the authoritative/reciprocal category, which signifies a child-centred approach where the carers are accepting, responsive and also firm in their control. However, parenting skills are shown in the context of two-way interactions between carers and young people (Quinton and Rutter 1988). If the relationship develops badly, there may be a change from positive to negative parenting patterns. The carers may reduce their commitment, withdraw warmth, become more authoritarian or possibly indifferent and uninvolved. Moreover, child-centred parenting is less likely to survive in overcrowded homes with heavy domestic pressures and little time for relaxed sharing of interests (Wilson 1974).

As previously noted, there are key areas in parenting a child in foster care that are different from the parenting task with birth children. These include understanding the implications of the child's background, previous parenting and any adverse experiences, acknowledging these experiences and losses, managing disturbed and difficult behaviours, adjusting to the child's defences and to their strategies for dealing with strong feelings, making relationships and developing attachments and maintaining links with the birth family. In addition, carers need to integrate a placed child with other children in the family.

Sinclair and his colleagues (2000) found that carers who received particularly high ratings on specific parenting skills had better success than others.

The parenting skills were: being caring, accepting, encouraging, clear in expectations; not easily upset by the child's failure to respond and capable of seeing things from the child's point of view. Success was also related to carers who were child-oriented, spending time with the children doing things that they liked. In contrast, the number of years of experience and training received were not linked to outcome.

Studies with systematic assessment of children's psychosocial functioning

There are few studies that use systematic evaluations of children's behaviour at placement and document changes prospectively. Tizard and her colleagues (Hodges and Tizard 1989a, 1989b; Tizard 1977) followed up a group of children who were in institutions in infancy and were placed with new families or restored to their parents after the age of two. The adopted children followed up in adolescence developed selective attachments to their new parents and showed a reduction in the restless, distractible behaviour exhibited at age eight. However, they still showed problems at school and had more difficulty in close relationships with peers. This difference in peer relationships was not shown by children restored to their birth parents, but otherwise, the latter group had poorer outcomes than the adopted group.

Rushton and his colleagues (Rushton et al. 1988, 1993, 1995) followed 18 boys from disrupted backgrounds over an 8 year period in their placements with unrelated foster and adoptive families. Poorer outcomes at one year were found for the older boys and for those who had experienced multiple changes of pre-placement environment. A modest reduction in problems in the first six months was followed by more rapid improvement by the end of the first year, accompanied for the majority by the steady development of affectionate relationships with the new parents. Restlessness and lack of creative play were persisting problems.

At the five year follow-up, two-thirds of the boys continued to show modest improvement but the remainder exhibited a high level of problems, which had either been present throughout or were associated with an upswing of difficulties in adolescence. Having spent a year pre-placement in residential care predicted disruption or poor outcome in placement. Very high quality and consistent parenting predicted better outcomes. The most common and persistent problem in continuing placements was restlessness.

A later study by some of the same researchers (Quinton *et al.* 1998) of children placed with 61 new families between the ages of 5 and 9 used a prospective, repeated measures design in which the type and severity of children's problems and the new parents' responses to them were assessed shortly after placement, again after six months and at the end of one year. The design was chosen to see whether parenting styles and social work support were related to the children's recovery.

Children singled out and rejected by their birth families made poor progress. In common with the previous study it was found that problems with overactivity and poor attention were a feature for many of the children at the outset and after one year. The new parents needed help to maintain their warmth and sensitivity and not to withdraw and reject the child. Parental responsiveness was related to the security of the placement through its relationship with the growth of children's attachment even though it did not have a noticeable effect on children's behavioural and emotional problems. Placements of children on their own into established families were at increased risk of poor outcome because of conflict between the arriving child and the children of the carers. The children who were having difficulties in forming relationships with their new parents also often had difficulties with their new siblings or peers. Placed children tended to show inappropriate social interactions with other children, for example insensitivity to the feelings of others, inability to keep to the rules of games or aggression with other children.

Over half of the new parents had difficulties with some aspect of the parenting role during the year. Usually, this took the form of difficulty in responding sensitively or expressing warmth to the child or in problems in day to day management. There was a close relationship between the children's behaviour, parenting style and placement stability, with the latter at risk where the child's behaviour deteriorated in the context of less sensitive parenting.

Howe (1996 and 1997) has reported on a retrospective study of 120 adoptive parents followed up when their adopted children were in early adulthood, a method which favoured continuing placements. The children who had had a poor start, that is, they had experienced inconsistent, neglectful, rejecting or abusive parenting, had the highest rates of behavioural problems and much poorer adoptive parent-child relationships at age 16. However, it was found that relationships improved when young adulthood was reached.

A prospective study of 19 children placed in long-term foster placements between the ages of 4 and 11 (McAuley and Trew 2000) showed that foster carers' ratings of the children's externalising behaviour early in placement predicted disruption at the two year follow-up stage.

This study too provides a prospective examination of the developmental progress of a sample of adolescents and relates this to the foster carers parenting approaches and to the stability of their placements over a one year period.

Such analysis of the skills and abilities which foster carers bring to the task of fostering adolescents and the kind of support they need should shed light on the issues of the recruitment, training, retention and support required by foster carers for this age group. Over and above this, there is a need to discover how far foster carers' parenting strategies and the supports they receive relate to the outcomes of placements for adolescents and what other factors within the placed child or the foster family relate to the stability and effectiveness of placements. It is these gaps in our knowledge that the study described in this book aims to fill.

Chapter Three

How We Designed
and Carried Out the Study

Main aims of the research

Given the lack of recent research on foster care and particularly on the foster care of adolescents, our main objective was to provide systematically gathered information on such placements which would uncover what makes them work well. There were a number of more specific aims:

- To analyse the parenting task for foster carers looking after adolescents with behavioural and emotional difficulties and to examine whether there are identifiable foster caring behaviours and skills which contribute to good outcomes with difficult adolescents.

- To determine which patterns of support, services and training for foster carers relate to good outcomes for adolescents, and to identify the formal and informal supports that foster carers actually use and those that they require.

- To assess the relative contribution to good outcomes of these factors and others, such as factors within the young people, their impact on foster family relationships and the presence or absence of external influences and stresses.

Design of the study

The study used a one year prospective, repeated measures design and was based on a consecutive sample of 68 newly placed young people aged between 11 and 17. Fourteen local authorities and two independent fostering agencies were selected to provide a mix of mainstream and specialist placements to ensure variation in parenting approaches and strategies among the foster carers and to allow an examination of differences in the levels of formal support provided. Specialist schemes generally offer enhanced levels of support and remuneration and sometimes also more training.

Three of the local authorities were shire counties and four were metropolitan districts with large multi-racial urban populations. There were also seven unitary authorities, including three cities and four towns. Four of the unitaries included rural areas. Together the authorities covered urban, suburban and rural areas.

The local authorities and independent agencies were asked to refer young people aged between 11 and 17 who had recently moved to a new medium- to long-term foster placement, regardless of where they were previously living. These were all young people about whom the reasons for admission included concern about their current behaviour and/or emotional well-being. Cases were referred to the study over an eighteen-month period. Certain types of placement and categories of young people were excluded, as the parenting skills necessary in these situations or the supports provided were considered likely to be markedly different from the target population. Young people in respite placements, mother and baby placements, placements with relatives or friends, and those remanded to foster care were not included. Young people with severe learning difficulties and asylum seekers were also excluded.

A series of meetings with senior management, practitioners and line managers was conducted to discuss relevant policy issues, to introduce ourselves and the study and to discuss the most suitable referral procedure.

Each authority and agency was asked to complete a referral form when a young person moved to a new foster placement. Parental consent for the young people to participate in the study was achieved by a nominated contact within the agency or authority. Once the consent of the young person's parents had been obtained by the agency, the referral form was forwarded to the research team. The social worker for the young person was then asked to help the researchers make contact with the young person and foster carers and to provide access to the young person's case file. Seven parents (3% of the total referrals) refused consent. Similarly, nine young people (4%) and sixteen foster carers (8%) declined to participate in the research and two social workers prevented access to the young person, in one case because there were ongoing legal proceedings involving the young person.

Five independent fostering agencies were invited to participate in the study but unfortunately only two young people and their carers were interviewed from two of these agencies. This was partly due to a low referral rate from the independent agencies, and partly due to problems in obtaining consent from local authorities that were not already participating in the study.

Ensuring continuous referrals from the agencies required substantial effort and involved regular liaison with the nominated contact person in each authority or agency. Nonetheless, some of the local authorities referred few cases to the study.

Unfortunately there was no administrative mechanism that could be used to determine whether or not all eligible cases were being referred to the research team by the authority, or whether there was any selection bias in the referral procedure. Some bias may have been introduced to the sample through either the young person's parents refusing to consent to involvement in the study, or the foster carer or young person themselves choosing not to participate. However, no consistent pattern to the refusals was discernible. The young people who did not participate in the study were not statistically significantly different from those who did, in terms of age, gender or ethnicity.

Data collection

Data for this study were collected in three ways: through a review of the young people's case files, through semi-structured interviews with the young people, their foster carers and social workers and through the use of standardised measures. Interviews were conducted 3 months after the date of placement and again after 9 months (that is 12 months after the date of placement), or at the point of disruption if this occurred earlier. Initial contact with the foster carers and young people was made by a letter from the researchers, requesting their participation in the study. The young people were given a small store voucher at both interview phases to thank them for the time they generously gave. The foster carers received a voucher after they had completed the second interview.

Case file scrutiny

The case files of all the young people referred to the study were scrutinised and information was recorded on pre-coded schedules. Data on the demographic and family background of the young person were collected, as well as information on their care careers, any history of adversities and the reasons for the current placement. This information allowed an examination of the factors which the young people brought to the placement that might influence the placement outcomes. For example, we needed to know whether the young person had attended school regularly and whether difficulties in learning had been identified, whether there were any medical conditions that might exacerbate behaviour or place an additional burden on the carers or whether the young person had experienced significant adversities in the past, such as abuse. These data were subsequently transferred to a computer database and analysed.

First interviews

First interviews were conducted 3 months after the start of the placement. This period was chosen because parenting behaviour assessed on the basis of data collected at an earlier point has not proved to be predictive of outcome at 12 months (Quinton *et al.* 1998).

The development of the interview schedules

The interview schedules were designed specifically for this study and covered a range of key areas. Three separate schedules were developed, one for each category of respondent. The schedules were designed to cover the same main issues, but each also focused on issues specific to the respondent. For example, the foster carers were asked about their training and preparation, whilst social workers were asked about their workload and opportunities for supervision. This design resulted in a more complete picture of the fostering process from each participant's perspective. It also enabled a comparison of different views on the same issues. During the development phase, the schedules were piloted and subsequently amended. Issues of reliability were addressed by cross-checking the interview recordings made by the researchers. These checks suggested that the quality of the data did not vary significantly according to who had conducted the interview.

The interviews were lengthy – the average foster carer interview was 2½ hours. All the interviews were conducted by the authors and followed an investigator-based approach (Brown 1983). This provides for the systematic but flexible coverage of topics of interest, using predefined coding. The interviews were tape-recorded and then summarised onto pre-coded schedules.

The coded information was then transferred to a database for analysis. Summaries of each case were written after the first and follow-up interviews. Care was taken to ensure that none of the participants, particularly the young people, felt pressurised to talk to the researchers. Particular attention was paid to ensure that the young people felt sufficiently in control of the interview to say if they did not want to answer any of the questions, or if they wanted to stop the interview. Whilst all of the interviews were confidential, ethical concerns about child protection led us to explain to the young people, at the outset of the interview, that if they told us anything which suggested that they or another child was at risk of harm that was not already known to the appropriate agencies, we would discuss with them what steps were needed to ensure their safety. In the event, this situation did not arise.

Interviews with foster carers

Interviews were conducted with 68 foster carers. Twenty-one of the foster carers were single carers, while the remainder had a partner. Where possible, interviews were held jointly with both foster carers, but this was not always convenient for the carers.

The carers' views on their approach to the caring task and their initial parenting behaviours were assessed through established investigator-based interviews of parenting (Quinton and Rutter 1988; Quinton *et al.* 1998), and through newly devised measures to cover carers' views and perceptions of their task. This part of the interview enabled researchers to rate the carers' parenting behaviour on established parenting dimensions, such as consistency, sensitivity to cues, flexible boundary maintenance, supervision and social and educational facilitation, and on dimensions of particular relevance to adolescents, such as dealing with their peer relationships, the management of sexuality and the encouragement of appropriate levels of independence. A rating of the foster carers' engagement with the young person was also used (see Farmer and Pollock 1998). These ratings were used to develop a profile of the parenting behaviours of all the foster carers in the sample. Detailed information was also gathered on the young people's behaviours in the placements and on a range of other topics relevant to our investigation.

Interviews with adolescents

Also at the 3 month stage, interviews were held with the placed adolescents to explore their views about why they were placed and their hopes and expectations of the placement and of the future. Other issues, such as their relationships with the other young people in the foster family, contact with their birth family, their peer relationships and educational arrangements were also discussed.

The young people were interviewed on their current behaviours and concerns using newly developed instruments and a modified version of the Child and Adolescent Functioning and Environment Schedule devised by Quinton and John for which community comparison information is available (Quinton, Messer and Ehrich 1996).

Interviews were conducted with 66 young people. The remaining two young people either refused to participate (although previously having consented to their involvement) or 'voted with their feet' and were repeatedly absent when the researcher visited the household.

Interviews with social workers

Telephone interviews were conducted with the social workers responsible for the young people in order to explore the plans made for the young people, contact issues, interventions provided in the past and currently and assistance of all kinds from any professionals to the foster carers and young people. Information about the preparation and planning for the placement was collected, including whether or not there was a choice of placement for the young person, and whether the study placement was considered suitable for the young person.

Sixty-seven interviews were conducted with social workers. It was not possible to contact one of the social workers, who had left the authority and had not been replaced.

The measures used

Both the young people and the foster carers were asked to complete a questionnaire which included a range of standardised measures, plus some new measures designed specifically for this study. The researchers were able to provide assistance with completion of the questionnaires where necessary.

FOSTER CARERS

The standardised measures the foster carers were asked to complete were:

- the Strengths and Difficulties Questionnaire (Goodman 1994), measuring the young person's behaviour and adjustment (SDQ)

- the General Health Questionnaire (Goldberg and Hillier 1979) measuring the carers' psychosocial functioning
- a questionnaire on the young person's social and psychological development used by Sinclair*et al.* (2000) and based on the summary measures from the Looking After Children Assessment and Action Records (Parker*et al.* 1991; Ward 1995).

The foster carers were also asked to complete a number of new instruments, assessing:

- the extent and content of training received
- the amount and quality of information they received before the placement about the history, characteristics and behaviour of the young person
- the types of support they had access to, utilised and found helpful, including specific questions about the family placement worker, the young person's social worker and foster carer groups
- the amount of contact the young person had with members of their birth family, the involvement of the carers in facilitating it and how this contact affected the young person and the foster carers.

Sixty-one carers completed and returned the measures.

YOUNG PEOPLE

The standardised measures the young people were asked to complete were:

- the Strengths and Difficulties Questionnaire (Goodman 1994), measuring the young person's behaviour and adjustment (SDQ)
- the Kovacs and Beck Child Depression Inventory (Kovacs and Beck 1977), measuring levels of depression
- the Loneliness and Social Dissatisfaction Questionnaire (Asher, Hymel and Renshaw 1984) which measures peer relationships and loneliness.

Sixty-seven young people completed and returned the measures.

Follow-up interviews

Interviews and measures were repeated 9 months after the first interview (that is 12 months after placement) or at the point of disruption if this occurred earlier. The interviews with each set of participants focused on their perceptions of the progress of the placement over the year and included sections (for the foster carers and social workers) on the strategies the carers had developed to care for and work with the children, how contact with the young person's birth family had been managed, the formal and informal supports that had been used or needed, and the levels of satisfaction with the placement. When placements had disrupted the foster carers, young people and social workers were in addition asked what had caused the breakdown and how it had been managed.

Sixty-two follow-up interviews were conducted with the foster carers. Only 19 follow-up interviews were completed with the young people, partly because they were sometimes hard to trace after placement disruption.

The young people were also asked to complete the same standardised measures as those completed at the first phase. Whilst only 19 interviews had been conducted with the young people at follow-up, 42 of them returned the questionnaires since social workers assisted by passing these on to them. The combination of measures the foster carers were asked to complete was altered slightly. The standardised measures the foster carers completed at the second phase were:

- the Strengths and Difficulties Questionnaire (Goodman 1994), measuring the young person's behaviour and adjustment

- the General Health Questionnaire (Goldberg and Hillier 1979) measuring the carers' psychosocial functioning

- a questionnaire on the young person's social and psychological development (Sinclair *et al.* 2000)

- changes in the young person's contact with their birth family

- changes in the amount of support available and utilised

- the Expression of Feelings Questionnaire (Quinton *et al.* 1998), measuring the foster carers' and young person's emotional closeness, the young person's openness in expressing feelings, willingness to share distress and the seeking and accepting of affection.

Forty-seven carers returned the measures; rather fewer than completed the follow-up interviews.

Fifty-eight interviews were held with social workers at follow-up. The number of interviews and questionnaires completed at each stage is shown in

Table 3.1. It should be noted that occasionally when a questionnaire was filled in a part of it was not completed.

Table 3.1 Number of interviews and questionnaires completed at each stage			
Type of measure	*Respondent*	*First stage*	*Second stage*
Interviews	Foster carer	68	62
	Young person	66	19
	Social worker	67	58
Questionnaires	Foster carer	61	47
	Young person	67	42

Outcomes

The intermediate outcome measures

We chose intermediate outcome measures that focused on a range of aspects of the young person's life. Some of these measures reflected the direction of change in certain behaviours and areas of social development which are particularly pertinent for adolescents. Ratings were also made about changes in the young person's psychosocial development, based upon the information gained from the questionnaires completed at the first and second interviews.

In summary, the intermediate outcome measures were:

- What was the direction of change in school attendance and attitude towards school?
- What was the direction of change in the adequacy of their peer relationships?
- What was the quality of their relationship with their carers, including whether or not there was a continuing positive relationship with at least one of the carers by the time of the second interview?
- What was the overall impact of the young person on other children in the household?
- Were the young person's major needs being met?

- Did the young person need specialist intervention which they were not getting?

- Had the young person been at risk due to their sexual behaviour? If yes, had the level of risk increased, stayed the same or decreased?

- Had the young person's behaviour put other children or adults at risk sexually? If yes, had the level of risk increased, stayed the same or decreased?

- Had the young person's behaviour put other children or adults at risk physically? If yes, had the level of risk increased, stayed the same or decreased?

- Had the young person's use of drugs or alcohol been a matter of concern during the placement? If yes, had the level of concern increased, stayed the same or decreased?

- Had the young person been involved in offending? If yes, had the level of offending behaviour increased, stayed the same or decreased?

- Did the young person show any new difficult behaviour within or outside the placement?

- Overall did the young person's behaviour improve?

- Were the aims of the placement, as defined by the social worker, met?

To these we added two more general outcome measures:

- Benefit of the placement. A rating was made of how beneficial the placement had been for the young person, which included an assessment of whether or not the young person's well-being had improved as a result of the placement.

- Satisfaction with the placement. The foster carers, young people and the social workers were all asked to rate their overall satisfaction with the placement.

The main outcome measures

Two main outcome measures were chosen to provide a broad overview of the placement. The first was placement disruption as this is an area that most people regard as important in ascertaining success. For this approach to outcome, the disrupted placements (27) were compared with those that were continuing after one year (34). The seven planned endings were excluded from the analysis as they fitted neither category and were therefore likely to distort the findings (see Table 3.2).

Table 3.2 Status of the placements after one year		
Status of placement	*Number of placements*	*Percentage of placements*
Disrupted	27	40
Planned ending	7	10
Continuing with many difficulties	9	13
Continuing well	25	37
Total	68	100

The second approach to outcomes focused on the quality of the placement for the child, since placements that end earlier than planned may be positive for the young person and a continuing placement may be detrimental. For these analyses good quality or successful placements were those that were continuing well or had had planned positive endings by the one year follow-up (32) and poor quality or unsuccessful placements were those that had broken down or were continuing but showing evidence of many difficulties (36).

The variables from the interviews and measures were run against these two types of outcome in order to distinguish the key factors affecting both placement disruption and the quality of the placement.

Analysis

The data collection approaches that we used bridged the normal qualitative/quantitative divide and provided data that were amenable to statistical analyses whilst retaining the richness of individual case material.

The case file material was coded, entered onto a computer database and analysed using Statistical Packages for the Social Sciences (SPSS for Windows). This information was important as it enabled an assessment to be made of the problems, difficulties and needs the young people brought with them to the study placement.

The material gathered in the interviews and the standardised measures were collated and used to form a composite view of the extent to which the young person's well-being had been promoted in the placement. Composite ratings of the parenting approaches adopted by the foster carers were related to the stability of the placement and their effectiveness in promoting the young person's welfare. Ratings of the support used by foster carers were also compiled and related to the outcomes of the placements. The data from the interviews and the ratings were also analysed using SPSS for Windows.

During the course of the study the three researchers met regularly to discuss the data collection and to share their views of the material and themes as they emerged. Discussions were also held at regular intervals with members of the advisory committee and others with helpful knowledge and experience. Cross-referencing several sources of data was useful in establishing some certainty about the occurrence of events and behaviour, as well as looking for similarities and differences in the perceptions of different participants. The numbers answering specific interview questions were sometimes a little less than the full number who had been interviewed as not all respondents answered every question. In the analyses small variations in sample size across tables are not commented on unless the reasons for the missing data are germane to the analysis. Significance was assessed using Chi-square or Fisher's exact test (two-tailed) and relationships were considered to be statistically significant where $p<0.05$, that is any association described as significant indicates a relationship beyond the 5% level of probability. Exact levels of probability will be used sparingly in the text.

In what follows, the names and some of the details of the individuals who are described have been changed in order to preserve confidentiality.

Chapter Four

Description of the Young People and the Foster Carers in the Sample

In this chapter, the young people's backgrounds and experiences prior to the study placement are described. This is followed by a description of the characteristics of the foster carers.

The case file records of all of the young people were scrutinised and information collected about the young people, their families, any adversities they had experienced, their placement histories and the reasons for their current placements. In a few instances, information about the young people was missing and the data had to be recorded as not known.

Characteristics of the young people

Boys and girls were represented almost equally within the sample, which included 35 girls (51%) and 33 boys (49%). The young people's age when they moved to this foster placement ranged from 11 to 17 years, with the majority aged between 13 and 15 years (71%).

Eighteen per cent of the young people (12 cases) were from minority ethnic backgrounds: nine young people were of mixed-race parentage, two were African-Caribbean and one was Asian. Eighty-three per cent of the young people were placed with foster carers of the same ethnic origin, and the remainder were placed with carers of different ethnicity. Whilst all but one of the white young people were placed with carers of the same background (a white girl placed with a dual heritage carer), 11 of the mixed-race parentage and minority ethnic young people were not. Two young people were placed in families of similar ethnicity (one white/African-Caribbean young person was placed with African-Caribbean carers and one African-Caribbean young person went to white/African-Caribbean carers). Nine black and minority ethnic young people were placed with white families. However of these, six were placed in households where there was an overlap between cultures. For example, an African-Caribbean boy was placed with a lone white carer whose own children were of African-Caribbean/white parentage.

Whilst the sampling criteria excluded young people with profound intellectual disabilities, 41% of the young people had some sort of health or developmental problems. These difficulties ranged from relatively minor treatable ailments such as eczema to more serious conditions such as asthma, epilepsy and cerebral palsy. Three of the young people (5%) had a serious learning disability of organic origin.

The young people's family backgrounds
Family composition
Only nine of the young people (14%) were living with both of their birth parents immediately prior to entering the care system. Thirty-four per cent were living with a lone parent (19 with a single mother and 3 with a lone father) and 46% with a step-parent (26 with their mother and a stepfather and 4 with their father and a stepmother). The remaining four young people lived with a grandmother, mother's partner, adoptive parent and legal guardian. For three children this information was missing. Nine of the young people had suffered the death of one of their parents. The death of a parent was significantly more common for the young people from a mixed-race parentage or minority ethnic background than for the white adolescents. A further three young people had experienced a failed adoption placement at some stage.

The young people from reconstituted families were statistically more likely than others to have a history of disruptive behaviour at home prior to admission to care. Within these step-family households, 22 young people (73%) had difficulties in their relationships with step-parents and these problems were often the main reason for their admission to care. The young people from reconstituted families were also less likely than others to have been in the care system before the index placement but were more likely to have had multiple separations from their main carer.

Adversities

As we would expect for a group of young people in foster care at this age, the case file records showed that the majority of them had experienced marked adversities during their childhood. This included family disruption, parental psychiatric disorder, physical and sexual abuse and neglect. The extent of the birth parents' problems is shown in Table 4.1.

Table 4.1 Birth parents' problems		
Parental problem	*Number of young people*	*Percentage of young people*
Domestic violence	25	38
Multiple house moves	21	32
Parent involved in drug/alcohol abuse	20	31
Parental psychiatric disorder	18	27
Parent involved in offending	17	25
Parental physical illness	9	14

ABUSE AND NEGLECT

Many of the young people had experienced physical or sexual abuse, neglect and/or emotional maltreatment, including being singled out for rejection (scapegoating). The figures in Table 4.2 are of confirmed incidents of abuse, as recorded in the case files. Obviously the actual rate of abuse may be higher, as incidents of abuse may not have been disclosed or recorded.

Table 4.2 History of abuse				
Form of abuse	*Girls*	*Boys*	*Total*	*Total percentage*
Physical abuse	15	13	28	44
Neglect	17	8	25	38
Sexual abuse	23	1	23	34
Scapegoating	9	3	12	20

As this table shows, 23 (34%) of the young people had experienced sexual abuse, and all but one of these were girls. Of the girls in the sample, 63% had been the victims of sexual abuse, which is broadly in line with Farmer and Pollock's findings (1998). In comparison, only 3% of the boys had experienced sexual abuse.

A number of young people were recorded as having suffered more than one kind of abuse. Fourteen young people had experienced both physical abuse and neglect, five had experienced physical abuse and scapegoating, and two had experienced physical abuse, neglect and scapegoating. Of the young people who had experienced sexual abuse, eight had additionally been physically abused, five had been physically and sexually abused and had suffered neglect, and one young person had a history of physical and sexual abuse, scapegoating and neglect.

In addition, a further six young people had siblings who had been sexually abused, although there was no evidence of sexual abuse to the study child and two young people who had not suffered physical abuse had siblings who had done so.

Overall, 52% of the young people were known to have been on the Child Protection Register at some point during their childhood, and 14% were currently registered. There had been some contact between social services departments and all of the young people prior to their current placement, often for a considerable period of time. Only five (8%) of the young people's families had been known to social services departments for less than one year, and only 13 (21%) for less than two years. Therefore, 71% of the young people had been in contact with social services departments for over two years, and for some, their family's involvement with social services departments went back much further, in some cases for many years before the young person was born.

However, in just over half of the cases (51%), as far as we could tell from the files, no professional work, in terms of social work help or therapeutic intervention, had been undertaken with the family either prior to or since the index placement had been made.

Placement histories

Not surprisingly, the young people in the sample often had complex care histories. Thirty-nine per cent of the young people (where information was available) had no previous experience of care before the start of the current care period, although some had been looked after by members of their family other than their parents.

The young people in the sample were classified according to the age at which they first entered the care system: those who were first looked after at the age of 11 or older ('teenage entrants') and those who had been in care earlier in their childhood, although not necessarily continuously ('non-teenage entrants'). Of the 68 young people, 42 had come into the care system for the first time as teenagers (62%) and 26 had entered the care system before the age of 11. Boys were significantly more likely than girls to have spent over two years in care prior to the current placement.

Since their first admission to care, the majority of the young people had experienced a number of placement changes, some moving between their parents' home, residential units, secure units and foster homes. Forty-one per cent of the young people had moved six or more times, 57% had experienced between one and five moves, and only one young person had as yet had no moves in care. Return home had been attempted for many of the young people in the sample, often on numerous occasions (see also Farmer and Parker 1991; Packman and Hall 1998). Three young people, however, had not lived with their birth parents for over a year, and eighteen others for over two years, including three young people who had not lived with their birth parents for more than nine years.

Emotional ties

Almost a third of the young people (31%) were rated by the foster carers as having little or no attachment to any adult at the start of the placement. This lack of emotional ties predicted later placement disruption. These were young people with a variety of disadvantages, including long periods in care and sometimes a failed adoption.

The reason for being looked after in this care period

The primary reason for entry into the care system at the start of the current care period was recorded (Table 4.3). Boys were more likely to be admitted because of their behaviour and girls because of sexual abuse or at their own request.

Table 4.3 Reason for being looked after in this care period				
Reason	*Girls*	*Boys*	*Total*	*Percentage*
Young person's behaviour	3	10	13**	18
Parent unable to care	4	6	10	15
Parents' request	4	5	9	13
Sexual abuse to young person	8	0	8*	12
Breakdown in relationship with parents	3	3	6	9
Young person's request	6	0	6***	9
Neglect	2	2	4	6
Physical abuse to young person	2	2	4	6
Neglect and physical abuse	2	2	4	6
Sexual abuse to another child	1	0	1	2
Schedule 1 offender in household	0	1	1	2
Unsatisfactory home conditions	0	1	1	2
Total	35	32	67	100

$n = 67$. No information on 1 case
Significant differences in the reasons for being looked after between boys and girls:
*Fisher's exact test, $p = 0.007$ *** Fisher's exact test, $p = 0.015$
** Fisher's exact test, $p = 0.023$

The move to the current placement

Seventeen young people moved to the index placement directly from their birth parents' home, and one from his adoptive parents' home (Table 4.4). Overall, 47% (32) of the young people moved to their current placement from parent figures, friends, relatives or guardians whilst 51% (35) arrived from a care setting, most frequently foster care, and one young person's history was unknown.

The reason for the current placement

The reason for the move to the current placement was also documented. For those who were already being looked after, this reason could be different from

Table 4.4 Residence before placement

Previous residence	Number of young people	Percentage of young people
Medium/long-term foster care	18	26
Immediate birth family	17	25
Other relatives	10	15
Short-term/temporary foster care	7	10
Residential unit	7	10
'Other'	4	6
Friends	3	4
Adoptive parents	1	2
Unknown	1	2
Total	68	100

the reason for their entry to care at the beginning of the current care period. Sixty-two per cent of the current placements were made as a result of a breakdown in the relationship between the young person and either their parents (35%) or foster carers (27%), frequently as a consequence of the young person's difficult behaviour. Some placement moves were planned (19%), for example, a planned move from a short-term foster placement to a long-term foster home. Three young people (4%) moved from their family to their current placement after having been abused, either physically or sexually, and a fourth moved after it was discovered that one of the adults in the household had previously abused another young girl. Three adolescents were placed in foster care because their parents became ill, either physically or mentally, and were therefore unable to cope. One young person was placed after her family became homeless and another when his grandparents became too old to look after him (Table 4.5).

Legal status at the time of placement
The majority of the young people in the sample (71%) were accommodated under Section 20 of the Children Act 1989 but a quarter were on care orders.

Table 4.5 Reason for current placement

Reason	Number of young people	Percentage of young people
Breakdown of relationship with parents (including the young person's behaviour and the young person's request)	24	35
Breakdown in relationship with foster carers	18	27
Planned move	13	19
Abuse	3	4
Illness of main carer (physical or mental)	3	4
Protection of young person (due to abuse of another child in the household)	1	2
Other	5	7
Unknown	1	2
Total	68	100

Placement with siblings

Thirty-three young people (49%) were the only children from their families who were looked after whilst their brothers and sisters remained at home with their parents. Twenty-one young people (31%) had siblings who were also looked after and two had initially been placed in their index placement with a sibling. Four had siblings but we had no information about where they were living. Eight young people had no siblings under the age of 18.

The past behaviour of the young people

Given the extent of the adversities in the young people's backgrounds, it is not surprising that a wide range of behavioural and emotional difficulties were recorded on the case files (Table 4.6).

Over three-quarters of the young people (76%) had a history of challenging and disruptive behaviour at home, and 68% had displayed disruptive behaviour outside the home. Previous difficult behaviour at home or outside the home (whether immediately prior to placement or some time in the past) and aggressive behaviour before the placement were all significantly related

Table 4.6 Emotional and behavioural difficulties

Difficulties	Girls	Boys	Total	Total %
Severe behaviour problems at home	24	28	52	76
Severe behaviour problems outside home	20	26	46*	68
Violent / aggressive behaviour	17	21	38	56
Caution or conviction for offending	9	18	27**	40
Drug or alcohol abuse	10	12	22	32
Self-harming behaviour	11	4	15	22
Risky sexual relationships	11	1	12***	18
Inappropriate sexual behaviour	4	7	11	16
Suicide attempts	7	1	8****	12
Sexually abusing behaviour	1	4	5	7
Cruelty to animals	0	2	2	3
Eating disorder	1	1	2	3

Significant differences in emotional and behavioural difficulties between boys and girls:
*Fisher's exact test, $p = 0.017$ *** Fisher's exact test, $p = 0.002$
** Fisher's exact test, $p = 0.013$ **** Fisher's exact test, $p = 0.033$

to placement breakdown, principally because previous disruptive behaviour tended to be repeated in the placement. Forty per cent had been cautioned or convicted of a criminal offence, including theft, joy-riding and assault. Significantly more boys than girls were recorded as being disruptive outside the home and had a caution or conviction for a criminal offence. Fifty-six per cent had shown violent or aggressive behaviour towards others, and two young people (3%) had a history of cruelty towards animals. There was no significant gender difference in young people who demonstrated violent or aggressive behaviour.

Five of the young people (4 boys and 1 girl) had a history of sexually abusing behaviour (of whom 1 had also disclosed sexual abuse). Eleven young people (4 girls and 7 boys) were recorded as having displayed inappropriate sexual behaviour, and 12 had been involved in risky sexual relationships, with girls significantly more likely to be at risk. One young girl had become pregnant and had had a termination.

Thirty-two per cent (22) of the young people had a history of drug or alcohol abuse. Fifteen young people (11 girls and 4 boys) were recorded as having deliberately harmed themselves, and eight (7 girls and 1 boy) as having shown suicidal behaviour, with significantly more girls than boys having attempted suicide. Two young people (1 girl and 1 boy) had histories of eating disorders.

The young people's behaviour at the time of placement

Not all of the young people were displaying evidence of their past behaviour at the time of the current placement. However the levels of difficult and challenging behaviour were still very high.

At the time of the placement on which we focused, 76% of the young people had still been showing disruptive behaviour either at home or in their previous placement. The number of young people demonstrating disruptive behaviour outside their home environment at the time of placement was slightly lower, with 61% of young people doing so. Four young people had recently sexually abused another child, and ten were behaving in a sexually inappropriate manner and/or in a way that put them at risk. Eleven had recently harmed themselves deliberately, with significantly more girls than boys having done so.

Past education

Rather worryingly, information about school moves was not documented on the case files of 30 of the young people, but from the information that was recorded it was apparent that many of the young people had had a disrupted education, with only 11 (16%) having had no unscheduled changes of school. Six young people had experienced over five unscheduled changes of school, including one boy who had attended at least 15 different schools. Forty-six per cent had been excluded from school on at least one occasion and the exclusion rate was significantly higher for boys than for girls. Two-thirds of the boys (68%) had been excluded as compared with just over a quarter (27%) of the girls. Fifty-six per cent (37) of the young people had also played truant from school on many occasions. One in five (14) of the young people had been made the subject of a statement of special educational needs, with 11 of these statements still continuing.

Educational provision in the placement

At the time of placement, 12 young people were permanently excluded from mainstream school. The details of the educational provision that had been made according to the case files are outlined in Table 4.7. The provision for three young people was not known, and four were over school age. Five young people were recorded as being in pupil referral units, four as having home tuition and no provision at all, it seemed, had been made for another two.

Table 4.7 Educational provision		
Type of provision	*Number of young people*	*Percentage of young people*
Mainstream day school	43	63
Special unit within mainstream school	1	1
Special day school	4	6
Pupil referral unit	5	8
Home tuition	4	6
Other	2	3
No provision made	2	3
Over school leaving age	4	6
No information available	3	4
Total	68	100

Links between adversities and behavioural difficulties prior to placement

A number of adversities were significantly related to the types of difficult behaviour demonstrated by the young people immediately prior to the study placement.

Having experienced multiple separations from the main caregiver was related to both substance misuse and the young person demonstrating sexually abusing behaviour (see Skuse *et al.* 1996). Exclusion from school was, unsurprisingly, related to a number of behavioural difficulties, for example, increased disruptive behaviour at home and outside the home, aggressive behaviour and offending.

Categories developed for analysis

In order to facilitate later analyses, the types and frequencies of previous adversities have been broadly grouped into the following categories. Whilst many of the young people might have experienced more than one form of adversity within the particular category, for simplicity, categorisation has been based on whether or not the young person experienced *any* of the type of adversity.

- *Physical adversities* – these include physical abuse to the young person, violence between the parental figures, and other violence within the household such as violence between siblings or violence by parents towards other children. Forty-four (65%) of the young people had experienced some form of physical adversity prior to the index placement. Having experienced some form of violence within the family was significantly related to the young person being less likely to demonstrate suicidal behaviour ($p = 0.001$). This is in contrast to other studies which have found a positive correlation between familial violence and suicidal behaviour (Beautrais 2000; Fergusson and Lynskey 1997).

- *Sexual adversities* – including sexual abuse to the young person or their siblings, sexual exploitation of the young person, and the young person witnessing the sexual activity of parents or carers. Thirty (44%) of the young people had suffered at least one form of sexual adversity. Sexual adversities were significantly more likely to have been experienced by girls than boys (Fisher's exact test, $p<0.001$), and were significantly related to the young person following a lifestyle that put them at risk sexually ($p = 0.018$).

- *Emotional adversities* – these include the death of a parent, failed adoptive placements, multiple separations from the main caregiver, neglect, scapegoating of the young person, and general harm to the young person's emotional development caused by the way they were managed. Ninety-one per cent (62) of the young people had experienced emotional adversities. Even if general emotional harm is removed from the analysis, the number of young people who had experienced other emotional adversities was still high (52 young people, 77%). Girls were significantly more likely to have experienced some sort of emotional adversity than boys ($p = 0.01$).

- *Parenting adversities* – these incorporate parental psychiatric or physical illness, parents who were involved in offending, drug or alcohol abuse, or prostitution. Fifty-nine per cent (40) of the young people had experienced parenting adversities.

- *Household adversities* – including many house moves, frequent changes in household composition, and dirty and unhygienic home conditions. These had been experienced by 41 (60%) of the young people. Again, in contrast to other studies which have shown a positive relationship, suicidal and self-harming behaviour were negatively associated with household adversities ($p = 0.015$).

- *Other adversities* – school exclusion, pregnancy and being bullied were included in this category, and had been experienced by 45 (66%) of the young people.

Only one young person had experienced only one category of adversity, whilst six young people had suffered at least one adversity from each category (see Table 4.8).

Table 4.8 Number of categories of adversity experienced		
Number of categories	*Number of young people*	*Percentage*
One	1	2
Two	7	10
Three	18	26
Four	18	26
Five	17	25
Six	6	9
Unknown	1	2
Total	68	100

High or low adversity groups

The young people were also categorised according to the total number of adversities they had experienced. Thirty-nine young people (58%) had experienced between no and seven adversities and this was categorised as low adversity. Twenty-eight young people (42%) had experienced between 8 and 15 adversities, categorised as high adversity.

Behavioural difficulty groups

The number of behavioural difficulties presented immediately prior to placement has also been grouped, again to facilitate later analyses. The *low behavioural difficulties* group includes young people who demonstrated two or fewer conduct problems immediately prior to placement. The *medium behavioural difficulties* group consists of young people who showed between three and five behavioural difficulties and the *high behavioural difficulties* group includes those who presented between six and nine conduct problems (Table 4.9).

Table 4.9 Number of behavioural difficulties presented prior to placement		
Number of difficulties	*Number of young people*	*Percentage*
Low behavioural difficulties (2 or fewer)	19	28
Medium behavioural difficulties (3–5)	28	42
High behavioural difficulties (6–9)	20	30
Total	67	100

$n = 67$
No information on 1 case

Young people who had experienced 'other' adversities, that is school exclusion, pregnancy or being bullied, were significantly more likely to present a high number of behavioural difficulties. This can be explained by the strong relationship between school exclusion (one of the 'other' adversities) and numerous behavioural difficulties such as disruptive behaviour at home and outside the home, aggressive behaviour, and offending.

Now that the young people have been described, we turn to look at the backgrounds, fostering experience and training of the foster carers, which might have equipped them to cope with these young people.

Characteristics of the foster carers and their households

The foster carers' interviews and questionnaires provided a substantial amount of information about the foster carers. The majority (69%) of foster carers in the sample were couple carers (47). Almost a third (31%) were lone carers (21) with 19 lone female carers and 2 lone male carers. In five couple carers the main carer was the man (10%). In some of these situations the male carer had been made redundant from his usual employment, had left work for health reasons or had retired.

Age of the foster carers

The ages of the main foster carers in the sample were spread widely, from 28 to 67 years. However, the majority were in their middle years, with over half (53%) of the primary carers between the ages of 41 and 50 and 81% (55) aged 41 to 60. Thirteen per cent of the main carers were under the age of 40 and a further four (6%) were over the age of 61 years.

Ethnic background of the foster carers

The majority (93%) of the main foster carers were white and of British origin (63); one was from a European background, two were African-Caribbean and two were of mixed-race parentage.

Foster family households

There was considerable variation amongst the foster family households, from a lone carer living with one fostered young person, to a large, busy household which included the foster couple, five fostered children and their own adult child.

Fifty-eight young people were placed in families where there were other children, either other foster children or the carer's own or adopted children or both. In a further three cases, there were no other children but the foster carers' adult offspring (aged 24, 31 and 33) were living with the family. Therefore seven young people were the only person other than the carers in the household and, of these seven, four were living with a single carer.

In addition to the immediate household, three-quarters (76%) of the foster carers (52) had grown-up children no longer living at home, who, in many cases, lived nearby and were actively and frequently involved with the fostering family. In one instance, the foster carer's daughter had been assessed as a temporary carer by the local authority, so that she could manage the household when her mother needed a break or a holiday. Many grown-up children were a great help and support to their parents who fostered. Nevertheless, there were also instances when carers' grown-up children disapproved of their parents fostering, were concerned for the safety of their parents or resented the amount of attention their parents gave to the foster child.

Fostering history and experience

As well as the composition of the family, carers were asked about their fostering background: what had attracted them to the work and what their preferences were in relation to the children they looked after. Other background history was also collected about how long they had been fostering, other relevant work and life experience and the training they had received.

Foster carers' preferences

Foster carers were asked during the interview whether they had any preference about the young people they looked after. They were asked if they favoured looking after boys or girls and if they had other preferences in terms of race, disability or age. Nearly half (48%) had no preference about the young person's gender. However, 28% preferred looking after boys and 24% favoured girls. Some of the lone female carers, for instance, expressed concerns about managing adolescent boys with difficult behaviour without a male presence and therefore chose to look after girls. Similarly, some of the male carers expressed concern about the placement of teenage girls within the home, particularly when the household was predominantly male.

Almost all the carers chose to look after teenagers, although two carers had no age preference and were willing to foster children of any age.

The preferences of the foster carers were met by the characteristics of the study young person in 86% (59) of cases, whilst 11% (7) were matched to some extent and 3% (2) were not matched with the characteristics specified by the foster carers.

In addition to these preferences, some carers expressed concern about looking after young people who might sexually or physically abuse other children. Their concern was to protect not only children living within the household but visiting grandchildren and other young relatives as well as the children of neighbours. Some also voiced concerns about not receiving enough information about young people to enable them to make an informed decision about whether they were suitable for their family situation. The issues around information given to, or indeed withheld, from potential carers will be explored more fully in later chapters.

Fostering experience and length of time fostering

The length of time this group of carers had fostered children varied from less than a year to nearly 36 years but overall they were a very experienced group of carers. Only 4% had been fostering for less than a year and a further 33% between one and five years. Nearly a quarter (24%) had been fostering for 5–10 years, 21% for 10–15 years and a further 18% for 15 years or more.

Main reasons for beginning to foster

The carers in the sample had many different reasons for beginning to foster children. The largest group (29%) were those who said that they liked a busy home life and the company of children and, in some cases, were feeling that their home was too quiet as their own children grew up and became inde-pendent (20). Eleven carers (16%) expressed a desire to help and felt that they had something to offer. Another group of ten (15%) knew a child who needed a family and five carers (7%) were unable to have children of their own. Seven carers (10%) were either brought up themselves as children of foster carers or they had other relatives or friends who fostered. Three (5%) said that they wanted to foster in order to benefit their own children and two carers (3%) had been in care when they were children. Ten carers (15%) said that their primary reason was that they wanted a job they could do at home and needed an income. Some of these carers had either left work because of ill-health or had been made redundant; others needed to earn an income but, at the same time, wanted to remain at home to look after their own children, and in one case, an elderly relative.

In most cases, when carers were part of a couple, both partners had wanted to foster, but in nine instances one carer primarily wanted to under-take the work whilst the other carer was initially less committed. In 60% of couple carers, the fostering task was regarded primarily as the woman's role and in some instances the male partner or husband played no part at all.

Indeed, one man had difficulty recalling the names of the children currently living in the household.

Carers employed as specialist teenage foster carers or mainstream carers

Just over a third (38%) of the foster carers were employed as mainstream foster carers, whilst 62% looked after young people under the terms of a specialist teenage fostering scheme. The specialist foster carers more often looked after black and minority ethnic children than their mainstream counterparts and more of their fostered children showed behavioural disturbance on the Strengths and Difficulties Questionnaire.

Education, experience and qualifications

Of the main carers and their partners for whom we had this information, 45% (37) had no formal educational qualifications. Thirty per cent of the carers (25) were educated to GCSE or 'O' level, 12% of the carers (10) to 'A' level, 6 had an NVQ (National Vocational Qualification), one had a HND (Higher National Diploma), 2 had a first degree and one, a higher degree.

Many of the carers brought to fostering considerable experience and sometimes qualifications from their working lives. In all, over half the main carers (56%) had work experience or qualifications relevant to looking after adolescents: experience that included social work, youth work of various kinds, teaching and counselling. In addition, almost one in five of the main foster carers (19%) had personal experience of losing a parent early in life or had suffered some form of abuse in their own childhood. Thirteen per cent had also had personal experience of the care system, having been in care or having a sibling or another relative who had been looked after.

The majority were very experienced carers with 82% having previously fostered four or more children. One in ten had also fostered informally for many years before entering the world of fostering for the local authority. Nevertheless, 18% were less experienced and had looked after three or fewer foster children previously. For two of the carers this was their first placement. Far from receiving less problematic young people, the adolescents placed with the two new carers had particularly difficult behaviour.

Training

Training prior to their first foster placement

Prior to their first placement, three-quarters (37) of the 50 main carers, who completed the relevant section of the questionnaire, had had local authority training of between 4 and 80 hours whilst approval for fostering was awaited. The mean length of training pre-approval was 22 hours but a quarter had received no training at this stage.

Recent training

Just over two-thirds (69%) of the 54 carers who completed the questionnaires had had some training in the 12 months prior to interview, although the remainder had had none. They had participated in between 2 and 70 hours of training during that time. The mean number of hours of training was 25. In most instances, training courses for foster carers included other workers such as social workers, although few courses included the foster carers' children.

Satisfaction with training

The majority of the main carers (87%) were either satisfied or very satisfied overall with the training they had received and 90% regarded the quality and relevance of the training as either satisfactory or very satisfactory.

Type of training received

Foster carers were asked whether they had received training on a wide range of training issues relevant to looking after teenagers in care. Some carers found it difficult, for a variety of reasons, to attend training events provided by the local authority, for example, because of lack of child sitters or transport difficulties. Furthermore, some carers were relatively new to fostering and had therefore not attended a wide range of training courses to date.

A substantial proportion of carers had attended training on some key topic areas (see Table 4.10). However, a large number of carers had not received training in areas that, one could argue, are very important in caring for young people within this age group. In particular, nearly half the main carers had had no training in dealing with depressed children and even fewer had attended training in dealing with young people who are withdrawn or suicidal. Similarly, approximately half of the carers had no training in dealing with young people who sexually abuse others or are aggressive. One carer commented:

Table 4.10 Local authority or agency training received by main foster carers

Training	Percentage of carers
Sexually abused children	82
Dealing with difficult behaviour	80
Safe caring	79
Sexuality	78
Physically abused children	77
The role of foster carers	75
Dealing with discrimination	74
Contact with birth family	74
Substance abuse	73
HIV/AIDS	71
Dealing with parents	70
The Children Act 1989	69
Local authority procedures	68
Loss and separation	67
Discipline	67
Child development	63
Letting children go	61
Allegations	60
Dealing with schools	60
Self-harming behaviour	60
Health care and first aid	59
Delinquency	58
Depressed children	55
Children who sexually abuse others	53
Children who are physically aggressive	46
Withdrawn children	45
Suicidal children	36
Disabled children	35

The training which I have undertaken was the general pre-approval foster care training. The reality of fostering young individuals has highlighted the great need foster carers have for more in-depth training specifically in the following areas – counselling skills, dealing with deliberate self-harm, anger management, physically/sexually abused individuals.

Another carer echoed this and said:

Training needs to focus on the day-to-day issues that are faced by foster carers i.e. occupying children who have no school placement, emotionally damaged children, loss and separation etc.

It is not clear from this information whether courses covering these issues had been provided by the local authority and not attended by these foster carers or whether courses on these topics had not been offered to them. As mentioned previously, some local authorities offered little training whilst some carers were either unable to attend training or did not feel the need to participate. One couple for instance said:

[We do not] see the need for foster carer groups or training. [There are] lots of meetings and courses but we don't get involved in that. Don't see the value of going to meetings to find out how to bring up children when you've brought up your own.

Single carers were significantly less likely than couple carers to have undertaken a range of training courses. The majority of single carers faced multiple difficulties in attending training which included child care difficulties, transport problems or training times clashing with work commitments.

Significantly more of the specialist than the mainstream carers had received high levels of training in the previous year.

Expectations and reality

Forty-five per cent of the foster carers had felt prepared for their first placement, 17% said they had not felt at all prepared, whilst 38% had not been sure what to expect. The reality of fostering turned out to be much as expected for three fifths (62%) of the carers. However, a fifth (22%) of the carers said that it was worse – including one who said she had expected to be looking after children who had no parent or carer temporarily as a result of a hospital admission or similar situation. A further 13% of carers said that it was better than they had thought it would be and two others said they had had no pre-conceived ideas about what it would be like.

How foster carers regarded their role

Few of the foster carers in the sample regarded their role with looked-after young people to be one of a substitute parent, although 12% did see their role in this way. For most, their task was seen as providing a family role model that was different from the one the children were used to (21%); to prepare young people for independence (20%) or to provide stability, security and a home whilst it was needed (18%). Other foster carers (12%) said that their role was to help the young person change their behaviour, and a few (9%) had not thought about their role. Two carers said their role was as a 'counsellor', another two, 'whatever they want me to be' and one to provide shared care with the birth parent.

Now that we have looked at the characteristics of the young people and the families to which they went, we turn to consider the planning and preparation that was made for the placements.

Chapter Five

Planning and Preparation for the Placements

A number of studies have suggested that lack of preparation for placement handicaps carers and may relate to less stable placements. We were therefore interested to examine the preparation provided to the placements in the study and to see if it affected the outcomes.

The social workers

At the beginning of the study we conducted telephone interviews with 67 of the 68 social workers who had responsibility for the young people in the study. Three-quarters were women and ten worked part-time. Just under half of the workers (48%) were responsible for children in six or more foster families and this included 16% who were supporting children in more than ten such placements. Amongst those who were involved with fewer looked-after children, over a third (37%) had responsibility for three to five foster placements and 15% visited one to two.

Over half of the social workers reported that they were working under heavy pressure and well over a third were under some pressure. Only one in ten said that they were working under little or no pressure. There were no significant differences between the authorities in the study in respect of the levels of supervision provided or the pressure under which practitioners were working.

At the 12-month follow-up point there had been a change of social worker in half of the placements. Four of the young people had had two changes of social worker and five, by this time, had no allocated worker.

Making the placements

The social workers said that almost two-thirds of the placements were made in an emergency and a third were planned. As Table 5.1 shows, the foster placements in the study were made as planned placements from care in a quarter of the cases, but such planning for adolescents admitted from their families was rare. The largest group of young people had emergency placements from home (38%) as a result of abuse, neglect or difficult behaviour and over a quarter (27%) were moved in an emergency from one care placement to another.

Table 5.1 Circumstances of the placements		
	Number	*Percentage*
Emergency admission from home	24	38
Emergency admission from breakdown of care placement	17	27
Planned placement from care	17	26
Planned placement from home	6	9
Total	64	100

No information on 3 cases

However, when asked in more detail it became clear that in some of the emergency admissions from home and care there was time for some planning. As can be seen in Table 5.2 the young people's social workers reported that over a third of the placements were made in a true emergency, that is that the workers had less than 48 hours' notice of the child's need to move. In another 17% of cases the workers had notice of between two days and one week whereas in as many as 45% of cases the placements were known about for more than a week. There was, therefore, an encouraging opportunity to prepare the young people and the carers for the placement in just under half of the cases.

THE CARERS' WILLINGNESS TO ACCEPT THE PLACEMENT

Carers were asked whether they had wanted to accept the young people at the time of placement. Almost three-quarters of the carers said that they had wished to accept the young person and that neither carer had had any hesitation about doing so. However, more than a quarter (27%) said they had

	Number	Percentage
Table 5.2 Planned or emergency placements		
Emergency placement	24	36
Short planned placement	11	17
Planned placement	30	45
SSD did not make the placement	1	2
Total	66	100

No information on 1 case

accepted the placement under pressure or that one or both of them had had concerns about the young person being placed with their family. Such reluctance to accept a young person was linked to foster carer strain during the placement which was, in turn, related to less effective parenting and poorer outcomes.

MEETING THE CARERS BEFORE GOING TO THE PLACEMENT

One in five (13) of the 66 young people already knew their foster carers, either through having stayed with them previously or through their existing social networks. However, for those who did not know their carers, only just over a quarter (26%) had the opportunity to meet them more than once before they moved in. Fifteen (28%) met their new carers once, whilst almost half (46%) did not meet their carers at all before moving to the placement.

A number of young people and foster carers talked about the need for meeting and getting to know each other before the placement was made. For example, one young person said:

> You should have more meetings before you move in, and to stay for the weekend and see if you'll get on.

Another said:

> Social workers should let you see the placement first, then if you don't like it you don't have to move in. The social worker tells you a bit and then takes you there straight away so you don't really get a chance to see if you like it.

One foster carer suggested a return to the system that was in place when he first became a foster carer:

> You originally had three or four weeks to get to know the child before making any decisions. You should have reception homes so you could get to know the kids before they moved in.

Unsurprisingly, significantly fewer young people who were placed in an emergency were able to meet the foster carers prior to the placement, although four did so. However, not all of those whose placements were known about for more than a week were given the opportunity to meet with the foster carers prior to the placement. If the young person cannot meet the foster family before moving in, it is important to provide the young person with at least some information about the foster placement beforehand.

The information given to the young people about the placements before they moved
The importance of giving up-to-date and accurate information about the young person to the foster carers prior to a new placement has been well documented. However, the need to give young people information about the foster carers has been given less attention. Children are always likely to find it difficult to move to a new placement, but this will be heightened if little is known about the people who live there. Having some idea of who lives in the household and what it is going to be like could reduce anxiety prior to the move.

The young people were asked if they were given any information about the new foster family before they moved in. Of the 53 young people who did not already know the foster carers and who answered the question, a worrying three-fifths (62%) said that they were given little or no prior information about the foster family (including 8 who had no information) and over a third (38%) received a moderate or large amount of information.

One young person said:

> I would like to have known more about Mary and Dan before I came here.

Another said:

> They should tell you a bit about it [the foster placement] before they just dump you there.

Placements in which the young person felt that they had been given adequate information about the foster carers and their family before the move had fewer disruptions, but this may have been partly because these were also the placements that young people wanted to be in and in some cases they already knew the carers. Nonetheless, young people emphasised that they considered it important to have advance information about the details of the people who lived in the family and about the family rules that they could expect. This is an area of practice that could easily be improved. A start could be made by ensuring that family placement workers supply regularly updated profiles of foster families for social workers to share with children.

The information given to the foster carers before the placement started

Given the importance in the literature accorded to preparation for placement, we were interested to see how much information the foster carers received about the young people before they arrived. We asked how well informed the carers had been about 16 different areas of information about the children. As can be seen in Table 5.3 the carers considered that they had had insufficient information about the emotional needs and education plans of a third or more of the young people, about the long-term plans, expected length of stay, the young person's behaviour, health and school attendance in between a quarter and a third of cases and about contact in one in five cases.

Other issues about which the foster carers were poorly informed included the young people's previous placements in care (16%), any previous counselling or other help provided (26%), the children's birth family and the children's birth parents (18%), and the cultural and religious backgrounds of the young people (25%). Given Farmer and Pollock's findings (1998) about the low levels of information passed to caregivers about sexual abuse or sexually abusing behaviour in the past we also asked specifically about this. Nine out of thirty-two carers (28%) who saw this as relevant had not been given the information they needed about sexual abuse in the young people's backgrounds and this was also the case for 9 out of 27 (33%) carers where sexually abusing behaviour was concerned. We also found that 6 out of 26 (23%) carers did not know when the last statutory medical health check on the young person had been carried out. In eight cases recommendations had been made, seven of which the carers were expected to follow up. In two cases these had not been acted on.

Overall, 40% of the carers told us that there was information that they needed which they did not have before the placement started. Almost a quarter (24%) considered that the information they had been given about the young people had not been accurate and up to date. One in five of the carers was overall dissatisfied or very dissatisfied with the information they had received. There were no statistically significant relationships between these gaps in information and whether the placement was made in an emergency or was planned. It appeared therefore that these deficiencies in information giving cannot be blamed on the fact that a proportion of placements were made at short notice.

Typical comments from the foster carers were:

We needed information on education, special needs, relationships with peers, siblings etc. and on anger management, plans to deal with low self-esteem, loss and separation. This appears to be standard practice now, to place young people within foster homes with the minimum of information. We consider this to be dangerous practice by a social services department.

After several weeks the social worker found out that Mark had supposedly sexually abused his brother and social services had been involved with this. This type of information should always be given when placing a child.

The information we needed was about educational problems, lack of concentration. We did not receive information that part of the reason why Maxine was in care was due to her parents' fascination with the occult and horror. Also we weren't told about problems with enuresis and nightmares.

This was an emergency placement so very little information was given. I never did receive the appropriate information on this child.

I had very little information on Nina. Needed details on how to care for a self-abusing woman and what to do! All I received was half a dozen lines on a piece of paper, although I did know it was an emergency placement.

To what extent do you agree that you received the information you needed about these issues?	Strongly Agree and Agree		Strongly Disagree and Disagree		Not Applicable or No Response
	Number	%	Number	%	Number
Emotional needs	35	61	22	39	11
Education or work plans	37	67	18	33	13
Background of sexually abusing behaviour	18	67	9	33	41
Special educational needs	34	68	16	32	18
Long-term plans	38	69	17	31	13
Expected length of stay	39	70	17	30	12
School attendance and progress	40	70	17	30	11
Plans for day-to-day care	40	71	16	29	12
Young person's behaviour	41	71	17	29	10
Background of sexual abuse	23	72	9	28	36
Young person's health	42	74	15	26	11
Counselling or other help	35	74	12	26	21
Cultural and religious background	41	75	14	25	13
Contact arrangements	44	81	10	19	14
Birth family	46	82	10	18	12
Previous care placements	37	84	7	16	24

Table 5.3 Information given to the foster carers before the placement

Note: Percentages in each column are of responses made or of those which are applicable.

The more experienced carers had developed the habit of telephoning other carers to seek information about young people before accepting a new placement, as they had found that social workers could not be trusted to give them full information. Indeed, one had been told by her worker, 'As a social worker it's our job to sell the child to you.' One foster carer said:

> I wish we had a little bit more knowledge about the backgrounds of these children. Sometimes we get a brief outline and then we find out later on. We learn a tremendous amount from other foster carers. We will ring up and they say: 'Did they tell you…?' 'No… They didn't tell me that one.'

There were significantly more disruptions when foster carers were not given adequate information about the young person's school attendance and progress, the plans for their education or employment or about the plans for their long-term care. The same deficiencies in information were significantly related to less successful placements as was a lack of information about the young person's health. Whilst there was a tendency for social workers to give less information about the children with the more disturbed behaviour, this alone did not explain these outcomes. It therefore seems that there are aspects of preparation that are extremely important. The lack of information given to carers led in some cases to high risk adolescents being placed in situations where they posed considerable sexual risks to other children in the family. Without prior knowledge about this, carers had been unable to take steps to keep their own (or visiting) children safe (see also Farmer and Pollock 1999b).

A particularly pertinent finding was that there were significantly fewer placement breakdowns when the young people had been no more difficult to manage than the carers had expected. This suggests that within certain parameters foster carers may be able to manage difficult adolescents as long as they take them with full knowledge of their difficulties.

Finding a placement

In over a third of the cases (35%) the social workers had had no difficulty in finding a placement for the young person. However, the young person's behaviour had made it hard to find a suitable placement for almost a quarter of them (23%) and this was significantly more often the case for boys than girls. For a further 31% of the young people the difficulties in placement finding were internal to the social services department concerned, such as a severe shortage in placements for all adolescents.

Choice of placement

A choice of possible placements had been available in only just over a quarter (28%) of cases and most of these involved boys. For the great majority (72%) no alternative placements were available. One social worker admitted he had been unable to take the young person's needs into consideration because of the lack of placements:

> I just could not find a placement. I know ideally I should take her needs into account, but I was so desperate I would have taken a place anywhere.

Another social worker said:

> It's gone past the days of being able to match a young person with a placement – it's just a question of finding a bed.

One young person said:

> They [Social Services] should have alternative placements lined up for young people so that if they are unhappy where they are they can be moved immediately, without having to stay there for another week.

The participants' understanding of the plans for the placement

In terms of the selection criteria for the sample it was not surprising to find that the social workers intended that for half of the young people the placement would be a long-term home. As Table 5.4 shows, for 12% it was to function as preparation for independent living and for another 8% it was to be short term while things were sorted out. The placements had a variety of other purposes, including to provide assessment, as preparation for another placement, to help the young person to change and to give the parents a break. It is worth noting how rarely placements were intended to assist in making reunification possible.

The foster carers' understanding of the care plans

It was interesting to find that the foster carers' understanding of these plans looked rather different. In a remarkable two-thirds (68%) of the cases the carers' understanding of the plans for the child did not match those of the social workers. Whereas the social workers viewed 5 of the placements as short term, the carers believed that this was the plan for 15 of these young

Table 5.4 Social workers' views of the purpose of the placements

Placement purpose	Number	Percentage
Long-term home	34	51
Preparation for independent living	8	12
Short-term home while things are sorted out	5	8
Help reunite young person and family	5	8
Preparation for another placement	4	6
Period of assessment	3	4
Help young person to change	2	2
Give parents a break	1	1
Other	5	8
Total	67	100

people. It was not surprising then to find that whilst the social workers viewed 34 of the placements as a long-term home the carers had only understood that they were offering a long-term placement to 23 young people. In almost one in five cases (18%) the carers did not know the plans for the child. Discrepancies of this sort could have arisen in a number of ways, but it did emerge in the interviews that some of the social workers had presented young people to the foster carers as a short-term prospect whilst hoping and indeed planning that they would stay long term.

Our research shows that adequate preparation can make a real difference to outcomes. When foster carers and social workers had the same view of the placement plans there were fewer disruptions and fewer carers felt under strain.

The young peoples' understanding of the care plans

The young people themselves, however, seemed even less clear about the purpose of the placement or about how long it was intended to last. Over a third (35%) of the young people did not know how long the placement was supposed to last, which left them with a considerable degree of uncertainty.

This suggests the need for fuller communication between social workers and young people.

Suitability of the placements

In spite of the lack of choices available, the placements found had been considered by the social workers as very suitable in over half of the cases and fairly suitable in just under a third. In only 9% of the cases was the placement considered fairly or very unsuitable for the young person, for example because the young person was placed at a considerable distance from their school and community, or with children of a similar age.

Expectations about the duration of the placements

The majority of placements were expected by social workers to last until the young person was independent (68%), with only 13% expected to last less than six months. The social workers' expectations about the duration of the remaining 19% of placements varied from over six months to more than two years.

The foster carers were often in the dark about how long the placement was intended to last. Almost a quarter (24%) of the carers did not know how long the young person was meant to be living with them. Carers also talked about not being given information directly.

One said:

> No one tells you what the plan is. We take it that he's here until he's 18. Social Services call it long term – just in conversations.

This suggests that more direct communication to foster carers about placement plans is needed.

The involvement of the young people and their parents in placement decisions

There was considerable variation in the extent to which the young people and their parents were involved in discussions about the placement before it was made. Parents had been involved in the plans in only a third of the cases (37%) and it was the black and minority ethnic parents who were most often excluded. The placement was discussed with them in only one of the twelve cases (8%) compared to 43% of white parents (see also Barn 1993). In only just under a third (31%) of cases had the social worker discussed the proposed placement with all the key players, that is, the young people, their parents and the foster carers; in 21% the move had been discussed with the young people and the foster carers whilst in 9% of cases the placement had not been discussed with any of them. In the remainder, the placement had been discussed with other combinations of the participants or with one participant alone, as Table 5.5 shows.

Table 5.5 The involvement of the foster carers, young people and their parents in discussions about the placement

Level of involvement	Number	Percentage
Discussed with all	21	31
Discussed with the young person and foster carers	14	21
No discussion	6	9
Discussed with the foster carers	3	5
Discussed with the young person and parents	2	3
Discussed with the young person	1	1
Discussed with the parents	1	1
Discussed with the foster carers and parents	1	1
Was not the social worker then	19	28
Total	68	100

The social workers said that the young people had been involved in the discussions in 78% (38 of 49) of the cases in which they had been the responsible worker at that time. However, the young people themselves felt much more excluded from the planning and decision making. Thirty per cent of the young people said that they had not been consulted at all about the move, and over half (52%) said they had only been briefly consulted about it. It may be that the young people felt that their role in any discussions or meetings was a passive one or that they had been unable to influence what was happening (see also Lipscombe 2003b). The young people frequently emphasised the need for social workers to listen to their views:

Social workers should involve young people in review meetings and make sure they have a voice in decisions made about them.

Social Services need to start talking and listening to kids in care. They shouldn't just read the files and then assume they know what the problems are. They should ask the young person as things may have changed. They should listen to their needs rather than dictating them.

Commitment to the placement

The young people were asked whether they wanted to be in this particular placement or not. Whilst almost three-quarters of the young people said that they did want to be in the placement, one in five said they would rather be at home, and four said they would rather be somewhere else entirely, such as living in their own flat or with friends.

The foster carers' commitment was greater, with 85% considered by the social workers to be fully committed and only one not at all committed, whilst the carers' own children were thought to have commendably high levels of involvement with two-thirds being seen as fully committed to the placements. However, 11 social workers admitted that they did not know what the foster carers' children thought about the placement. The birth parents were seen as showing less enthusiasm for the placements. Only just over a third (36%) were seen as fully committed to what had happened and one in five (20%) were not at all committed to the placements working. Interestingly, the parents of boys were considered to be more fully committed to the placements than those of girls. This was partly because parents were often committed to the placements of young people who were admitted because they were beyond control (mostly boys) and rarely committed when the admission was because of sexual abuse (all girls).

Long-term plans

Over a third of the young people were expected to move to live independently after this placement. Almost a quarter were considered likely to return home, and 11% were expected to move to another foster home. None of the young people were thought likely to go into a children's home. Other plans had been made for six young people including, in one case, going to live with friends. For 15 (22%) of the young people, no long-term plans had been made. Return to parents was more often considered for the boys than the girls, partly because the largest group of planned returns were in respect of young people looked after because they were beyond parental control (7 out of 13) and most children in this category were boys.

One of the young people commented on the need for more consideration to be given to long-term plans so that preparation for independent living could begin earlier:

> You need much more time to plan for leaving care, not just in the last few months before it happens.

What the social workers did during the placements

Visiting frequency

During the placements in our study 85% of the social workers reported that they visited the young people *alone* monthly or more often, including 22% who said that they visited weekly. Seventy-nine per cent of the workers said that they visited both the carers and the young people monthly or more often, with 13% visiting weekly. Almost all the workers also made contact in other ways, for example by telephone. These findings were interesting in view of the criticisms of some of the foster carers about absent social workers and unreliable visiting. However, one explanation is that only a minority of the social workers (22%) saw their primary role as supporting both the foster carers and the young people, with many more (61%) seeing their role as supporting just the young people. A minority conceived the role as principally one of case coordination (12%) or managing statutory requirements (5%).

The social workers' views of their help to the young people

The social workers with whom we spoke had a variety of views of how they had best been able to help the young people. Twenty-one per cent thought that this had been through moving them to a safe environment, 17% through their availability and 16% through organising services. The remainder of the responses included listening and understanding, forming a positive relationship with the young person, keeping them informed, communicating with the family, acting as the child's advocate, challenging their behaviour and helping to arrange suitable education.

The social workers' contact with birth families

A third of the social workers were in touch with the birth parents less often than monthly and 12% had no contact at all. However, almost half (49%) of the social workers said that they were in touch more often than once a month. More frequent contact (monthly or more often) was made with the parents of the younger adolescents (under the age of 14½). We were also interested to discover how often the practitioners undertook any work with the parents. The majority of the social workers (61%) were doing no work with family members but 39% were working with one or both of the parents, with most working with just the birth mother.

The social workers' views of the placements

The great majority of the social workers were very positive about the placements and 91% thought that the child's main needs were being met. They pointed to the main benefits of the placements as the provision of stability (23%), nurture (18%), clear boundaries (15%), clear boundaries and nurture (28%) and also separation from the birth family, the carers' commitment to the young person and the experience of a 'normal' family.

Well over half of the social workers (57%) thought that there were no shortcomings in the current placement. The shortcomings that were described included lack of boundaries or nurture, lack of a male role model, bedroom sharing, the distance from school, other children in the household, the carers' negative view of the birth parents and insufficient independence given to the young person. The foster carers were credited with a variety of parenting skills, including providing patience, honesty and openness, nurture, support, security, humour, gradually increasing autonomy, someone in whom the young person could confide and showing commitment. Their parenting skills were seen as very well matched with the young people's needs in 82% of cases and the match was seen as particularly good with the younger adolescents.

Thirty-nine per cent of the social workers reported considerable improvements in the young people since the placement had started and 45% some improvement. Only 14% saw a mixed picture or no change and just one reported a deterioration. In line with this, well over half of the social workers reported no difficulties with the placements. The difficulties mentioned included those between the young person and other children in the placement and difficulties with school, problems with friends or in relationships with the foster carers and also difficulties with the birth family.

Specialist and social work help for the young people

Over half of the young people (52%) had seen a specialist professional for help before the placement. Almost a quarter (23%) had seen a clinical psychologist, 11% a counsellor and the remainder had consulted educational psychologists, psychiatrists, family counsellors or a number of these professionals. The proportion who were seeing a specialist during the placement dropped to 37% of the young people. As a result of this help at both stages, 6% of the young people were thought by the social workers to have changed a lot for the better and 53% a bit for the better. Over a third (35%) were not thought to have changed.

The social workers themselves had worked with a quarter of the young people before the placement and since the move this proportion had risen to a third. In addition, they had arranged services for just under half of them but had been unable to provide the appropriate service or were still waiting for a resource for 12% of them. In addition, five young people had refused a service and for a quarter no services had been thought to be necessary.

When asked how much difference their help was making to the foster carers, over half (52%) of the social workers thought that it helped to keep them going, while another third thought that their help was not much used but that the carers managed well without it. These findings are shown in Table 5.6 below:

Table 5.6 Social workers' views of the impact of their help on the foster carers		
Social Workers' views	Number	Percentage
Help well used and it helps to keep the carers going	31	52
Help well used, but carers would be fine without it	9	15
Help not much used but carers fine without it	20	33
Total	60	100

No information on 7 cases

In relation to the young people 72% of the social workers thought that their assistance made a real difference to the young person, whilst 25% thought that their help was not much used by the young person and, of these, that 7% of the young people were struggling to cope.

Overall then, the interviews with the social workers suggested that they were fairly positive about the foster care placements and were sanguine about the help which they themselves were providing. However, in practice there were serious gaps in the information given to carers about the young people and this was related to poorer outcomes. The strong message for practitioners is that it is vitally important to share fully with the carers all the information they have about young people before placements start and that this has an impact on the progress of the placements. There is also a need to involve young people more in placement decisions and to give them more information and contact with foster carers before a new placement is made. The foster carers' views of the support provided by the social workers proved to be very different from those of the social workers as will be shown in the chapters that follow.

Now that the preparation for placements has been described, we look in the next chapter at what happened when the young people arrived.

Chapter Six

The Young People's Behaviour in the Placements

In this chapter, the young people's behaviour in the placements will be discussed, as will the effect that they had on other children in the family. The educational provision made for the young people and their peer relationships will also be explored. The chapter will also look at changes in the young people's behaviour by follow-up and the impact of their behaviour on placement outcomes.

Foster family relationships

Relationships with the foster carers

At the time of the first interview, 18% of the young people said that they were not settled or were only beginning to settle into the placement, with 82% feeling settled or very settled. Those who were less settled in the foster family had a significantly increased chance of placement disruption by follow-up. Four-fifths (81%) of the young people said that they felt close to the main carer at this stage.

However, by follow-up, the relationship between more than a quarter of the young people (26%) and their carers had deteriorated markedly, with the relationship between a further 15% having got slightly worse. There was no change in the relationship for a quarter of the young people and their carers, whilst 12% experienced some improvement and 22% experienced a marked improvement in this relationship.

Young people who had abnormal or borderline total scores on the SDQ, measuring behaviour, were more likely than others to experience a deterioration in their relationship with the carers ($p<0.05$). Not surprisingly, there was a close relationship between good outcomes and situations where the quality of the relationship between the carers and the young person had improved or stayed the same.

Relationships with other young people in the family

Twenty-seven (48%) of the 56 young people living with other children who were interviewed said that they shared very few activities with the other children in the household. In some instances this was due to the large age difference between them (for example, a 16-year-old foster child placed with carers' own children aged 4 and 5), but in six cases the young people reported being excluded by other children in the family. From the accounts of the foster carers one in five of the young people were excluded by other children in the family, and a third excluded themselves from them.

The best relationship the young person had within the household was seen by the carers as being with either another foster child (33%) or with one of their own children (31%). However, in 11 cases (16%), the worst relationship was considered to be with another foster child. Some young people had very good relationships with other children of the same age within the family, sharing activities, helping each other and confiding in each other. However, others did find it hard to get along with young people of their own age, including a 15-year-old boy who was placed with a 14-year-old fostered girl, even though he had requested not to be placed with other children of his age.

The findings of the study show the close link between placement outcome and the impact of the fostered adolescents on the carers' own children (see also for example Quinton et al. 1998; Triseliotis 1989) and other fostered young people. By the time of the follow-up interviews (Table 6.1) the number of young people who had a negative or very negative impact on other children in the family had risen from 4 to 28. Only one instead of ten was by then thought to have had little impact. Those young people who by follow-up had emerged as having a negative impact on the other children in the placement had poorer outcomes on both of our outcome measures (see also Chapter 11).

Not surprisingly, young people who had medium to high levels of behaviour difficulties often had an adverse effect on other children in the family. Moreover, the emergence of new difficult behaviours and demonstration of high risk sexual behaviour (adolescents who put themselves sexually at risk) were related to a greater risk of placement disruption, primarily because of the negative impact these behaviours had on other children in the household.

Table 6.1 The impact of the fostered young people on other children in the household by follow-up

	Number	Percentage
Young person had a very positive impact	2	3
Young person had a positive impact	31	50
Young person had little impact	1	2
Young person had a negative impact	20	32
Young person had a very negative impact	8	13
Total	62	100

$n = 62$
No information on 6 cases

The analysis at follow-up identified two other behavioural changes that were related independently to both placement disruption and to an adverse effect on other children in the household. These were deteriorating peer relationships (that is young people who became involved in negative peer groups or who had noticeably fewer friends by follow-up) and behaviour that worsened during the course of the placement. When either of these occurred in combination with the adolescent having a negative impact on other children in the family there was an increased risk of placement disruption. However, when young people had a positive impact on the other children in the fostering household, worsening peer relationships or behaviour did not significantly relate to disruption. Thus, it appears that foster carers may be able to cope with a certain range of difficult behaviours as long as their own (or other fostered children) are not badly affected.

It was interesting to find that when, by follow-up, young people had had a negative impact on other children in the placement, foster carers had shown poorer parenting to them in a number of ways. They liked these adolescents less, they showed more aggression in their attempts to discipline them, lower levels of warmth and commitment and had less control over their behaviour. Carers had also made less effort to assist with the friendships of these young people.

Favouritism

Of the 56 young people fostered in a placement with other young people, only two (4%) thought that the foster carers treated their own children more favourably than they did the fostered young people. This was particularly evident for Tiffany who had to do her own washing and ironing whilst the foster carer's daughter, Amy, who was the same age, did not. Tiffany also thought that it was unfair that the foster carer's own children received extravagant Christmas presents whilst Tiffany was given a cheap nightdress and that the foster carer refused to take Tiffany to singing lessons until Amy said that she wanted to go as well.

The young person's behaviour

The carers were asked to give a detailed picture of the behavioural and emotional difficulties presented by the young people, both within the home and outside the placement. The problems described have been broadly categorised below according to the type of difficulty (for example, conduct disorder or emotional difficulty), and the severity and frequency of the episodes (Table 6.2).

Table 6.2 Frequency and severity of behavioural and emotional difficulties reported by the carers as occurring within or outside the home

Problem category	Minor, infrequent	Serious, infrequent	Minor, frequent	Serious, frequent	Total
Conduct problems	62	39	51	27	179
Emotional problems	21	18	13	3	55
Overactivity	11	0	14	5	30
Sexualised behaviours	1	3	1	3	8
Total	95	60	79	38	272

Conduct problems

The number of young people who showed specific conduct difficulties is shown in Table 6.3. The most frequently occurring behaviours were disobedience, defiance, uncooperativeness and lying.

Table 6.3 Types of conduct difficulties demonstrated within the home

Type of behaviour	Number of young people demonstrating behaviour		Total
	Girls	Boys	
Uncooperativeness	12	14	28
Defiance	12	15	27
Lying	16	10	26
Disobedience	10	14	24
Running away	13	8	21
Theft	8	6	14
Aggression	5	9	14
Soiling	1	0	1
Animal cruelty	0	0	0

Nineteen (28%) young people showed no difficult behaviours within the home, 20 (30%) showed only one or two difficult behaviours. No young people demonstrated all nine conduct difficulties, but two (3%) showed six types of behavioural difficulty, and two showed seven (Figure 6.1).

The range of behaviours covered also included verbal and physical aggression or assault outside the placement (3 and 4 young people, respectively), and more serious criminal offences such as theft (8 young people), taking a motor vehicle without the owner's consent (TWOC) (1 young person), vandalism (4 young people), breaking and entering (3 young people), and fire-setting (1 young person). No young people were reported to have been involved in cruelty towards animals, although the examination of the case file records revealed that at least two young people had been previously.

The young people who had been rated as demonstrating high behavioural difficulties prior to the placement were significantly more likely to be disobedient once there than others and were also more likely to lie or run away. Previous exclusion from school was significantly related to young people being more disobedient ($p = 0.008$), defiant ($p = 0.001$) and uncooperative ($p<0.001$) in the placement, although these differences were not related to current exclusion from school.

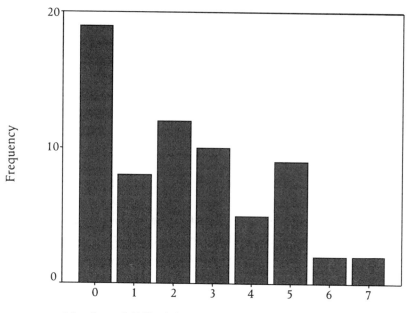

Figure 6.1 Number of types of difficult behaviour shown by the young person within the home

Changes in the young people's behaviour (at home, school and outside the home) were measured at the follow-up stage. There was a marked improvement in behaviour for some young people (37%), a corresponding deterioration for others (35%) and maintenance of problems for a few (12%). A small number (16%) maintained problem-free behaviour throughout the placement.

Conduct problems in the placement at the first interviews predicted poor outcomes at follow-up. Not surprisingly, young people whose behaviour worsened also had an increased risk of poor outcome on both of our outcome measures (disruption and success). Deterioration in behaviour however was much less common among those young people who had high levels of emotional problems on the SDQ. (This sub-scale includes questions about whether the child has somatic symptoms, many worries, is often unhappy or fearful, shows anxiety or lack of confidence.) On the other hand, behavioural deterioration was more common among young people who had a history of disruptive behaviour at home or outside the home and was associated with having links with a negative peer group.

New difficult behaviours

A quarter of the young people showed a new type of difficult behaviour during the placement. For example, Zoe started to lie about herself and her history, making up stories apparently to attract attention and sympathy for herself, for example, telling people that she had suffered a miscarriage. She also demonstrated some potentially dangerous behaviour (for instance removing the rubber sealant from around the oven door) which the foster carer struggled to understand, although she thought it might be because Zoe wanted more drama and excitement in her life. Two young people began to abscond from their placements, and at least three began to take drugs (substance abuse is discussed in more detail below).

The emergence of new behavioural difficulties was significantly related to poor outcomes, in part because of the impact this behaviour had on other children in the placement. Young people who demonstrated new behavioural difficulties often had a history prior to this move of truanting and non-attendance at school and had become involved in more negative peer relationships by the second interview.

Emotional difficulties

Emotional difficulties included episodes of depression, problems with sleeping and eating, self-harm and suicide attempts. Carers reported that two-thirds (45) of the young people experienced episodes of depression, that three had caused themselves deliberate self-harm and that three had made at least one suicide attempt. Young people who had experienced violence within their family, either as a victim or as a witness, were significantly more likely than others to have episodes of depression ($p = 0.046$).

However, self-harming behaviour often was not known to the carers – eleven young people admitted to having self-harmed recently and nine as having made suicide attempts as compared with the three incidents of each which the carers knew about (see also Farmer and Pollock 1998). About a third of the carers had had no training in dealing with suicidal or self-harming behaviour in adolescents, which might have increased their level of awareness and knowledge of the signs to look for.

In addition, problems with eating were reported by half of the carers, ranging from being a fussy eater to showing signs of anorexia or bulimia (2 young people). Some carers thought that issues around food might be related to previous experience of neglect, for example, young people who ate excessively or took food from the cupboards and hid it in their rooms.

Difficulties with sleeping were reported by 20 carers, such as nightmares (3 young people), bed-wetting (1 young person) and difficulties in falling asleep (13 young people) and three could only sleep with the light on.

Aggression

Nineteen (28%) of the young people had been physically aggressive to other children or adults during the placement. Ben, for example, twice brutally attacked the foster carers' eight-year-old son, hitting and kicking him. Ben also threw stones at the other children and became aggressive towards the foster carers. Of these 19 young people, the risk presented by 14 had increased during the course of the placement, for four the risk had decreased and for one the risk had stayed the same. The potential for aggression did not significantly relate to the likelihood of placement breakdown. However, it was significantly related to the success of the placement, with over half (55%) of those who were not physically aggressive experiencing successful placements compared with only a quarter (26%) of those who were ($p = 0.03$).

Young people who had previously been excluded from school were more likely than others to be physically aggressive ($p = 0.02$). Of course, some of these young people may have been excluded from school precisely because they had shown aggressive or violent behaviour.

Overactivity

The category of overactivity included difficulties in concentration, restlessness and distractibility and the carers considered these to be problematic for 30 (44%) of the young people. Only two (17%) of the minority ethnic and mixed-race parentage young people were seen as having problems with poor concentration and restlessness compared with 28 (51%) of white young people ($p = 0.03$).

Concentration problems included, for example, not being able to sit still, tapping the arms of the chairs and constantly flicking through the television channels, which could all prove irritating for the other members of the family. One carer described the 16-year-old boy she fostered as being 'like a dripping tap' which she found difficult to cope with. He found it difficult to sit still for more than a few minutes, and would jump up and rush off through the house, allowing doors to slam behind him. He needed constant reminding to do things, for example clearing up after he had eaten, and had to be 'nagged' to finish things he had started. This carer said it was easier to manage one big explosion of difficult behaviour than to deal with constant minor irritations.

Although foster carers were not reporting that hyperactivity had much effect on the family at the first interviews, by follow-up most had sought help from social services because they found these young people so difficult to contain.

At the first interviews 35% of the young people had hyperactivity scores in the abnormal range on the foster carers' SDQ questionnaires and this rose to almost half (47%) by the follow-up stage. Another 12% at the first and 13% at the follow-up stage scored in the borderline hyperactive range. Thus, by follow-up, as many as 60% of the young people had problems of hyperactivity. Hyperactive behaviour at the first interviews strongly predicted poor outcome by follow-up.

Sexualised behaviour

The sexualised behaviour category included inappropriate sexual behaviour such as openly masturbating and talking sexually (7 young people), and sexually abusing behaviour (1 young person at the first interview stage). The latter was a 13-year-old girl who had inappropriately touched a four-year-old girl whilst in the placement and who had a history of sexually abusive behaviour towards younger girls.

Two-thirds (66%, 45) of the carers had established specific house rules, in order to avoid the risk of any allegations being made against them. A few carers had additional safeguards to protect children in their households, particularly when the young person had demonstrated inappropriate sexual behaviour or was seen as being a risk to the other children. For example, the carers of a 12-year-old boy who had previously sexually abused two younger children had to install a downstairs toilet so that visiting children did not need to go upstairs. Another carer tried to arrange respite provision for the young person so that her grandchildren could visit safely but this was not agreed by social services. The grandchildren still came to visit but the carer felt she could not let them stay overnight.

One carer spoke about feeling shocked when she and her partner had to accompany the fostered boy to the police station. He had been charged with sexually assaulting a six-year-old child in his previous foster placement and had to attend the police station for fingerprinting and DNA testing. The carers felt that a social worker should have been with them at the police station.

By follow-up, five (7%) young people had put others at risk due to their sexual behaviour. For example, one 16-year-old boy, Joss, sexually abused a younger fostered boy whilst they were on holiday, and a 12-year-old boy,

Alan, exposed himself to a girl at school. Of these five, the risk presented by three young people had increased during the course of the placement. For one young person the risk had decreased and for one it had stayed the same.

Interestingly, young people who were a sexual risk to others were no more likely to experience disruptions or to have unsuccessful placements than those who were not.

Sexual risk to the young people

Thirteen (19%) of the young people were considered to be at risk due to their sexual behaviour, with significantly more girls (11) at risk than boys (2). The risk to the two boys decreased during the course of the placement whilst the risk to the girls stayed the same for four girls but increased for seven girls. For example, prior to the study placement, Wendy was in a relationship with a much older man. This relationship ended soon after the beginning of the placement and she started seeing an 18-year-old boy. Whilst still not ideal as Wendy was only 13, this relationship was safer for Wendy as it was monogamous and could be monitored by the foster carers. However, that relationship was short-lived and Wendy then became increasingly sexually active, having sexual intercourse with anyone she wanted. She started absconding from the placement so the carers were often unaware of where Wendy was or with whom. An ex-fostered girl told Wendy's carers that she had seen Wendy having sex with a middle-aged man at a bus stop. Wendy refused to attend her medical appointments to have contraceptive injections and contracted a number of sexually transmitted diseases. The placement ended as a result of Wendy's behaviour and she moved to another foster placement. Wendy has since been in contact with the study foster carers and told them that she is pregnant.

There were higher rates of disruption for the young people who were at risk due to their sexual behaviour. Seventy-three per cent (8) of those who were at such risk experienced a placement breakdown, compared with 38% (19) of those who were not ($p = 0.039$). Again, as with the young people showing a new type of difficult behaviour, the factor influencing disruptions appeared to be the negative impact that young people who were at risk had on other young people in the placement, rather than the fact that they were at risk *per se*. The adolescents who placed themselves at risk due to their sexual behaviours had often been sexually abused ($p = 0.001$) and quite often had difficulties in their peer relationships ($p = 0.039$).

Standardised measures of the young people's psychosocial problems

Standardised instruments were used to supplement the information provided during the interviews about the young people's emotional and behavioural difficulties. The young people and carers were asked to complete the Strengths and Difficulties questionnaire (SDQ) (Goodman 1994) and the young people the Child Depression Inventory (Kovacs and Beck 1977).

Sixty-six of the sixty-eight young people in the sample completed the SDQ, with two girls failing to respond. The SDQ was also completed by 58 of the foster carers. The different number of respondents for each set means that comparisons between them can only be approximate, but where relevant these comparisons have been made.

The Strengths and Difficulties Questionnaire

The Strengths and Difficulties Questionnaire is scored on five categories: the prosocial scale, hyperactivity scales, emotional symptoms, peer problems and conduct problems, plus an overall total score of difficulties (which excludes the prosocial score). The level of strengths or difficulties indicated by the score is divided into normal, borderline and abnormal categories as shown in Table 6.4.

Table 6.4 Scores used to classify the Strengths and Difficulties Questionnaire			
Category	*Normal*	*Borderline*	*Abnormal*
Total difficulties score	0–13	14–16	17–40
Emotional symptoms score	0–3	4	5–10
Conduct problems score	0–2	3	4–10
Hyperactivity score	0–5	6	7–10
Peer problems score	0–2	3	4–10
Prosocial behaviour score	6–10	5	0–4

THE FOSTER CARERS' RATINGS

The young people tended to normalise their behaviour and social adjustment on this measure. This is in line with John's finding (1997) in a large cross-national study of adaptive social functioning, that children (aged 7–18) with the most serious social and other problems were more likely to underrate their difficulties than were their well-functioning peers. For this reason only the foster carers' ratings are reported here.

As would be expected with a group of looked-after adolescents and, as can be seen in Table 6.5, the young people had quite high levels of emotional and behavioural difficulties. The foster carers rated young people who had previously been excluded from school as having more conduct difficulties and as having more overall difficulties than those young people who had not been excluded from school ($p<0.001$).

Table 6.5 The foster carers' scores on the Strengths and Difficulties Questionnaire at the first and second interviews

Category	Normal		Borderline		Abnormal	
	First interview (%)	Second interview (%)	First interview (%)	Second interview (%)	First interview (%)	Second interview (%)
Prosocial score	50	51	24	9	26	40
Hyperactivity score	53	40	12	13	35	47
Emotional symptoms score	57	60	9	8	34	32
Peer relationships score	38	28	12	19	50	53
Conduct difficulties score	33	21	12	9	55	70
Total score	35	32	12	4	53	64

Although, with the exception of the emotional symptom scores, more young people were rated by the foster carers as 'abnormal' at the second interview (see Table 6.5), only one sub-scale showed a statistically significant change. Using a Paired Samples T test there was a significant increase in peer difficulties by the time of the second interview ($p<0.05$). All of the sub-scores, with the exception of the hyperactivity sub-score, were significantly correlated, that is if the young person had an abnormal score at the first interview, they were likely to have an abnormal score at the second interview ($p<0.05$). This suggests that the young people's psychosocial functioning and behaviour were largely static over time. This is similar to the findings of Quinton and his colleagues (1998) when adoptive parents were asked to complete the Rutter A2 questionnaire (Rutter, Tizard and Whitmore 1970).

The questionnaires completed by the young people showed a similar stability of scores, with the exception of the emotional symptoms score. The mean score for emotional symptoms was 3.46 at the first interview, but 4.34 at the second interview ($p<0.05$). This means that the young people felt that they had more emotional difficulties by the time of the second interview than at the beginning of the placement. However, the young people also completed the Kovacs and Beck Child Depression Inventory (1977) at the first and second interviews but this showed no significant changes over time.

The lack of psychosocial change shown by the SDQ may mean that significant change is too much to expect. Adolescents' psychosocial functioning and behaviour is in part based on their temperaments and in part on their previous experiences, which in this case often included emotional, physical or sexual abuse, neglect and poor educational attainment. To realise change might require considerable time and intervention, which was not provided for most of them (see also Quinton *et al.* 1998; Sinclair *et al.* 2000).

As previous research has shown and as previously noted, the behaviours at the first interviews that particularly predicted poor outcomes were hyperactivity (see also Quinton *et al.* 1998) and conduct problems in the placement itself. In contrast, those young people who had shown psychological or emotional distress in the past had a much greater chance of *not* experiencing placement breakdown, probably because they turned their difficulties inwards rather than acting them out.

The Kovacs and Beck Child Depression Inventory

This questionnaire showed the levels of depression suffered by the young people and was completed by 67 of the 68 in our sample (33 boys and 34 girls). In five cases (one boy and four girls) five or more questions were left unanswered by the young person. It is important to note, therefore, that the true level of depression within this group of young people is likely to be greater than the scores reflect.

Twenty-eight young people (42%) showed no signs of depression whilst a further 28 (13 boys and 15 girls) exhibited depression to some degree. However, 11 (16%) exhibited clinical levels of depression which indicated that intervention was necessary. This group consisted of eight girls but only three boys. Thus 58% of the young people experienced some level of depression.

As already noted, there were no significant changes in the depression scores by follow-up.

The carers' view of depression among the young people

Forty-five young people showed signs of depression according to foster carers. Of these, two (5%) of the foster carers felt that the young person's depressed behaviour had had a significant impact on the family. In both of these cases the young people (both girls) had made suicide attempts and one of the girls had also been cutting herself. Eleven per cent (5) felt that the depressed behaviour had some impact on the family, including one girl who frequently announced she was 'fed-up and depressed' and would interrupt conversations, demanding attention. Thirty per cent (13) thought that the depressed behaviour had only a minor effect on the family, and 54% (24) felt that there was no effect on their family life.

Educational provision for the young people

It will be recalled that lack of information to carers about the educational histories and needs of the young people prior to placement was related to poor outcomes on both of our outcome measures. Many of the young people had had a disrupted education. Only 16% had had no unscheduled change of school. Almost half had been excluded from school on at least one occasion, over half had often shown poor attendance and one in five had been the subject of a statement of special educational needs at some stage.

Almost one in five of the young people were not in full-time education during the placement (Table 6.6) and this placed an additional burden on the carers.

Table 6.6 The young people's educational provision in the placement

Provision	Number	Percentage
Full-time education	53	78
Part-time education	5	7
Pupil Referral Unit part-time	2	3
Home tuition only	3	4
No provision	1	2
Over school age, working	2	3
Over school age, not working	2	3
Total	68	100

Almost two-thirds of the adolescents were attending a mainstream school, with a further six attending a special school (for example, a school for children with learning difficulties or an EBD school). Twelve had been excluded from school. The local authorities in the study varied considerably as to how they dealt with young people who were looked after and not attending school. In some, a minimum of home tuition (a few hours a week) was provided, leaving foster carers with the young person at home all day. In others, imaginative packages of activities were developed. The independent fostering agencies in our study took a particularly active role in providing appropriate educational facilities for the children in their schemes and ensured that the foster carers remained very actively involved in liaising with the schools. One young person had no educational provision made at all, having not attended school since she was 12 years old. Various attempts to reintegrate her into education had failed, as had attempts to involve her in voluntary work.

A third of the young people had changed school when they moved to the placement and it is important to note that for almost all of them this was seen as positive, for example, in giving them a fresh start or in removing them from negative peer influences. Problems in relation to schooling continued in placement, with a third showing attendance problems and nearly half demonstrating conduct difficulties in school. Twelve per cent of the young people had been involved in bullying other young people at school, and 29% had been the victims of bullying at school. In some instances, bullying resulted from the young people confiding in others about their past sexual abuse or their current sexual behaviour. Given these levels of difficulty, it was encouraging to find that, at the outset, half of the foster carers were actively involved with schools on the young person's behalf but the other half were much less involved – including twenty who reported having no contact with the young people's school teachers.

Once placed, school attendance improved for just under one-third of the young people but worsened for a quarter. Just under half showed no change in attendance. Worsening school attendance was related to both a decrease in the number of friends the young people had by follow-up and to involvement in negative peer groups. Interestingly, school attendance itself did not relate to outcomes. Two factors that were evident at the first interviews, however, did. Low confidence in schoolwork was significantly related to disruption and lack of confidence in social relationships at school was significantly related to low success rates in placements.

The findings of the study show that attention to the young people's education was very variable not only in terms of local authority provision and interest but also in relation to the efforts made by foster carers and the young people's social workers. The risk is that the education of looked-after adolescents is seen as a rather low priority particularly as they approach school-leaving age. Some practitioners worked hard to arrange suitable education or other activities to enable young people to have some relevant work experience and occupation. However, many education departments gave little priority to these vulnerable young people. There was also confusion about whether arranging a suitable educational placement for an accommodated young person was the responsibility of the birth parent, the child's social worker or the foster carer.

Activities and interests

The acquisition of skills learned through hobbies and activities has been shown to increase the self-confidence of children and young people, thereby enabling them to proceed to further achievements (Rutter *et al.* 1983). The Looking After Children report to the Department of Health (Ward 1995) found that parents of young people in the community generally emphasised the development of non-academic skills such as playing a musical instrument, learning to swim or to ride a bike, but that these skills were given little attention with looked-after children.

The young people were therefore asked whether they were involved in any leisure time activities, for example sport, art, music or drama. Twelve per cent (8) of the young people were not involved in any activities, and 22% (15) were involved in only one. Thirty-nine per cent (26) took part in two activities, 21% (14) in three and 6% (4) in four or more activities. This measure was somewhat crude as it did not take into account the extent of the young person's involvement in the activity, but it does provide some information about the lack of participation in non-academic activities by these young people (Table 6.7). Twenty-three per cent (15) of the young people said that they would like to learn a new hobby or activity; however these tended to be young people who were already involved in a range of other activities.

Only 27% (18) of the young people read books for pleasure, with 39% (13) of the 33 young people who had previously been excluded from school

Table 6.7 Participation in activities

Type of activity	Number of young people involved in activity	Percentage of young people
Sport	43	65
Art or music	22	33
Reading	18	27
Dance or drama	13	20
Computer games	8	12
Organised club*	8	12
Making things	6	9
Writing stories or poetry	3	5
Watching films	3	5
Collecting	2	3
Other activities	2	3

$n = 67$

No information on 1 case

* includes youth clubs, Guides, Cadets, in-care groups

doing so. This echoes the concern expressed by Ward and her colleagues (1995) that young people were not being encouraged to read even though research has shown a link between encouragement to read at home and educational achievement (Tizard, Schofield and Hewison 1982; Tizard *et al.* 1988) and looked-after children frequently have poorer literacy skills than their peers (Garnett 1994).

Young people who were not in full-time education or employment were neither more nor less likely to be involved in non-academic activities than those who were in full-time education or employment, with the exception of dance or drama. All of the young people who did take part in drama were in full-time education and it is likely that they participated in a school-based drama society.

Interestingly, the young people who had a particular skill or interest (that may have been developed at school or at home) had an increased chance of having a successful placement.

The young person's friendships

Since many of the young people were involved in few activities or hobbies, school was often the only opportunity that they had to make new friends. The foster carers said that 10 of the young people (15%) had no friends, 23 (34%) had casual friends but no close friends, 8 (12%) had close friends but not a wider social network, and only a third had both close friends and more casual friends. Four carers (6%) did not know whether the young person had any friends or not.

The girls were significantly more likely to report having 'normal' friendships, with 17 (52%) of the girls having both close friends and a wider social network compared with only 9 (28%) of the boys ($p = 0.047$). However the girls were also more likely to admit to feeling lonely, with more than half of the girls (55%) saying they frequently or sometimes felt lonely, compared with less than a quarter (24%) of boys ($p = 0.011$). The young people who admitted feeling lonely were more likely than others to have experienced some form of sexual adversity in their past ($p = 0.038$).

By follow-up, well over a quarter of the young people (28%) had more friends but a quarter had experienced a deterioration in the quality and number of their friendships. For instance, at the beginning of the placement Katie had a group of close friends at school. However, she began truanting from school and made friends with a group of young people who were also truanting. This group had a very negative impact on Katie's behaviour and she began drinking to excess, taking drugs, and absconding from her foster placement to stay with these friends.

Young people whose peer relationships deteriorated or became more negative were significantly more likely to experience a placement disruption ($p<0.01$), and were significantly less likely to experience successful placements ($p<0.01$), than those whose peer relationships remained the same or improved.

On the other hand, young people who, at the outset, had difficulties in making and maintaining adequate relationships with peers (as measured by the SDQ) had significantly *fewer* disruptions and *more successful* placements. Other findings supported the idea that such difficulty in sustaining peer relationships assisted in maintaining the placements. Those with these peer difficulties, for example, were less likely to get into trouble than other teenagers in the sample, more likely to have beneficial relationships with their foster carers, to have their major needs met by them and they had an increased chance of behavioural improvement. These rather immature young people sometimes got on well with much younger or much older children in the placements.

The young person's sexual relationships

Two-fifths (42%) of the young people said that they currently had a boyfriend or girlfriend. The majority (78%) were dating young people of the same age but three (11%), all girls, were dating men five or more years their senior.

Eleven (16%) of the carers thought that the young person could potentially be at risk of sexual exploitation. Carers expressed concern about almost half (47%) of the girls' relationships but about only just over a quarter (27%) of the boys', but this difference was not statistically significant.

The carers who were concerned about the young person's relationships responded in different ways. Two (8%) took no action. Eight (32%) said they monitored the situation closely, and 14 (56%) discussed their concerns with the young person and/or encouraged more contact with other young people whom they were less concerned about. One carer (4%) was particularly worried about the young person's sexual behaviour and arranged for the young person to see a psychologist to discuss her sexual relationships. This was a 13-year-old girl who demonstrated very sexualised behaviour and who sought sexual attention from numerous men, many much older than herself.

The foster carers were significantly less at ease in talking about sex and relationships with the boys than with the girls ($p = 0.022$). Twenty (30%) of the carers said that they had open discussions with the young person about sex and sexuality and 18 (27%) said there was some discussion, but more than two-fifths (43%) said that they had little or no discussion about sexual health, contraception or normal sexual development with the young people. This is of some concern, particularly as many looked-after young people do not attend or play truant from school and may therefore also miss sex education lessons at school. Furthermore, it cannot be assumed that the young person will have been able to talk about issues of sex or sexuality with their parents.

One foster carer talked about having been criticised by a social worker for encouraging the young men in her care to use condoms. The social worker felt that by buying condoms for the boys the carer was encouraging them to have sex. The carer, however, knew that she would not be able to stop the boys from being sexually active but realised that providing them with condoms and information about contraception and sexual health could help prevent unwanted pregnancies and sexually transmitted diseases. Another carer said that the social worker had asked her not to talk to the young girl in her care about her sexual behaviour as the social worker intended to do so, whilst working with her around the sexual abuse she had experienced. The carer was quite concerned as Nicky had a very limited ability to keep herself safe sexually, and had poor knowledge of contraception and sexual health. She only saw her social worker once a fortnight and there was little evidence to suggest that much time had been given to dealing with either the abuse or Nicky's sexual behaviour.

Offending behaviour

Twelve (18%) of the young people were involved in criminal behaviour during the placement that was sufficiently serious to warrant police action. The level of the offending behaviour of five young people increased during the placement, stayed the same for one young person and decreased for six young people. More boys than girls offended. All but one of the young people who did commit an offence during the placement had previously been involved in criminal activity ($p<0.001$). This is in contrast to the increased levels of offending by non-offenders in Sinclair and Gibbs' (1998) study of children in residential care.

The type of offences these young people committed included shoplifting, theft, joy-riding, fraud and drug-dealing. Whilst for some young people their offending was a one-off incident, others were more prolific. In spite of this, offending behaviour was not significantly related to the likelihood of place-ment disruption or the likelihood of experiencing a successful placement.

Young people who had previously been excluded from school were more likely to be involved in offending behaviour ($p = 0.028$), as were those with a history of truanting and non-attendance ($p = 0.03$).

Alcohol and drug misuse

Eleven (17%) of the young people admitted during the interviews to smoking cannabis. Small numbers of young people admitted to having taken other drugs in the past. One young person admitted to still using glue or other solvents occasionally. This is likely to be an underestimate of the level of drug use and information obtained from the case files indicated that at least 26 (39%) of the young people had been involved in drug or alcohol abuse prior to the current placement.

Twelve carers knew that the young person used drugs, and of these, eleven carers reported some degree of difficulty with it. For example, one carer said that using drugs made the young person devious, underhand and deceitful, which had an adverse effect on the other members of the family. Eight (67%) said that they disapproved of and discouraged the young person from using drugs, but three (25%) said that they did allow the young person to use soft drugs. One carer had sought specialist advice and arranged for the young person, who admitted to having used ecstasy, cannabis, amphetamines and cocaine, to see a drugs counsellor on a fortnightly basis.

The young people admitted more alcohol use, with 3 (4%) saying that they drank regularly, 16 (24%) drinking socially, 14 (21%) drinking occasion-ally, for example at parties, and a further 15 (22%) drinking on special occa-sions. Young people in the older age group were significantly more likely to drink alcohol regularly or socially than those in the younger age group. These findings are comparable with the results of the Youth Lifestyles Survey 1998–99 (Harrington 2000) which found that frequent drinking became more common with increasing age.

Only 28 (41%) of the carers knew that the young person drank alcohol (compared with the 48 young people who told the researcher that they drank). Thirteen of these carers (46%) said that the young person's alcohol use had caused them difficulties. In one case, a 12-year-old girl had been brought home by the police, so drunk that she could not remember where she had been. The foster carer had to put her to bed and then make regular checks on the young person during the night to make sure she did not choke on her own vomit.

At follow-up the foster carers expressed concern about the young person's use of illegal substances or alcohol in 17 (25%) of the placements. The level of concern increased for 11 of the young people during the placement, it remained the same for three young people and decreased for three. Young people about whom such concern was expressed were more likely to experience a placement disruption than those for whom there was no such concern ($p = 0.043$).

Alternative adult support

The young people were asked if there was another adult, apart from their parents or foster carers, whom they could turn to for help if they needed it. Half said that there was someone else they could ask for help and support but a third (36%) said there was not, and nine (14%) were unsure. Those who did have someone who could help them had more successful placements by follow-up.

Young people's views of professional support

Young people expressed considerable satisfaction with their placements. Although none were very satisfied, 92% were satisfied, with only 8% dissatisfied and none very dissatisfied. They were asked in the interviews about their views of the support they received.

Most of the young people (74%) were satisfied with the frequency of the social workers' visits, but almost one in five (18%) felt that they saw too little of them and five young people (8%) too much. Almost three-quarters of the children (73%) found their social workers helpful, but over a quarter (27%) saw them as unhelpful. When asked what social workers did that was helpful, nearly a quarter (24%) saw the social worker as providing them with general support, and 22% said that they had arranged the placement, almost one in five (19%) mentioned being listened to and understood, 14% said arranging contact and the same proportion arranging activities for them. Five per cent talked about work with their family, and one young person said that he had been helped by discussion of coping strategies.

Typical comments were:

She asks me how I'm feeling and what I want to see changed. Nothing more anyone can do.

She's trying to find out about my past as lots of things are missing.

Talking to me about things. Talking to me about meetings and what's going to happen.

Picks me up. Makes sure I'm settled and calm. She says things that help me in school and helps me out with Mum. Suggests things to help.

Supported me through everything that's happened.

Everything! He is the person I depend on most.

It was interesting that finding placements was quite often suggested as helpful. This could mean that the young people trusted the worker to sort things out if the placement was not working out:

If I'm not going well in a placement he will find me another placement.

However, it could mean that this was the only role in which the social worker was seen as active:

Finding placements – that's all really. Finds houses.

Put me here and that's it really.

The young people were also asked if the social workers had done anything that was unhelpful. Over two-thirds (67%) had nothing to report. The remainder mentioned finding the worker difficult to contact or late for appointments (5), being subjected to unwanted placement changes (4), the worker not doing things they had said they would (3), not listening (3), breaking promises (1), telling them off or bossing them around (2) and being the wrong gender (1):

Taking me away from here and putting me back home.

She's difficult to get hold of.

Often doesn't do things. I often have to do them myself because she hasn't time. Sometimes slow in acting.

> I can't talk to him as he's a man. He's always late which is annoying, especially when I want to go out.

> Doesn't do much.

> He didn't listen before I ran away - he's learned from it now!

Just under half (44%) of the young people said that they did talk to the social worker when things were worrying them, but over half (56%) said that they did not.

Finally, we asked the young people for their suggestions about what would make things easier for other children joining new families. The young people suggested giving more information about the foster carers (6), organising introductions to the carers (5), giving more reassurance (4) and involving them more in discussions (3):

> Let them see the placement first. Then if they don't like it they don't have to move in. Social services tell you a bit and then take you there straight away so you don't really get a choice.

> Need to encourage young people more – building their confidence – more information about where they're moving to. More information about the foster carers.

> Letting them meet [the foster carers] first. My second placement was planned and much easier then.

> Have more meetings before, stay for a weekend and see if you'll get on.

> Involve young people in review meetings and make sure they have a voice in decisions made about them.

> Tell you a bit about it before they just dump you there.

We also asked the young people if they had seen any other professionals for help in the past. Twenty-eight (42%) of them said that they had done so. Twenty-one (32%) reported that they were seeing a specialist at that time. These included individual counsellors (5), psychologists (4), psychiatrists (3), psychotherapists (2) and a family counsellor (1). Four were unsure of the type of professional they were seeing and two were seeing more than one kind.

When asked about such help both past and present, two-thirds had found the specialist helpful but a disappointing third had not. The young people cited a number of aspects of counselling as helpful, including being listened to and understood (14) and getting help to sort things out (3):

> Lots of flashbacks. It helped me get things sorted out.

> It was helpful but upsetting afterwards. I wanted to forget it all but the sessions kept bringing it all back.

> Could talk, get things off my chest, get the anger out.

> See things differently. Increased my self-esteem.

They were less specific about what had been unhelpful to them but they mentioned finding it upsetting (3), not feeling they were being helped (2) and the professional being the wrong gender (1):

> I hate psychology...does my head in. Can't stand people judging me, assessing me.

> I can't talk to him because he's a man. Maybe if I could see a woman it would be helpful.

> Said that nothing could be done and I just had to keep busy. Made no useful suggestions, no help.

> Talked about abuse – brought it all back. I didn't know if it was a dream or real. It was very upsetting.

When young people were seeing a specialist for counselling their carers tended to feel better supported. Conversely, when foster carers considered that a young person needed specialist help and it was not provided, this did much to make them feel unsupported. Over and above this, there were fewer disruptions when appropriate therapeutic help was provided for young people (or was not needed) and more successful placements when young people reported that they were receiving such assistance.

Three wishes

The young people were asked what they would wish for if they were given three wishes. Some wanted money, fast cars and big houses, which seemed fairly typical wishes for the average adolescent. However, 18 of the young people wished for changes within their family, for example wishing for their parents to get back together, or for them to be able to return home (see also Sinclair *et al.* 2000). One 12-year-old girl said her only wish was that:

> We could all live at home with Mum.

Another teenage girl wished that:

> All stigmas about being in care would go and people would see us as individuals.

Clearly, young people harboured a range of concerns about the families from which they were separated.

Now that we have looked at the behaviour of the young people in the placements, we turn to consider in the next chapter the strains on the foster carers caused by such behaviour and those that arose for other reasons.

Chapter Seven

Foster Carer Strain

In this chapter we look at the strains on the foster carers in the study, the impact of such strains on their parenting practices, what intensified or alleviated stress and its overall impact on placement outcome.

General areas of potential stress in the context of foster care

We discussed with the foster carers the impact on them and their children of a number of issues that form a context to current foster care.

Fear of allegations

We asked fosters carers if they had any fears of an allegation being made against them by the children they fostered. Almost half (49%) had some fears and 11% had many fears. One in ten of the carers had had an allegation made against them at some time in the past (3 against individual carers and 3 involving both carers) and two others had close friends who were foster carers who had experienced allegations. Of the six who had experienced an allegation, three reported that it had had a significant impact on them and three that it had had some effect (see also Wilson *et al.* 2000). It is worth noting that, of those who had had an allegation made against them, far fewer now felt an important member of the professional team, and this might suggest that the methods of dealing with allegations at that time were very unsatisfactory for carers (see also for example Verity and Nixon 1995).

Safe caring

In order to forestall allegations against them, particularly from young people who showed sexualised behaviours, foster carers are advised to adopt 'safe caring' practices. Most had done so. Two-thirds (66%, 45) of the carers had established specific house rules, for example having to knock before entering anybody else's bedroom and no one being allowed to walk around in their underwear or nightclothes (see also Farmer and Pollock 1998; Devine and Tate 1991; Macaskill 1991). In just under half of the families with such rules (20) the carers felt that they had a negative effect on the carers themselves, for example, restricting their feeling of liberty in their own homes. Forty-two per cent (19) of the carers with such rules also felt that they had a negative impact on the other children in the house, for instance, making young children aware of sexual issues earlier than would otherwise have been the case.

Experiences of criticism or hostility because of fostering

It was interesting to find that well over a third (38%) of the carers reported that they had experienced criticism or hostility because they fostered. As we included hostility from anyone, this is higher than the quarter of foster carers in the study by Sinclair and his colleagues (2000) who said that they had experienced some criticism or hostility from neighbours. In our study, neighbours were also the biggest source of criticism of foster carers. Some neighbours were reported to dislike living next to foster children, to see carers as unable to control their fostered adolescents or occasionally to feel intimidated by them. A number of carers also had members of their extended family who criticised them for fostering, either because they felt that the children had taken over their lives or that their parents were simply working too hard.

What contributed to strain for the foster carers?

Specific child behaviours that had a negative impact on the foster family

We discussed with the carers the impact on the whole foster family of a range of specific emotional and conduct difficulties, including theft, aggression, lying and running away. The researchers then rated the extent of the impact of each behaviour on the family. Taken individually, none of these emotional and behavioural difficulties was seen as having a major effect on the family, except uncooperative behaviour (Fisher's exact test, $p = 0.001$). The cumulative number of behaviours did, however, have a significant impact on the family. The young people displaying the greatest number of conduct difficulties were most likely to have a negative effect on the foster family (Table 7.1).

Table 7.1 The impact of emotional and conduct difficulties on the foster family					
Effect of behaviour on foster family	*Number of behaviours shown in the home*				*Total*
	0	*1–2*	*3–4*	*5+*	
No effect	18	12	5	0	35
Negative effect	0	9	10	13	32
Total	18	21	15	13	67

Chi-square = 33.02, df = 2, $p<0.001$
No information on 1 case

In addition, most of the carers who looked after young people who were misusing drugs reported that this created difficulties, as did half of those with adolescents who were misusing alcohol, who were depressed or who had problems with concentration or distractibility.

Contact difficulties

The young people's contact with family members was discussed at some length during the interviews. It emerged that problems with contact arose, in particular, when parents were unreliable in their visiting patterns, when there were inappropriate amounts of contact, when parents showed persistent rejection or neglect or when the adolescent was not safe during contact with family members. The difficulties often led to disturbed acting-out behaviour, including violence and defiance by the young people which continued for some time after contact and had a considerable effect on the whole foster family. Such difficulties in contact with the young people's families were rated by the researchers as having a negative impact on 41% of the carers and as having repercussions for the other children in the family in 21% of cases. As we will see, by follow-up foster carers felt under increased strain when there were considerable difficulties in the young people's contact with family members.

Factors related to strain

In addition to asking foster carers about a range of issues relating to fostering that were stressful for them we examined which factors from our statistical analyses were most strongly implicated in increasing or decreasing strain and the effects of strain on the carers' ability to do their job. We investigated strain in three different ways.

1. Stressful life events in the six months prior to the study placement

First, we asked foster carers about a variety of life events during the six months preceding the placement that could have caused them stress. For some these stresses were also ongoing. Not surprisingly, there had often been movements in and out of the families. Two-fifths (41%) (28 families) had incorporated a new person into the family during this period, either a child (23), an adult (4) or both (1). In more than two-thirds (69% or 47 families) someone had left the family during this period, either a foster child (39 in a planned move or disruption), a birth child (4) or in one case the carer's partner, whilst three families had seen a combination of such moves. In addition, five families had moved house. Seven carers reported relationship difficulties with their partners, four had suffered a bereavement and two a relationship breakdown with someone who had been important to them. Over a third (37%) of the families had had to cope with the serious illness of a family member or other relative, including in seven cases the foster mother and in six the foster father, in five one of their children and in two cases another relative. An accident had affected one foster father, one child and three relatives, whilst a quarter of the carers (17) had experienced changes at work such as increased working hours or responsibilities or redundancy. Eighteen per cent of the carers (12) reported financial worries during this period and 17% (11) had had concerns about their grown-up children.

In addition, in the previous six months, 45% (27) of the 60 foster carers who had been fostering other children had been through a placement breakdown and in another 18% of the families a previous foster child had shown difficult behaviour, so that, in all, almost two-thirds (63%) of families had been affected by such previous placement difficulties. Thus the events connected with previous foster children provided a background of stressful events even without allowing for the many other life difficulties that the carers encountered. Overall, only five (7%) of the families had not experienced any of these stressors. Over half (52% or 34) had suffered from one to three such stresses, almost a third (32% or 21) had been through four to six and a further 9% (6) had experienced seven or more such stresses over the previous six months.

2. Strain during the placement measured by the general health questionnaire

We also assessed carer strain during the placement by administering the General Health Questionnaire (Goldberg and Hillier 1979) at the first and follow-up interviews. As can be seen in Table 7.2, over a quarter of the carers who completed the General Health Questionnaire (GHQ) at the first interviews had scores in the clinical or sub-clinical range, suggesting that they were under a great deal of strain and this fell slightly to one in five at the second interviews. When the sub-scores on the GHQ were scrutinised it was found that half the carers showed some somatic stress symptoms at both stages, over a third (38%) showed some signs of anxiety at the first interview, rising to nearly half of the carers by the follow-up stage, but few carers had depressive symptoms at either point. There were very high levels of difficulty in social functioning at both the first (81%) and follow-up stage (98%). This meant that carers were not functioning well day to day, did not feel that they were coping adequately and were not enjoying their daily activities. There was also a statistically significant increase in difficulties in social funtioning between the first and follow-up interviews.

Table 7.2 General Health Questionnaire – Changes over time				
	First interview questionnaire		Second interview questionnaire	
	Normal range (scores 0–4)	Sub-clinical and clinical range (scores 5–21)	Normal range (scores 0–4)	Sub-clinical and clinical range (scores 5–21)
Somatic symptoms	22 (52%)	20 (48%)	21 (50%)	21 (50%)
Anxiety symptoms	26 (62%)	16 (38%)	22 (52%)	20 (48%)
Social functioning	8 (19%)	34 (81%)	1 (2%)	41 (98%) ***
Depression symptoms	41 (98%)	1 (2%)	40 (95%)	2 (5%)
Total scores	30 (71%)	12 (29%)	33 (79%)	9 (21%)

$n = 42$
*** Significant differences $p < 0.001$ Paired Samples T test

3. Strains during the placement reported by the foster carers

Our third approach to considering foster carer strain was by asking the carers at the first interviews how much strain they felt that they were under during the placement. It was important to capture their subjective experience of strain, particularly as it was somewhat different from the scores on the GHQ. Thus, as Table 7.3 below shows, of the 15 carers who were in the clinical range on the GHQ, 6 (40%) reported feeling no strain, whilst of those who showed no problems on the GHQ, 18 (42%) reported themselves as being under strain. Clearly, self-perception of strain is rather different from scores on this clinical measure.

Table 7.3 The relationship between the strains reported by the foster carers and the results of the GHQ

	No strain		Strain		Total
	Number	*Row (%)*	*Number*	*Row (%)*	*Number*
Normal range on the GHQ	25	58	18	42	43
Clinical range on the GHQ	6	40	9	60	15
Total	31		27		58

n = 58

Missing information on 3 of the 61 carers who filled in the questionnaires

At the first interviews three-fifths of the 68 carers said that they experienced no undue strain in looking after the fostered adolescents. Over a third (35%) reported some strain on one (15) or both (9) carers, whilst 6% (4) declared that they were under such significant strain that their ability to cope was seriously impaired.

The factors that increased strain for the foster carers

Using these three approaches to strain levels we explored which factors were significantly related to foster carer strain. Interestingly, there was no relationship between the young people's scores on the Strengths and Difficulties Questionnaire (SDQ), which measured the young person's behaviour and adjustment at the first interview, and foster carer strain. On the other hand, perhaps not surprisingly, more carers who *considered* that the young people they were looking after had behaviour problems did show strain on the GHQ ($p = 0.05$) or reported feeling under strain ($p = 0.05$). Indeed, carers showing strain on the GHQ at the first interviews had often been reluctant to accept the placement of the young person in the first place.

Three other factors were related to high strain levels for foster carers. First, carers who were looking after young people who were violent to other children reported high levels of strain at the first interviews ($p = 0.05$). Second, strain on the GHQ was particularly evident by follow-up for foster carers who were looking after young people who were hyperactive (on the SDQ). Clearly, hyperactive behaviour makes particularly heavy demands on foster carers (see also Quinton et al. 1998). Third, strain levels on the GHQ at the one year stage were also markedly high when difficulties in the young people's contact with their parents and relatives had affected the whole foster family ($p = 0.031$).

One very important finding was that significantly more of the carers in the clinical or sub-clinical range on the GHQ at the first interviews (93%) found the young person's social worker difficult to contact as compared with the carers in the normal range (64%) ($p = 0.04$). Of course the link may work in either direction: difficulties in making contact with social workers may increase strain or strained carers may be more vulnerable to feeling that professional contact is unsatisfactory. However, the burden of findings in the research would suggest the former. This was backed up by the finding that there was also a significant relationship between carer strain on the GHQ at follow-up and the experience of at least one change of social worker ($p<0.05$). Changes of social worker had been noted from the case review and were not therefore affected by carer perception. This finding emphasises the importance of the social work role to foster carers and suggests that discontinuities make accessing their services more difficult.

One reason why difficulty in contacting the young people's social workers increased foster carer strain is probably that children's social workers provide the only access point for essential services for the young people, such as referrals for counselling, for permission for various actions such as overnight stays and holidays, for issues relating to the child's family and for any difficulties shown by the young person. There are therefore frequent occasions when their services are needed and where a lack of contact means that a problem has been left unresolved.

Whilst frequency and ease of contact are very important, the manner in which professional help is provided is also crucial. We found that more of the carers showing strain on the GHQ felt that their views were not taken seriously by professionals (33%) as compared with those not showing such problems (16%), although these results did not quite reach significance.

The factors that alleviated strain for the foster carers

Help from friends emerged as an important antidote to strain. There was a significant relationship between having friends who provided useful help and fewer feelings of strain on both the GHQ (p = <0.05) and on self-reported levels of strain ($p<0.01$). It seems therefore that the availability of supportive friends is an important buffering factor in reducing strain. This is likely to be because friends are generally more available and accessible than professionals and may be able to assist with tasks in ways that provide immediate practical and emotional benefits. In addition, since support from friends was by no means universal for foster carers, those who could count on such help were likely to have particularly robust social support networks. For single carers who cannot turn to a partner for assistance, support from friends emerged as especially crucial.

Moreover, those carers who had access to help or advice from non-social services professionals (such as a GP or counsellor) also had somewhat lower levels of reported strain. It was interesting to find that social workers both visited the carers alone and made visits to the young person more frequently when the carers were *not* under strain than when they were. This suggests that attentive social work reduces strain or that strain increases when there is too little visiting or both. It may also be that visiting the less strained carers was less demanding and more rewarding for social workers and therefore occurred more.

The impact of strain on the foster carers' parenting

Whilst foster care would generally be broadly viewed as a stressful occupation, we found that high strain levels had a considerable impact on specific aspects of the parenting that carers were able to provide and on their fulfilment of caring tasks.

The foster carers more often disliked the young people when the stresses on them prior to placement had had an intense impact on them ($p = 0.015$) or they felt under strain during the placement ($p = 0.01$). They also showed lowered levels of sensitive parenting during placement when prior stresses had had a significant effect on them ($p<0.05$) or they had been under stress during the placement ($p = 0.04$). The ability to respond to the young person's emotional age when it differed from their actual age, a factor that measured an aspect of sensitive parenting, was considerably reduced among carers where stress prior to placement had had an intense impact on them ($p = 0.004$) or they were under current stress during the placement ($p = 0.02$). Many of the young people had an emotional age that was much younger than their chronological age and some foster carers provided regular opportunities for play and nurture that was appropriate to a much younger child to meet these young people's earlier unmet needs. Strained carers did this much less often than others.

Of course, it could be that the carers with high prior strain scores were those whose poor parenting had led to previous placement breakdowns and where this cycle was starting again with difficulties in the placement occasioned by poor parenting and their dislike of the young person leading to further parenting difficulties, that is, that their parenting deficits had caused the prior strain rather than the prior strain leading to current parenting difficulties. We checked to see whether the foster carers with the high prior strain scores or those where previous stresses had had an intense impact on them had experienced a high number of previous placement breakdowns. We found that, on the contrary, more previous breakdowns had occurred for the carers with lower previous strain levels. It seems, therefore, that prior strain led to parenting difficulties rather than the other way round.

We should also note that poorer parenting skills were associated not with higher numbers of prior stresses *per se* but with situations in which prior stresses had had an intense impact on the carers. When we looked more closely at this we found that whilst most of the carers with a high number of previous stressors had also experienced these as having a major impact on them, the majority of carers who had found that prior stressors had had an intense impact on them had experienced lower numbers of stressful events. Thus, whilst carers who had suffered a very high number of previous stressful events were likely to be affected and parent more poorly than others, poorer parenting occurred when one or more prior stresses had made an intense impact on the carers leaving them without access to all their usual emotional resources. This probably connects with the finding we come to in a moment that carers who had suffered a significant impact from such stressors also often scored in the clinical range for social functioning on the GHQ.

Foster carers who felt very strained also parented the fostered young people less well in other ways. We rated commitment to the young people as high when foster carers had a long-term commitment to them, considered that the placement would have a considerable impact on them and often acted as their advocate. Significantly few carers who reported that they were under strain were highly committed to the young people ($p<0.05$). High engagement was rated as present when the carers showed high levels of acceptance, support and concern for the young people and a degree of understanding of their inner emotional world. Such carers encouraged open communication about difficult feelings and issues and had a general concern for the young people's long-term welfare. Again, few foster carers who were under strain were highly engaged with the fostered young people in this way ($p<0.05$). By follow-up the carers under severe stress on the GHQ were also less effective at providing consistent appropriate limits.

These strained foster carers had made less effort than other carers to help the young people to fit into the foster family ($p=0.02$) and were also less active than others in ensuring that the young people's various needs, for example for counselling or appropriate education, were met ($p<0.05$). Those who reported feeling under strain also provided the young people they looked after with little preparation for independence. Moreover, fewer of the placements of the carers under strain on the GHQ ($p<0.05$) or from self-report ($p<0.05$) were rated by the researchers as beneficial overall for the young people.

In addition, those carers who reported that prior and sometimes ongoing stressors had had a significant impact on them markedly more often scored in the sub-clinical or clinical range for social functioning on the GHQ at both time points. This meant that they were not functioning well day-to-day and had difficulty in taking decisions or enjoying their normal activities. Carers with this reduced day-to-day functioning also expressed significantly higher levels of dissatisfaction with the placement right from the beginning ($p=<0.05$) and fewer of the young people in these placements showed improved well-being ($p=0.005$). Carers with higher prior strain levels (four or more stressors in the previous six months) also more often than others felt unsupported during the placement ($p=0.04$).

Thus it can be seen that the resources of these strained carers were exhausted and their parenting capacity reduced. They were less committed and engaged with the young people, less sensitive to them and took a more limited view of the caring role than less strained carers. The carers also felt more dissatisfied and less well supported. Overall, these placements provided less good environments for meeting the needs of the placed adolescents than those with less strained carers.

The effect of carer strain on placement outcome

The importance of carer strain emerged even more strongly when we examined its links with placement outcome. Higher disruption rates were associated with the placements of the young people whose carers had experienced high levels of stress prior to their arrival and this association was on the borderline of significance ($p = 0.058$). This may be linked to the poorer and less sensitive parenting that these carers provided, their reduced day-to-day functioning or to the carers' dissatisfaction with the placements (which was itself related to placement disruption) or to a combination of these factors.

Disruption rates were also higher for carers with high prior stress levels, when those strains that were related to previous placement breakdowns and moves were excluded, although the relationship did not quite reach significance. This suggests that the previous strains that are linked to later placement disruption are often a mix of difficulties with previous placements and other stressful life events but can be caused by stresses unrelated to fostering and relate to an accumulation of prior stresses.

As already noted, foster carers who were under strain during the placement were significantly often unable to respond sensitively to the young people's emotional age and frequently disliked the placed young people. At the outset of the placement the first of these factors predicted later placement breakdown whilst, by follow-up, dislike of the young person was also linked to placement disruption. In addition, the young people placed with foster carers whose social functioning on the GHQ was impaired did less well overall in placement: their well-being less often improved and their major needs were much less likely to have been met.

These findings make clear that when foster carers are under strain, whether from events prior to the child's arrival or because of placement difficulties, placement outcomes suffer. This suggests that family placement workers should review the personal situation of foster carers (for example, whether they are looking after an elderly parent or sick relative, have had a recent bereavement or a difficult placement ending) and the resulting effects of stress on the foster carers before each placement is made, in order to match those who are under a great deal of strain with less demanding adolescents or to offer them enhanced levels of support or both.

There are strong indications in the study of the importance of a careful consideration of foster carers' reactions to the prospect of a new placement. Carers felt under more strain when they had only accepted a young person reluctantly or under pressure. The initial reactions of the foster carers to the young people often continued and affected the course of the placement. Carers who were under strain prior to the placement often expressed dissatisfaction with the placement at the outset and most of these placements had disrupted by follow-up. Reluctance to take a young person or early expressions of dissatisfaction should therefore be taken seriously and appropriate action taken when possible.

Strain was also related to looking after hyperactive, violent or uncooperative young people and to an accumulation of conduct difficulties. This suggests that the placements of young people with conduct difficulties, and particularly hyperactivity, need enhanced levels of support if they are to succeed. It may be that integrated packages of support geared to the needs of these particular children and their foster families are required.

Importantly, a number of findings suggest that enhanced support can attenuate the experience of strain, in particular, the regular and reliable availability of the young person's social worker, continuity of social work help and taking the foster carers' views seriously.

In the next chapter we will examine the supports that were available to the foster carers in the study and how effective they were.

Chapter Eight

Support for the Foster Carers

In this chapter we will consider the supports that the foster carers were receiving from all sources, both professional and from within their own networks. We will then explore the important question of how far good support leads to better placement outcomes. In addition, we will examine what changes were made to the services provided over the one year follow-up.

Administrative support

First we will consider the adequacy of arrangements for pensions and payment and the efficiency of the administrative arrangements made by social services departments.

Ineligibility for pension schemes, lack of sick pay or of paid breaks between placements

A number of carers talked about the need for sick pay and for a pension scheme. Many foster carers said they were ineligible for private pension plans as fostering was not considered to be 'work' but that they could not join the social services pension plans as social services considered them to be self-employed. This was a major concern for some carers, particularly those who had spent the majority of their adult lives as foster carers and were not therefore part of any other pension schemes. In addition, only six foster carers had paid breaks between placements. Given the adverse outcomes associated with placements where foster carers were under strain, shown in the previous chapter, wider use of paid breaks might have led to fewer placement breakdowns.

Pay and financial support

The foster carers were asked how satisfied they were with their pay and with the process by which they were paid. A third (35%) of the carers were dissatisfied with the amount that they were paid. For example, one carer said that she had worked out how much she earned from fostering per hour:

> The pay works out as about 60p per hour. It is not enough for a 24-hour job, dealing with young people with extreme behaviour.

In spite of this, neither the rate of pay nor the carers' satisfaction with payment significantly related to placement outcomes, but both were the cause of many complaints and criticisms from the foster carers. The evidence from other studies on financial issues has been mixed but there is wide agreement that payment is not the principal determining factor in terms of recruitment or retention (Bebbington and Miles 1990; Chamberlain et al. 1992; Denby et al. 1999; Kirton 2001).

As many as 30% of the carers (20) were dissatisfied or very dissatisfied with the payment methods of their authority or fostering agency. One carer said that there had been only one month in the year when her pay had been correct and that she often had to wait for three months to get paid. She took emergency placements but poor social work recording meant that some of the children had not been reported as staying with her and no payments made. Some foster carers were understandably critical about this, particularly when it meant that they had to subsidise the children's activities over long periods from their own pockets. Other carers said that it could take as long as six weeks after placement for payments to be started. One carer actually reported:

> …some hostility and snide comments from the Wages Department at the Civic Centre when asking for wages that haven't been paid to me. In reply you hear 'You're lucky receiving some money, you get paid more than me'.

Organisational inefficiency

A major criticism was of the organisational inertia of social services departments. There were frequent delays in responding to even simple requests and in making administrative arrangements of all kinds, including payments to carers. There were particular criticisms when young people could not stay overnight or be looked after by others in a crisis because the response to the request was given well after the event.

When we asked the foster carers what one thing they would like to change about fostering, one spoke for many when she said:

> Fostering is not the problem but frustration with social services is. You can't even get the basics for the [young people]. We've had difficulties even getting school uniform for Harry.

What was most helpful and unhelpful from their sources of support

Asked what they found most helpful from any source of support, foster carers emphasised the *availability* of the people they approached (see also Triseliotis *et al.* 2000). More than two in five (44%) emphasised the importance to them of family placement workers who were available and almost a quarter (24%) mentioned the accessibility of other foster carers. Typical comments were:

> [What really helps] is knowing that there's help on the end of the phone.

> Being able to gain help and advice 24 hours a day.

At the same time, some carers said that they needed not just telephone advice but a visit out of hours if things were difficult.

In line with these findings, difficulty in contacting social workers was the main problem identified when we asked carers what they found most unhelpful (32%). Also, one in five of the foster carers (19%) had encountered professionals or other helpers who showed a lack of interest, were critical or patronising or even reacted negatively or critically to their requests for help. Other difficulties included professionals who rarely visited (13%) or lacked an adequate understanding of fostering (13%).

The family placement workers

We asked specifically about the assistance provided by the family placement or link workers. All of the foster carers had a family placement worker. Only 29% had known the link worker for less than a year, another 26% had worked with them for between one and two years, 18% had known them for two to three years whilst the remaining 27% had worked with their link worker for four years or more. These relationships were clearly very long-lasting, unlike those with the children's social workers.

Fourteen per cent of the family placement workers visited either weekly or fortnightly, well over half (58%) visited monthly, 18% were seen every two months and 10% every three months or less frequently. All except two foster carers also had telephone contact with the link workers. Half of the carers said that it was always easy to contact their link worker, over a third (36%) occasionally found it difficult whilst 14% reported having problems making contact sometimes or always.

When family placement workers were especially helpful they listened and gave advice (61%), were supportive (22%), visited when needed and always responded to phone calls or rang back (24%). They were people who showed understanding, with whom carers could talk through problems, who made practical suggestions and took the actions they had promised. They had sound opinions, could see both sides of an issue and be impartial and truthful. Several carers commented on how important it was that if they could not reach their own link worker they could talk to one of the other family placement team workers.

Carers wanted to feel respected and on the same level as the family placement worker – indeed to feel part of a team. A sense of humour, providing reassurance and positive feedback to carers were all valued qualities. Link workers who knew the whole family were valued, especially when they were aware of the needs of individual family members and looked after the foster carers' needs for training:

> [The link worker] is the most important support we have. She has an overview of all our family's needs as well as the placement's. She respects and empathises with us and always shows an awareness of our own needs. [She's] extremely experienced and skilled. She gives us the benefits of this while enabling our own view and strengths to develop.

Several (10%) mentioned the skills and expertise of the family placement workers who really understood the problems of fostering, often attributing this to their previous experience as residential workers, workers in an adolescent unit or foster carers. One carer who was very positive about her link worker said:

> Sometimes he is the only reason why we stay fostering. A ready ear, a calming influence, always available – even out of hours, though we have never done this. [He's an] experienced foster carer himself. Down to earth, realistic, avoids social work speak. Is always honest!!

Another responded:

> [She is] very caring and supportive. Doesn't promise what she can't do!
> Sorts out any difficulties I may have. Listens!! Very understanding of
> problems concerning fostering. Good knowledge.

A third said:

> Pam and I have known each other for a long time now. I trust her judge-
> ments, her advice and I value her very much as part of my support system.
> I feel that I can ring Pam any time, any place. She listens and advises and
> is very knowledgeable. She has once fostered too and that does help.

Family placement workers were occasionally mentioned as people who could
liaise with the district social workers if the carers were 'hitting a brick wall'
with them.

When asked how satisfied the foster carers were with their family placement worker almost two-thirds (63%) said that they were very satisfied, just
under a quarter were satisfied (23%), 5% were dissatisfied and 9% very dissatisfied.

The young people's social workers

We also sought the carers' views on the children's social workers. All but one
of the fostered young people had an allocated social worker, although another
two only had a social worker allocated after some time. In addition, another
two social workers passed on the case and no social worker was allocated for a
period. In most cases the carers would have met the social workers only quite
recently when the young person joined the family. In effect this meant that the
carers had to deal with a constantly changing group of social workers.

The social workers have a broader role than the family placement workers
since they have overall responsibility for the young people and they also have
varied caseloads which may make pressing demands on them. Two-fifths of
the carers (40%) saw the social worker's role as supporting the young person,
just 4% as supporting the carers but over half (54%) considered that it was to
provide support to both.

Well over a third of the social workers visited the young person weekly or
fortnightly (38%), 41% did so monthly, 10% every two months and 11%
three-monthly or less often. The foster carers saw the social workers without
the young people present weekly or fortnightly in 38% of cases, monthly in a

quarter, every two months in 6% and less than three monthly or rarely in almost a third (31%). These figures show that whilst two and a half times as many social workers as compared with family placement workers visited and saw the foster carers alone weekly or fortnightly, at the other end of the spectrum, three times as many social workers rarely visited and saw the carers alone when compared with the family placement workers.

All except five foster carers also had telephone contact with the social workers. However, only 30% of the carers said that it was always easy to contact the social workers, 41% found it occasionally difficult, 22% sometimes hard and 7% always difficult. These figures are in stark contrast to the ease of contact experienced with the link workers (see also Department of Health 1995). This suggests that the services provided by the social workers were more variable than that of the family placement workers.

The qualities which were found helpful by the carers were the ability to work with, or to provide understanding and advice about, the young person (26%) and keeping the carers informed about the young person's family (9%). One foster carer said that what was most helpful was the social worker:

> Being there for Simon. Simon knows he has her all the time. She talks to him when I'm not around. I find that unusual because I haven't had that before. She likes to spend time with him on his own.

Again, the carers appreciated the workers who listened, advised and showed support and understanding (39%), who discussed issues with the carers (5%) and who sorted out practicalities (17%). They also appreciated it when social workers would always ring back quickly when they telephoned (17%) and would always respond if the young person needed to see them.

Again, several carers commented that they wanted to be respected and to feel part of the team looking after the young person. A typical positive response was:

> [She] responds quickly to requests, always takes action that has been agreed. Feeds back information. Discusses issues with us and generally supports the placement positively. [She] works very much as a team with us. Treats us as fellow professionals.

Another wrote:

> She respects us as professionals and listens to and acts on what we have to say.

A third commented:

> She listens, advises and shares her knowledge. Always does her best to answer your questions and solve problems.

When asked what social workers did that was unhelpful only 22 out of 61 answered the question. The greatest criticism that was made of social workers was that they did not respond to phone calls and only phoned back if there was a crisis (see also Triseliotis, Borland and Hill 1999; Triseliotis *et al.* 2000). Half of the carers who answered this question experienced this difficulty. As one carer said:

> With all my placements I have had huge difficulty in contacting or seeing their [the young person's] social workers as often as they were needed – some not at all unless by the complaints procedure.

Another echoed this comment:

> She doesn't respond to phone calls – [she] only responds if there's a crisis. She doesn't see that the young person needs positive intervention. She is always difficult to contact [and] only visits in a crisis.

Another said:

> They [social workers] are generally unavailable or more often non-existent.

A particular difficulty reported by almost a third (32%) of the carers who had criticisms was that no work was undertaken with the young person (or occasionally with the young person's family), an issue to which we will return. They also reported that social workers did not telephone or visit enough. One carer said that in order to get her social worker to provide the services they needed, she:

> Had to get nasty with her

and added:

> But it's horrible to have to get nasty to get things done.

Foster carers were particularly upset when they thought that the young person needed specialist help but it had not been provided. In one of these situations the carer commented ruefully:

We've been told she's not old enough yet!

which contrasted with the explanation given to another carer that the young person was too old. One foster carer put it like this:

> I am sometimes disappointed with the area offices, as no work was done with Clive's family and hardly any contact with Clive. Even though he's been in care for some months [there's been] no review yet.

Considerably more foster carers felt very satisfied with the support offered by the family placement workers (63%) as compared with the social workers (44%), although when the satisfied and very satisfied ratings were combined the proportion who felt satisfaction with both services was almost the same (86% and 88%).

Being treated as a team member

In spite of the current emphasis by social services departments on partnership with users it emerged that professionals have a long way to go before partnership with foster carers is achieved (see also Ramsay 1996; Strover 1999; Triseliotis *et al.* 2000; Waterhouse 1992). The reluctance to treat foster carers as partners was also shown in a study by Farmer and Pollock (1998) where carers were rarely allowed to see children's case files, in contrast to residential workers. The foster carers in this study made it clear that they wanted to be regarded as full members of the team which had responsibility for the young person. Somewhat under half (46%) said that they felt that they were an important member of the team, whilst 31% only sometimes felt they were and just under a quarter (23%) felt unimportant. More specifically, although over half of the carers (56%) thought that their views were usually taken seriously, a quarter considered that this was the case only some of the time and worryingly almost one in five (19%) found that their views were not taken seriously. That means that a sizeable group – about half – were unhappy with the way in which the professionals treated them.

As one carer said:

> [It's a] 'them and us' situation – that's how it feels. We're the amateurs and they are the professionals.

Access to other professional help

In the interviews we also asked the foster carers whether they had access to any professionals, other than social workers or family placement workers, for help or advice in a crisis. Well over half (57%) had no such access. Thirteen per cent (9) said that they would use the services of their GP, 7% (5) a counsellor, 5% (3) a psychiatrist, 3% (2) a clinical psychologist, 6% (4) other professionals while 9% (6) were unsure.

The experience of strain was significantly related to whether the carers had access to outside professionals. Of those who had such access only 20% felt under strain whereas 53% of those without access to other professionals felt under strain. There was also a relationship between foster carers feeling satisfied with the young person's social worker and obtaining access to other professionals for help or advice. This may be because it was often the social worker who had arranged the provision of help from other professionals.

Of the carers with poor social support only 8% had access to professionals as compared with 46% of those with some or substantial social support. It appeared that carers who already had good social networks were also skilled at ensuring that supports from the wider professional network were forthcoming.

Respite care

In recent years respite care has been developed (see for example Aldgate 1993; Bradley and Aldgate 1999; Webb and Aldgate 1999) and we had expected that it would be an important ingredient of support in some of our placements. However, this did not prove to be the case. At the outset respite care was planned for 4 of the 68 placements, but in practice in only one was regular respite care actually provided. As the study progressed, in one case respite stays were provided too late to stave off disruption but in another respite care was used successfully to prevent a placement breakdown. This suggests that whilst respite care is rarely used to support the foster placements of adolescents, consideration might be given to testing its effectiveness in preventing placement disruption.

Foster carer groups

Foster carer groups are another important source of help for carers and 84% knew about their local group. Attendance was compulsory for just nine carers, all of whom worked for a specialist scheme, and tied to their fees in four of these cases. Over half of the carers attended a foster carer group (one carer attended in 42% of cases and carer couples in 10%). The remaining 48% rarely attended. Attendance was higher for couple carers, almost two-thirds of whom attended (63%), than for single carers (29%). This suggests that lack of adequate child care arrangements may be a barrier for many single carers.

Satisfaction with the groups was fairly high with 14% very satisfied and 61% satisfied, but a notable minority (26%) were either dissatisfied or very dissatisfied. Carers commented on 'extremely useful' sessions on subjects such as prostitution and also on the support which carers gave each other. For example, one carer said:

> This group is very supportive to each other. It's possible to be completely honest, to complain, to get advice, but we also laugh!

Of those who did not attend, 26% had child care difficulties, for example, they could not find or afford sitters for the children; almost one in five was too busy (17%); the same proportion thought the groups were not worth attending (17%); whilst for 5% the groups were at an inconvenient time of day and 35% had other problems or a combination of difficulties. These figures suggest that more carers might go to groups if help was offered to deal with any obstacles to attendance.

However, of those who were not keen to attend, some complained that the groups were cliquey or competitive, or that:

> The same few people turn up. Problems that arise are rarely solved.

One carer commented that:

> Social workers frowned on any negative comments even though it is supposed to be a support group – can cause more stress than support.

This carer said that, as a result, the foster carers talked to each other about the real problems they faced during the coffee breaks rather than during the group sessions.

Contact with individual carers

Of the 43 carers who answered the question, 86% had contact with individual foster carers for advice or practical help. Foster carers are clearly an important source of advice and help to each other. This underlines the importance of foster carer groups and training in making and cementing these relationships.

It is important to note that more couple than single carers had this helpful contact. Of the couple carers 92% had such contact as compared with 78% of single carers. This is probably related to the fact that more couple than single carers attended the foster carer groups.

Out of hours services

Arrangements for out of office hours help, advice and support varied considerably. Almost one in five carers (19%) could call on a specialist team, 3% could contact a family placement worker, whilst the majority (67%) had to rely on the general emergency duty team which provides all out of hours services for the local authority. Twenty-six per cent of the carers were very satisfied and 48% satisfied with these arrangements. On the other hand, 17% were dissatisfied and 9% very dissatisfied with this cover. Thus an important minority (more than a quarter) had reasons for dissatisfaction with the out of hours arrangements in their authorities.

Foster carers often commented that the emergency duty teams would try hard to take no action when called and rarely came out. As one carer said:

[They are] never that helpful. Always seek to do nothing if possible. They are more likely to be asking us to do something, for example provide emergency placements.

Another carer said:

People on the line are often distracted or sound rather bored or put out by your call.

In one case distressed foster carers who reported that a young person was sitting on the front lawn at 2 a.m. refusing to come inside were told by the emergency social worker to take her to McDonald's. In another case, when the police contacted the emergency duty team at midnight to say that a foster child who had run away was at the police station the response was that since the child had got herself there under her own steam, she could get home under her own steam too.

There was a significant relationship between carers feeling well supported and feeling satisfied with out of hours support. Feeling an important member of the professional team was significantly related both to satisfaction with out of hours support and, as already noted, with having access to a specialist out of hours service.

Foster carers' own children

We were interested in how much support and help birth children provided to their parents who were foster carers. Over a quarter of the carers (27%) said that they got a lot of support from their children, 53% some and one in five none. The carers' own adult children often played an important role in supporting the placement, either through direct help to the carers or through the relationships they made with the fostered young people. Carers' younger children or grandchildren or other fostered children in the household too were sometimes good playmates or confidantes for placed adolescents.

Carers' own children (whether living in the family or outside it) were often seen as mediators between the foster carers and the fostered children. One foster carer explained it as follows:

> My immediate family – especially my son Philip when he's at home – has supported me throughout my fostering career [and] has a profound understanding of the issues. There are no problems about confidentiality. Also he's a valuable go-between, being within the peer group of the young people fostered.

In a similar way, a few carers said that a foster child was particularly helpful to them, as one explained:

> The oldest and youngest foster children help with any problems (although sometimes the oldest causes them).

Occasionally though, the carers' children had less positive effects on the placements, such as when the demands of visiting children and grandchildren deprived adolescents of the individual attention from carers which they needed or when relationships between the adolescent and another child in the placement turned sour, and these could then be factors in placements ending.

The availability and usefulness of sources of help

We asked the foster carers to rate the usefulness of a number of sources of help both professional and informal, including family, friends and institutions such as the school or police. When useful help was checked against the availability of such assistance, the realities of useful help actually received by the carers can be seen in Table 8.1.

Table 8.1 Availability of useful support	
	Useful support which was regularly available (%)
Family placement worker	85
Own children	82
Other foster carers	71
Partner	69
Young people's social worker	64
Friends	57
School	54
GP	38
Foster carers' parents	36
Psychologist/psychiatrist	36
Other relatives	36
Police	34
Work colleagues	33
Neighbours	25
Religious organisation	7

In practice, the highest proportion of carers drew useful help from their family placement workers (85%) and their own children (82%), followed by other foster carers (71%), a partner (69%) and the young people's social workers (64%). About half of the carers made use of their friends (57%) and the local school (54%). Around a third received valued help from their GP (38%), their own parents (36%), a psychologist or psychiatrist (36%), other relatives (36%), the police (34%) or work colleagues (33%). Far fewer received such help from neighbours (25%) or from their faith (7%).

Dimensions of support

From this analysis a number of key dimensions of support to foster carers emerged. One is the availability of support, that is, how readily and reliably such help can be accessed. In the case of professional help this depends on practitioners always responding quickly to requests for help. An added issue is availability if needed on a 24-hour basis. A second dimension is the usefulness of the support that is provided. Support may be available but not useful or vice versa. People with particular skills, knowledge and experience were highly valued. A third dimension is the suitability of different people to act as supporters, so it seems that the church and neighbours are often not very suitable, partly through lack of knowledge and partly because of issues of confidentiality, whilst children are, through their accessibility and close knowledge of the situation. Finally, a fourth dimension might be the foster carer's feeling of having the right to request help. They feel they do have this with other foster carers, partly no doubt because such help may be reciprocal and partly through having a current shared experience of the fostering task. They may not feel this so strongly with other professionals, such as GPs.

Availability of specialist help for the young people

Finally, we looked to see how often the young people were receiving help from other professionals, as it had emerged during interviews that an important aspect of support for foster carers is gaining access, when needed, to outside professional help for the children they foster (see also Butler and Charles 1999). When foster carers considered that a child needed specialist help and it was not provided this could do much to make them feel unsupported. The foster carers reported that over half (54%) of the young people in our study were not receiving any specialist help and the remainder (37%) were or had been seeing a variety of specialists including a psychiatrist (4), a psychotherapist (3), an individual counsellor (3), a clinical psychologist (2), family counsellor (2), educational psychologist (1) and family centre worker (1) or another professional (6), whilst three children were visiting more than one such specialist. Six young people were awaiting an appointment (9%).

Significantly more of the boys were seeing a specialist (52%) than the girls (23%) There was a connection, which did not quite reach significance, between carers feeling better supported and the young person seeing a specialist. Of the cases where the young person was seeing an outside professional, 44% of the carers felt well supported, compared with only 26% feeling well supported when this was not the case. More young people who received specialist help also received frequent social work visits.

Ten foster carers had themselves searched for individual help for the young people but only five had been successful. The carers who had looked but could not find help for the fostered young person often also had infrequent social work visits. It appeared that social work activity in making appropriate referrals for outside help was linked to the extent of involvement with the fostered young person as measured by the level of social work visiting.

Differences in the preparation and support provided for specialist and mainstream foster carers

Carers who worked for specialist schemes were more satisfied with their income from fostering and with the placement itself than others and more often felt very well supported, but these differences did not quite reach statistical significance. In addition, fewer specialist than other carers showed evidence of strain on the GHQ. They also more often had access to a counselling scheme for foster carers and were significantly more often very satisfied with out of hours arrangements than mainstream carers and found social workers easier to contact. Many more specialist foster carers (51%) had access to professional help or advice if they needed it as compared with mainstream carers (14%) and more felt included in the help their fostered child received.

The specialist carers more often attended the foster carer groups organised by social workers than their mainstream counterparts and, as we have seen, for a few (9 out of 42) attendance was compulsory. Overall, the specialist carers tended to receive higher levels of local authority or agency support and received significantly more social and community support as compared with mainstream carers.

Shortfalls in support for single carers

A somewhat worrying finding was that on a number of ratings of support single carers did less well than couples. As one carer said:

> I sometimes feel that it is not appreciated that being a single foster carer has problems of its own.

This carer felt the need for a child-sitting service to enable her to go out. Without this she felt isolated and that she would never make a new adult relationship.

Lone carers were significantly more likely than couple carers to have low support scores across all the dimensions of support – support from family members, friends, community professionals and from social services. In particular, they were significantly less likely than carers in couple relationships to have much useful support from members of their families. Over three-quarters (77%) of lone carers had low family support scores, whereas less than half (42%) of couple carers had these low scores.

Furthermore, lone carers regarded the support received from professionals such as psychologists, counsellors and therapists for the children they cared for as being less useful than did couple carers. In spite of these shortfalls, lone carers reported getting more useful support from friends than couple carers ($p<0.05$).

As previously mentioned, lone carers were also less likely to attend foster carer support groups. Among those who attended groups, almost two-thirds were couple carers (63%) whilst only 29% were lone carers. Possibly as a result, lone carers made slightly less use of individual carers as sources of help than couple carers. In addition, we have already noted in a previous chapter that single carers had been involved in less training than couple carers.

These findings suggest that the lone carers in our sample generally received less support from almost all potential sources than couple carers, although they did receive more useful support from friends. One issue was that lone carers found it difficult to get sitters for the children in order to access support services or to get out to develop their social networks. One way to increase the numbers of foster carers would be to recruit more single carers. However, their particular needs for support and the barriers to accessing services will need considerably more attention if this is to be successful.

Overall levels of support

Towards the end of the first interviews we asked the foster carers how well supported they felt overall. As can be seen in Table 8.2, just under a third (32%) said very well supported, almost half (49%) quite well supported and almost one in five (19% or 13) not very well supported. Clearly in spite of evidence of very skilled and dedicated practice there was still a worrying minority of foster carers (almost one in five) who lacked adequate support.

	Number	Percentage
Table 8.2 Foster carers' overall perception of support at the first interviews		
Not well supported	13	19
Quite well supported	33	49
Very well supported	22	32
Total	68	100

Not surprisingly, we found that there was a significant relationship between carers' feelings of being supported and their experience of strain ($p = 0.03$). Of those who felt poorly supported, half reported feeling under strain whereas of those who felt very well supported only 23% did so. On the other hand, it was interesting that total GHQ scores and feelings of support were not significantly related.

We checked to see if there were other variables which related to the foster carers' feelings of being well supported. The carers' perceptions of how well they were supported were significantly related to how easy it was to contact the young people's social workers ($p = 0.05$) but not the family placement workers. This is probably because there were relatively few contact problems with the family placement workers. Of those who felt well supported around half (53%) found the social worker difficult to contact but of those who felt poorly supported more than three quarters (78%) found the social worker hard to contact. Low frequency of social workers' visits to the young people and to the carers was also connected with carers feeling poorly supported.

Significantly more of the carers looking after young people with severe behaviour problems on the SDQ felt unsupported ($p = 0.02$). Similarly, significantly more of the carers who considered the young people they looked after had difficult behaviour felt unsupported, as did those who considered the young person's behaviour was having an adverse effect on the foster family. As we have seen, another important finding was that carers' experience of being supported was also significantly related to their satisfaction with out of hours arrangements. Of those who felt well supported, 94% were satisfied with these arrangements, but of those who felt poorly supported only 66% were satisfied. Carers also more often felt well supported when the young people were seeing a specialist.

Interdependence of the different parts of formal support systems

We had some concern that the foster carers' ratings of support did not seem to reflect what they had told us about the quality of the individual services they received. We therefore mapped in detail all the types of services each carer received against their satisfaction with these services and then looked to see how these matched their ratings of overall support from social services departments.

When the whole pattern of support was scrutinised it emerged that foster carers experienced support systems very much like nets. If one part was weak then their overall ratings were low, even when the other supports for them were strong. For example, a carer who was very satisfied with the family placement worker and the foster carer group and satisfied with the social worker was very dissatisfied with the out of hours service supplied by the emergency duty team and rated herself as overall 'not well supported'. Yet another carer who was very satisfied with the family placement worker, social worker and out of hours services was very dissatisfied with the local foster carer group which was rather competitive and was displeased by the lack of information about the young person given by the social worker. As a result her overall rating of support was 'not well supported'.

The implication of this finding is that all the key formal support services need to be in place if carers are to feel adequately supported. Authorities in which changes have been made to strengthen one part of the service at the expense of another, such as by increasing pay but removing family placement workers, are likely to find their foster carers very dissatisfied.

Were supports provided to those who needed them most?

We were keen to discover whether the carers who were most in need of support were the ones to receive it. We found that the young people's social workers made more frequent visits to the children who had the more severe behaviour problems. In contrast, as previously noted, social workers visited to see the carers and the child least often when the carers were *most* under strain. This could mean that attentive social work reduces strain or that strain increases when there is too little visiting. Either or both of these are likely since the carers who felt well supported also found the children's social workers easy to contact and had frequent social work visits.

However, this means that when carers felt most stressed the children's social workers actually visited less. We know that foster carers felt keenly about the variable service that they received from the young people's social workers. As one carer put it, 'A different social worker can make a hell of a difference'. It may be that visits are more rewarding with the less strained carers or that these less stressed carers are better at eliciting the services they need.

There was also a surprising and statistically significant relationship between low levels of local authority support and poor social and local professional support and between high support of both kinds. Clearly, this relationship is not in the direction that we might have hoped. One kind of support is not compensating for the other. It is likely that in the local authorities with higher support levels, there is less general strain on resources and more referrals are made to local GPs, schools and other agencies. It may also be that carers who are well supported by professionals gain a feeling of competence and mastery that carries over into their social life and vice versa.

However, this was not a one-off finding. A number of other findings suggested similar accumulations of support or lack of it. For example, we also found that the young people's social workers and the family placement workers saw the foster carers with good social and local professional support *more* frequently than they saw the carers with more fragile social support systems ($p = 0.01$). It could be that the more frequent visits had helped to create better general support for the carers or that these better supported carers knew how to get a better service from the local authority professionals. Similarly, a significantly higher proportion of carers who had good social and community support (38%) also found the young person's social worker easy to contact, as compared with those with poor social support (7%). It could be that those with good general support had less anxiety about any difficulties they encountered in contacting social workers or that they drew higher response levels from them.

However, it also turned out that more of the experienced carers had substantial social and community professional support than the less experienced carers. More experienced carers will have had longer to establish good social and community networks that support their fostering but it is also quite likely that they are also more skilled at eliciting, or perhaps demanding, the support that they need. More single foster carers had poor social and community support (33%) than couple carers (17%). We have already noted the higher social support levels enjoyed by couple carers. Interestingly, couple carers (60%) also had somewhat higher levels of local authority support than single carers (43%) although the difference did not quite reach statistical significance.

These findings may suggest that rather than services being tailored to meet the individual needs of the carers, those who already have fairly good support systems get more help than those who are vulnerable. It may well be that social workers and family placement workers need to find out more about foster carers' support systems and ensure that services better match needs. Certainly, we found some carers who lacked the confidence to ask for help when they needed it and who feared that needing help might be interpreted as a sign that they were not coping. In all, 22% of the foster carers had minimal or little social and local professional support. These carers had little access to informal foster care support, were isolated from family and social support networks and had little positive contact with professionals.

Changes in the support provided over the one year follow-up

Requests for help during or after the placement

We found that the foster carers who were looking after young people with either conduct problems or hyperactivity had great difficulty in containing these young people on their own. A significant proportion of foster carers were clearly dissatisfied with the placements at the time of the first interviews and as the placement went on four-fifths asked for help, primarily for the young people but also for themselves. Of those who requested help in looking after a young person with conduct problems fewer than two-thirds received any assistance and of these the help was effective in only half of the cases. For the remainder, the service arrived too late or was insufficiently tailored to the needs of the young people and their carers. It is not surprising therefore that hyperactivity and conduct problems at the first interviews predicted poor outcomes on both of our measures.

Foster carers rarely asked for help for themselves when a placement ended in an abrupt or painful manner. Nonetheless, they told us that they would have greatly appreciated an opportunity to talk through what had happened. One said:

> Since Julie left the placement we no longer receive the support we were receiving from Julie's individual worker. Since Julie's removal from the placement was quite traumatic I feel that we could have used some additional support at this time to help us make sense of what had happened.

Only one carer couple had received an appropriate service to assist them after a placement breakdown. This seems an unfortunate gap (see also Quinton *et al.* 1998). Social services departments too would benefit from an analysis of why placements end in order to refine subsequent placement decisions, whether through disruption meetings or by some other means.

Overall levels of support

At the second interviews we rated how well supported foster carers were overall. As Table 8.3 shows, a third were rated as not well supported, over a third quite well supported and more than one in five very well supported. When these ratings were compared with those from the first interviews a somewhat worrying picture emerged. Those considered to be poorly supported had increased from 19% to 34%. In practice, 6 of the foster carers were considered to be better supported than at the first interview and 14 less well supported. For the majority (47) there was no change in the support provided.

Table 8.3 Foster carers' overall levels of support at the second interviews		
	Number	*Percentage*
Not well supported	23	34
Quite well supported	25	37
Very well supported	19	29
Total	67	100

No information on one case

Interestingly, poor support at follow-up did not itself directly relate to poor placement outcome. The carers who felt poorly supported one year after the start of the placement were those where, at the outset, both the initial information and preparation for the placement had been deficient. The other factors that related to carers feeling poorly supported by follow-up were that, at the start of the placement, the mental health needs of the young people had not been adequately addressed, other interventions needed by the young people had not been provided, the carers had found the social worker difficult to contact and the worker had not been willing to take their views seriously.

Factors that related to carers feeling well supported by follow-up were that the initial care plan had made sufficient provision to support the placement; the carers had access to help from a GP, psychologist, counsellor or psychiatrist; had not been under strain at the start of the placement; had been satisfied with out of hours support from the outset and had always found the social worker easy to contact. The striking thing about these findings is that many of the factors that are linked to how well supported foster carers feel after a one year period relate to the early preparation and help provided in the placement. Clearly, if things are done well from the beginning this augurs well. In contrast, trying to provide help later in the placement is much less effective.

The foster carers with substantial social networks and local professional support at follow-up had an increased chance of being satisfied with the placements by that stage. They also offered more warmth to the young people than more poorly supported carers and the young people they looked after had a significantly increased likelihood of having their major needs met and showing improved well-being.

The relationship between support and placement outcome

We were interested to examine how far support related to placement outcome. Some studies have found very few or no links (see for example Quinton *et al.* 1998; Sinclair *et al.* 2000). However, one advantage of our methodology was that we were in a good position to tease out these associations. We found that a number of areas of support from the first interviews were significantly related to placement outcome and could therefore be useful as predictors. The carers who had a lot of support from their own children (including adult children) had fewer disruptions (see also Ames 1993 in relation to placements of children with severe learning disabilities). More recognition is needed of the important role played by the carers' children in supporting placements. These children wanted their views to be listened to and their difficulties acknowledged, including feelings of jealousy and lack of attention.

As previously mentioned, there were also fewer placement breakdowns when young people had appropriate therapeutic help, that is when the carers did not consider such assistance necessary or where the young people were already receiving such help. Successful placements (using our other outcome measure) were significantly more frequent when the young people reported that they were receiving counselling and there were more failed placements when carers thought that the young people needed therapeutic help that had not been forthcoming. In addition, there were significantly more successful placements when the carers were receiving substantial support from family members (principally their parents, partners and children), their social networks and from local professionals, such as doctors and teachers. Finally – and this finding links to a number of others – support from the young person's social worker (including through arranging services) was significantly related to the success of the placement.

In summary, the supports that make a difference to adolescent placement outcomes are from both the informal system (support from children, other family members and social networks) and the formal. Foster carers benefited from support from local professionals, but in addition, they needed appropriate therapeutic help for the young people and good support from the children's social workers. The encouraging message from these findings is that good professional help is related to better placement outcomes, so local authorities and agencies can make changes that are likely to improve outcomes.

Given the unrelenting pressure on children's social workers it will be difficult to improve the service they provide without arranging for much greater specialisation or considerable task reallocation so that routine tasks such as permissions for overnight stays are devolved to foster carers. In addition, given the shortage of therapeutic services for adolescents, local authorities may need to consider employing therapists or paying privately for their services. The other key message from these findings is that good early preparation and service planning has positive effects throughout the placement.

We end the chapter with some case examples that illustrate some of the ways in which support relates to placement outcomes.

Case example 1: Poor support is linked to placement disruption

Carl, who was aged 17, had moderate learning difficulties and had been in and out of care for most of his life. His foster placement with Pat and Jim was meant to continue until he was 18. The foster carers believed that, due to his learning difficulties, he would never be able to live completely independently but would need some form of supported accommodation. However, making the arrangements for this had been left almost entirely to the foster carers.

Pat had to locate and visit suitable accommodation and then fill in all of the forms outlining Carl's difficulties and needs.

Carl had had three different social workers in the previous 12 months and his case was then unallocated. Pat's requests for respite, for a sessional worker for Carl, and for activities for him during the holidays had been ignored. Carl's family criticised the carers for asking for respite whilst their grandchildren visited, saying that they thought Pat was putting her family before Carl. Pat spoke to her link worker about this situation as she felt she should not be put in that sort of position, but again she received no support in dealing with Carl's family.

Eventually Pat asked for the placement to be ended as she felt she was being given no support from social services in caring for Carl day-to-day, making arrangements for his future or for dealing with the hostility from his family.

Case example 2: The provision of support does not influence placement disruption

Phil by the age of 15 had been in numerous foster placements, residential care and a STEPS (short-term emergency placement service) placement before being placed with Mary. He had a great deal of support from social services, including seeing his social worker twice a week, plus sessional workers, two social workers from the STEPS project and a counsellor. He had activities organised for him after college and during the holidays. Mary is a Senior Fostering Officer and has fostered for almost 36 years but said that she had never seen so much support provided for any other young person. This level of support for Phil caused some resentment from the other boys in the placement as they had much less support from social services.

Mary said that the support for her was also excellent, both from Phil's social worker and the duty team at social services. Even with this support, however, the placement broke down. Phil was not at all committed to making the placement work and was not prepared to take responsibility for his behaviour or the impact that his behaviour had on the foster family. Both Mary and Phil's social worker felt that nothing more could have been done to make the placement work unless Phil was prepared to change.

Case example 3: Proactive support prevents placement disruption

Craig was placed with Marion and John after leaving secure accommodation, to which he had been sentenced following a number of offences, including burglary and assaults. The foster placement was frequently difficult due to Craig's temper and rapid resort to violence. Craig had a very difficult relationship with his mother, who alternated between accepting him and rejecting him, and his violent episodes were often preceded by some form of contact with her.

The placement almost broke down after Craig had an argument with the foster carers' daughter, Sarah. Craig hit Sarah and stormed out. He was moved to a children's home for a fortnight whilst Marion, John and Sarah decided whether they wanted to continue the placement. The independent fostering agency arranged for John and Craig to go on a short fishing holiday together so that they could sort things out. After a few days, Marion and Sarah joined them so that they could all spend time together in a neutral atmosphere. All four decided that they did want to give the placement another chance and were all committed to making it work.

The fostering agency also arranged for Craig to have home tuition as he was unable to settle at school, even in the agency's own school. A combination of work experience with John, who was a farrier, and home tuition seemed to work well for Craig. By the follow-up stage he planned to go to college to train to become a farrier himself.

Now that the supports available to the carers and their effectiveness have been examined, in the next chapter the parenting approaches of the foster carers in the study are considered.

Chapter Nine

The Parenting Approaches of the Foster Carers

Few studies have attempted to measure the parenting skills that are important in looking after adolescents. One of the aims of this research was to conduct a detailed assessment of the parenting approaches and strategies used by the foster carers in the study.

The method of assessment used was based on well-established techniques developed in other studies of parenting (Quinton and Rutter 1984, 1988; Quinton *et al.* 1998). During the initial interviews, foster carers were asked to give detailed descriptions of their responses to various issues or episodes that had arisen at home, in school or outside the placement. For example, the carers were asked for information about how they managed or disciplined incidents of difficult behaviour, and about how they responded to the young person's concerns or anxieties. The carers described the extent to which they facilitated the young person's social development, including education, leisure activities and peer relationships. Areas of development relating specifically to adolescence, such as the management of sexual relationships and sex education, were also discussed. The carers explained how they managed contact between the young person and their birth family and how they dealt with any difficulties that arose from such contact.

The parenting approaches used by the carers were rated again at the second interview stage on the same dimensions as at the start of the placement. The changes in the parenting styles and approaches were noted and related to the changes in the young people's behaviour. It is difficult to state categorically whether the carers' parenting styles altered in response to changes in the young person's behaviour, or the young person's behaviour changed as a result of changes in the carers' parenting approaches. The true picture is likely to be a combination of adjustments by both parties. Previous research suggests that parenting quality is maintained or improved when the carers are rewarded by positive changes in the young person's behaviour. Conversely, where the behaviours are unaffected by the carers' efforts, the ability to continue with strategic approaches to manage behaviour seems to dissipate (Quinton et al. 1998).

The descriptions given by the carers were used to make summary ratings for each carer on key dimensions of parenting. The degree of consistency between carers was also measured where both carers were interviewed; in general, both carers gave similar accounts. Whilst this may have been a result of interviewing them together, the young people reported that the carers usually dealt with them consistently and it was clear that the majority of the carers made a concerted effort not to let any disagreements affect their responses to the young people.

The relationship between the child's characteristics and parenting

Quinton and his colleagues (1998) suggested that, in the early stages of a placement, the young person's characteristics, previous experiences and behaviour will not greatly influence the parenting strategies employed by the carers but they may do so at a later stage. To check this, each dimension of parenting was run against the young people's gender, age, ethnicity, admission history, their previous experience of adversities and the levels of difficult behaviour which they had demonstrated immediately prior to the placement (see Chapter 4). As expected, none of these characteristics were related to parenting behaviours at the start of the placement.

We then investigated how far the initial parenting approaches of the foster carers were predictive of later disruptions or the quality of the placement for the young people. The complex relationship between the young people's background, their characteristics and behaviour, the effects of family contact and the foster carers' situation probably explains why only a small number of initial parenting strategies were predictive of outcomes for the young people. The parenting styles at the beginning of the placement that did predict outcome are important to note. They were: responding to the young person's emotional as well as chronological age, the level of supervision of young people when outside the placement, the extent of preparation for independent living and the management of contact with the young person's birth family. These will be discussed later.

There were, however, substantial changes in the parenting approaches used by the second interview stage. These appeared to be related to the behaviour of the young people during the placement and were significantly related to the likelihood of disruption and to the success of the placement.

Parenting strategies and approaches

The majority of carers were very experienced and provided a good standard of parenting for the adolescents, which is described below. None of the carers' characteristics, such as age, gender, ethnicity or length of fostering experience were related to either the likelihood of disruption nor the overall quality of the placement. However, placements were more likely to be of a high quality if the foster carers had other relevant work experience, such as nursing, teaching or social work.

Control and discipline

Summary ratings were made for each carer on areas of control and discipline, including levels of indulgence, aggression and supervision. One of the areas of discussion used to make these ratings was the carers' understanding of limits and of the need to set and maintain appropriate boundaries for the individual young people, particularly those presenting difficult behaviour. Suitable boundaries for the young people needed to be established so that their behaviour could be contained without being too restrictive or permissive, taking into account their emotional and developmental age. If the boundaries were too limiting or rigid, particularly for a young person who had not had boundaries set before, the young person was likely to rebel against them and possibly abscond. On the other hand, if boundaries were not set the young person might continue to behave in an unacceptable or risky manner. Furthermore, some young people who have experienced neglect may like firm boundaries as it makes them feel secure and part of the family (Youniss and Smollar 1985).

Ways of achieving the right balance between care and control varied from carer to carer. In some instances carers were clear about broad rules at the beginning of the placement, outlining what was expected of themselves and the young person within the placement. In other cases, the carers said that there were no stated rules or regulations when the young person first moved in, but that the young people learned through experience what was or was not acceptable.

Judging where to set the boundaries for these particular young people is very difficult. In some ways it is the reverse of normal child development where boundaries are established early and gradually relaxed as the child grows. Many of these teenagers had not had consistent boundaries set before and were likely to respond negatively to too many restrictions on their behaviour. The carers sometimes needed to establish a few loose boundaries to begin with and then gradually establish more boundaries to bring the young person into a more normative range – at the same time as encouraging the young person to become independent. For example, Joss had been living almost as a street child for many years. He had lived alone with his mother, a heroin addict, who allowed Joss virtually total freedom to come and go as he pleased. The foster carers began to set basic rules, for example, instead of enforcing a rigid bedtime which Joss would have resented, the carers stipulated that he had to be able to get up in the morning in time to go to college, giving Joss responsibility for his own bedtime. The carers also established a 'reward' system where Joss got extra money on a Friday evening if his behaviour during the week had warranted it.

The majority of carers had either good or average control over the young person's behaviour, but just over 7% had poor control, making only intermittent, irregular or ineffective attempts at control, with the young person generally being able to get their own way. At the opposite end of the spectrum, 4% of carers were over-controlling and restricted the young people's behaviour to their possible detriment, for example not allowing them opportunities for exercising initiative or developing control over their own relationships and environment.

Supervision

Another element of control is the level of supervision of the young person, the awareness of where the adolescent is, who they are with and what they are doing. Adolescents are more likely to succumb to environmental pressures to engage in activities of which adults disapprove when their parents or carers are either very strict or very lax and when there is little monitoring of the young person's activities (Rutter, Giller and Hagell 1998). The carers were rated on their supervision of the young person both within and outside the placement. Generally, supervision within the placement was higher than supervision outside, with 16% of the carers showing low or very inadequate supervision outside the home. For example, one young person had been involved in and convicted of various vehicle-related crimes, including driving without a licence and taking without the owner's consent, yet the carer was rarely aware of where he was, who he was with or what he was doing. The carers of another young person who was seen as at risk of prostitution often did not know her whereabouts. Low levels of supervision outside the placement at the first interview predicted unsuccessful placements ($p<0.05$) whilst, by follow-up, low levels of supervision of activities outside the placement were significantly related to placement breakdown ($p = 0.001$) and fewer successful placements for the young people ($p = 0.03$).

By the time of the follow-up interviews, carers provided less supervision within ($p<0.05$) and outside the placement ($p<0.01$) for the one in five young people (mainly girls) who were at risk due to their sexual behaviour. In addition, the carers were less involved in facilitating these young people's activities and showed less encouragement of their hobbies and leisure pursuits. Both of these factors may of course contribute towards an explanation of why the young people continued to be at risk due to their sexual behaviour during the placement as they were neither being effectively supervised nor encouraged to participate in more appropriate activities. On the other hand, young people who engage in high risk sexual behaviour may not be readily amenable or available for involvement in other activities. It seems that there is lack of knowledge or expertise about how to manage this specific group of teenage girls who display inappropriate sexual behaviour (see also Farmer and Pollock 1998). This is discussed in more detail below.

Carers were significantly more likely to increase their supervision within the home if they were concerned about the young person's use of drugs or alcohol ($p<0.05$). There were no significant differences, though, in the levels of external supervision of these young people, which suggests that the carers' increased concern may be related to the protection of other children in the family, or it may be that the carers do not see their role as extending to supervision outside the placement. Behaviour within the home is in a domain in which carers can more easily have an influence and the young people, of course, are likely to be more amenable to control within the placement than they are outside it. However, these young people were often at risk outside and it may be important for foster carers to try to extend their monitoring role beyond the confines of the home.

Sensitive responding

Responsiveness and receptivity to the child are important parenting attributes in caring for fostered children (Quinton *et al.* 1998). Sensitive responding has been defined as 'the degree of understanding and sympathy with which parents handled both anxiety and distress and defiance and misbehaviour' (Quinton *et al.* 1998, p.190). Sixteen per cent of the carers in this sample were rated as being insensitive and were unable to recognise or respond to the young people's anxieties or worries. For example, one carer showed a clear lack of awareness of the boy she was fostering. She described him as very self-confident and arrogant and was ignorant of his interests, needs or problems. At the other end of the scale, 50% showed above average or very sensitive responding, being able to recognise and respond to non-verbal cues and to anticipate anxiety-provoking circumstances.

A key element of sensitive responding was found to be the ability to recognise and work with the young people at their emotional or developmental age, rather than just their chronological age. Twenty-nine (43%) of the young people showed evidence of behaviour and needs appropriate to much younger children (see also Farmer and Pollock 1998). For example, one 15-year-old boy whose mother had died when he was 9 desperately missed physical attention. Although the carer said she felt uncomfortable with it, she allowed him to have a cuddle and suck his thumb for a while, as a younger child would, before encouraging him to act in a more age-appropriate way. In contrast, a 13-year-old girl appeared physically much older than she was, and behaved in a manner more typically shown by older teenagers. She was well-developed, outwardly confident, smoked, was sexually active and appeared very mature in her outlook. As a result, some adults had tended to treat her as a much older teenager, and had expected her to take on responsibilities not suited to someone of only 13. Her carers responded in a way that took into account her previous experiences and expectations, yet encouraged her to revert to behaviour more suitable for a young girl, such as playing with dolls and drawing. Whilst two-thirds (19) of the carers of these young people responded to the young person's emotional age as well as their chronological age, some carers were unable to do so. Placements in which the carer did not respond to the young person's emotional age were significantly more likely to break down ($p = 0.049$).

TALKING ABOUT THE PAST

Another aspect of sensitive responding is allowing the young person to talk about the past (Macaskill 1991; Farmer and Pollock 1998). Young people who were able to talk about the more negative events in their backgrounds with the foster carers or other important adults had significantly fewer placement disruptions than those who were not able to do so ($p = 0.018$). Whilst this is partly dependent upon the young person's readiness to speak about distressing events, it requires sensitivity and receptivity by the foster carers and a willingness to make time for the young person to share these difficulties. The carers who demonstrated the capacity to hear painful past events had, in some instances, developed specific strategies for eliciting and dealing with the young person's anxieties and concerns. For example, one carer set aside an hour's 'bubble time' every week, during which she enabled the young person to 'burst the bubble' and talk about any past or current issues that were causing her distress.

Warmth

Warmth is also a parenting attribute that has been found to be important in previous research (Quinton *et al.* 1998) but a minority (13%) of the carers showed no physical or verbal warmth or affection towards the young person. Fifteen per cent showed some warmth but found it somewhat difficult or problematic to do so. Carers found it significantly harder to show warmth towards young people who had difficulties with their peers (for example, young people who either had no friends or could not sustain relationships) as measured by the SDQ ($p = 0.041$). Nelson's study of adoption (1985) found that the most important factor in poor satisfaction for parents was if the new parents thought that the child was isolated in the sense of having few friends, being mistrustful and holding people at arm's length. Similarly, Sinclair and his colleagues (2000) found that children who were 'aloof' or childishly attached were more likely to experience a placement disruption.

The young person's attitude towards physical and verbal affection was also rated – whether they would like more or less than their carers offered. Carers often tried to adjust the amount of warmth or affection shown to what they perceived the young people to want. In 90% of the cases in the sample the carers did seem to have an accurate perception of the young person's desire for affection, but 5% of the young people would have liked more affection and warmth, and 5% would have liked less than they received.

Liking the young person

The researchers made a judgement on whether or not the carers appeared to like the young person in their care. Some carers talked of experiencing an instant 'bond' with the young person and getting on very well with them (see also Sinclair *et al.* 2000 and Schofield *et al.* 2000). However, 15% of the carers appeared either to dislike or very much dislike the young person. These placements were characterised by the carer showing less warmth and engagement towards the young person, being less sensitive to their needs and providing less intervention for their needs. Carers were less likely to like young people who had been rejected and scapegoated by their families ($p = 0.013$) or who had experienced multiple separations from their main caregiver ($p = 0.015$). It may be that, in light of their relationship histories, these children found it harder to build a relationship with a new caregiver. These findings echo those of Quinton and his colleagues (1998) who found that children who had been rejected by their birth parents made poorer progress with their new adoptive or foster families.

Facilitation of activities and friendships

The extent of help and encouragement the carers gave the young people with their leisure activities was measured. Many of the young people did not see themselves as requiring assistance with activities and this may have deterred the carers from helping, but there was clearly scope for more encouragement of constructive activities. Whilst a fifth of carers were highly involved in arranging or suggesting activities and encouraging the young people to take up new sports or hobbies, such as ice-skating, swimming or Sea Cadets, two-fifths (43%) did not do so. Levels of involvement in the young people's activities did not appear to be related to the age or gender of the young person. It is important to note that the young people in the study who had some special skills or interests of their own at the start of the placement were more likely to have good quality placements than those who did not. Young people who spend their time in positive activities also have less time to become involved in anti-social behaviour. In addition, carers who are involved and interested in young people's free time are likely to have more awareness of their activities outside the home and thus more ability to supervise them outside the placement.

Similarly, the carers were rated on their facilitation of friendships, for example allowing friends to visit or stay, helping with transport arrangements and so forth. Establishing and maintaining good peer relationships is an important aspect of adolescent emotional and behavioural development, yet many of the young people in this sample had problematic peer relationships. However, only 27% of the carers played an active role in encouraging or helping the young person to make and sustain friendships. Three per cent of the carers (two carers) were rated as discouraging, where they limited the amount of positive contact the young person could have with their friends. For example, one carer would not allow any other young people into the house so the fostered girl started meeting her friends out on the streets and hanging around the city centre instead. The majority of carers (48 carers, 70%) were generally encouraging of the young person's friendships, but were not involved in actively facilitating these relationships.

The level of facilitation of activities and friendships was generally fairly stable over time and was not related to either the likelihood of disruption or quality of the placement for the young person. However, the development of positive relationships and activities is important to the promotion of self-esteem and confidence, and can help to expand opportunities available to the young people. This is, again, related to the view that carers have of their role and whether or not their caring responsibilities extend beyond the boundaries of the home.

The management of contact

As early as the first interviews it was clear that, for those young people who saw family members, some aspect of contact was problematic for the great majority (see Chapter 10; see also Sinclair *et al.* 2000). The foster carers considered that half of the young people had difficulties in their contact with family members and for most adolescents there was remarkably little improvement in contact during the placement.

Difficulties with contact, as we will see, were significantly related to higher disruption rates. In addition, there were fewer successful placements when at the first interviews carers were highly involved in attempting to manage the contact between the young person and family members. Carers were involved in contact issues in this way when young people had particularly difficult histories, problematic contact and showed the kinds of disruptive behaviour that related to placement breakdown. Their ability to assist in resolving contact issues, however, was circumscribed unless the young person's social worker took action to intervene.

The effects of strain on parenting

As we have seen, when foster carers were under stress, their parenting capacity was reduced and this could lead to poorer outcomes for the young people. The carers were asked about their experiences of difficult or stressful life events (for example, relationship difficulties, family illness or bereavement, accidents, work changes or people joining or leaving the family, including foster children) in the six months prior to the start of the placement. They were also asked about strain during the placement and the GHQ was used to measure the effects of the strain they experienced (see Chapter 7). Notably, carers on whom prior stress had had an intense impact were significantly less likely than others to show very sensitive responding ($p<0.05$) or to like the young people ($p = 0.015$). They were also significantly less likely to respond to the young person's emotional age than the less strained carers ($p = 0.004$).

These findings showed that placing a young person with carers who are currently experiencing or have previously experienced a high level of stress may put the young person at a considerable disadvantage early in the placement. This suggests that consideration needs to be given to the strain that carers are under when a placement is being made in view of the reduced ability of stressed carers to recognise or respond to the young person's emotional or developmental needs.

Routine omissions in foster care practice

There were a number of omissions in routine foster care practice, particularly relating to the facilitation of education, the discussion of sexual health and contraception and the development of life skills, which suggest that there may be a lack of clarity about what is expected of foster carers, or a lack of training and support in these areas. There were also examples of reduced sensitivity to the needs of fostered girls. The overall high standard of care suggests that these deficits were not due to the carers' inability to parent the young people but that a significant minority of carers did not view their role as extending to these areas.

Facilitation of education

Like many children within the care system, the majority of the young people in the sample had experienced high levels of educational disruption, with 46% (30) having been excluded and 56% (37) regularly playing truant from school. A lack of educational skills makes care-leavers particularly vulnerable to unemployment and is associated with involvement in offending behaviour (Farrington 1996). The level of involvement carers had in facilitating the young person's education was therefore rated. Thirty-six per cent of the carers were highly involved, encouraging the young person to attend school and showing interest in their achievements. Where the young people were not attending school, these carers were actively involved in finding alternative educational provision. Fifty per cent showed average involvement in the young person's education, being moderately encouraging of their educational activities and providing some practical help and support. However 14% showed little or no facilitation, being unaware of the young people's educational progress or of any problems they had at school. In addition, 20 of the foster carers reported having no contact with the young people's school teachers. Single carers were significantly less likely to be involved in the young person's education than couple carers and may need additional support and assistance if they are to do so. Given the educational disadvantages of looked-after young people, this highlights an area where routine practice needs to change.

Development of life skills

For many of the young people, a return home was not envisaged so they were likely to have to become self-sufficient and independent at a much earlier age than most teenagers. The extent to which carers encouraged the young people to develop life skills and self-efficacy was measured, as was the management of appropriate levels of independence, for example tidying their own room, helping with household chores, cooking, budgeting and managing public transport. For both ratings, consideration was given to the young person's chronological and developmental age, for example a 12-year-old would not be expected to develop the same skills as a 16-year-old. Gilligan (2000) has suggested that foster care can promote resilience through giving young people a secure base and by enhancing their self-efficacy. However, over 40% of the carers showed no or little encouragement to the young people to develop appropriate life skills. These levels were worryingly low, given the likely future for these young people. Encouraging the development of lifeskills could also affect the quality of the placement for the young person. This is discussed in more detail later.

Discussion of sexual health and development

As adolescence is typically a time of increasing sexual awareness and sexual activity, the carers' management of the young people's sexual relationships was also rated. Most carers were aware of whether or not the young person had a partner, although not necessarily whether it was a sexual relationship. A significant proportion (20%) had little or no knowledge of or control over the young people's involvements. Only 8% of the carers were rated as showing a high level of management of the adolescents' relationships, having good knowledge of them, establishing appropriate rules concerning contact and being sympathetic if the young person was upset about a relationship.

Over half of the foster carers were concerned about the young people's sexual relationships but few actually talked to them about their concerns. As previously mentioned, two-fifths of the carers did not discuss sexual health and sexuality with the young person and they were less at ease discussing sexual matters with boys than girls. Many looked-after young people are poorly informed about normal sexual development, sexual health or contraception (see for example Farmer and Pollock 1998) and need the opportunity to talk about these issues and about their relationships. There was considerable confusion over whose responsibility it was to talk to the young people about sex and sexual health. Some carers believed that the social worker would assume this responsibility yet this was not happening. The high levels of young people leaving care who are either pregnant or who already have children (see for example Speak 1995) is testament to the fact that these young people may need greater advice and support in managing their sexual relationships than they currently receive.

A small proportion (6, 9%) of young people were demonstrating inappropriate sexual behaviour, ranging from having sex with much older men (one 12-year-old girl was having a sexual relationship with a 30-year-old man), to a girl inappropriately touching a younger girl. The carers' management of this behaviour varied, with a quarter of the carers who had to deal with inappropriate sexual behaviour showing poor management, for example trying to shame the young person into changing their behaviour or not enforcing appropriate boundaries around their behaviour. This suggests that inappropriate sexual behaviour may be a particularly difficult area of management for carers (see also Farmer and Pollock 1998). It is notable that almost half of the carers (47%) had not received training on caring for children who sexually abuse others and that this was an issue of concern for a number of carers. How the carers adapted their approach to dealing with such behaviour during the placement is discussed later.

Fostering teenage girls

As noted above, there were particular issues relating to parenting teenage girls. For example, carers were significantly less sensitive to the needs and anxieties of girls than boys, which may be due to boys' tendency to demonstrate their anxieties through their behaviour whilst girls internalise their anxieties more (see for example Colten and Gore 1984; Lerner 1985). This was reflected in the level of communication between some of the girls and their foster carers. One of the ratings we made took account of discrepancies between the carers' and the young people's perceptions of the placement, which in some instances were marked. In four cases (6%) there were major differences in the account given by the young women and their carers. For example, during the interview a 15-year-old girl said that she was very happy in the placement, yet the carers stated they actively wanted the placement to end. Another 15-year-old girl was extremely unhappy with her placement but the carer thought that she was content. The latter was a particularly busy household, with eight children and young people living in the house and many ex-fostered young people making regular visits. The carer was therefore often involved with other children and the young woman in the study felt that the carer did not have time for her. However, she did not have the self-confidence to speak out about her distress to the foster carer or her social worker.

There are a number of issues relating to fostering girls which may have an impact on the relationship they have with their carers. For instance, some carers may find it difficult to cope with a girl's emergent sexuality, particularly when inappropriate sexual behaviour is shown. They may see the girl as a sexual threat or they may become concerned about the risk of allegations against their partner or children. O'Neill (2001) found that staff in local authority secure units had a more negative attitude towards working with girls than with boys. Girls were regarded as more difficult and demanding to work with and were seen as potentially 'dangerous' because of the risk of allegations against male staff. The male staff in these units abdicated responsibility for girls so that the female staff were expected to deal with everything for the girls. A similar negative attitude to girls has been found to prevail among male residential workers in children's homes (Farmer and Pollock 1998).

Clearer policies, training and support might lead to greater involvement by foster carers in these four areas with considerable benefit to placed young people.

The effect of parenting strategies on placement outcomes

Some of the specific parenting strategies at the first interviews had a significant impact on the placement outcomes for the young people, both in terms of the quality of the placement and the likelihood of the placement breaking down. Identifying these strategies is therefore important. Skills which have a positive impact should be encouraged whilst intervention may be needed where parenting approaches which have a negative impact are employed. For example, the degree of supervision outside the placement at the first interview was significantly related to the success of the placement, although the level of supervision within the placement was not. Carers who provided average or good supervision outside the home were significantly more likely to have successful placements than those who provided very inadequate or low supervision ($p =<0.05$). Supervision outside the home can be increased by offering young people lifts, by talking to them about their friends and intervening if children make contact with high risk individuals. Whilst some young people may not be amenable to this, it appears that some foster carers do not see their role as extending to supervision outside the placement. These carers need to be encouraged to view the fostering task more widely and to consider the management of the young people's friends and activities outside the placement as part of their role (see also Farmer and Pollock 1998).

The level of encouragement of appropriate life skills and independence was related to the overall quality of the placement for the young person. Carers who, at the first interview, involved the young people in an average level of preparation for leaving care were significantly more likely to provide good quality placements for the young person overall compared with those who involved the young people in either little or high levels of preparation ($p<0.05$). Lack of help in developing self-efficacy and life skills would put the young person at a disadvantage when they left care but perhaps too much of an emphasis on independence meant that the young person did not settle as well within the placement or that the placement was never seen as more than a short-term bridge to independence.

The foster carers' ability to respond to the young person's emotional age as well as their chronological age at the first interview was significantly related to the likelihood of placement disruption. Seven of the eight place-ments (88%) in which the carer did not respond to the young person's emo-tional age at the beginning of the placement disrupted, compared with 8 (44%) of the 18 placements in which the carer did respond to the young person's emotional age ($p = 0.049$). This has implications for the training needed by carers and suggests the need for a greater focus on child develop-ment and an increase in awareness of the potential disparity between a child's chronological age and their emotional or developmental age.

Whether the foster carer liked the young person at the beginning of the placement did not directly affect the likelihood of placement disruption but was related to poorer parenting in a number of areas. Carers were more likely to show a decrease in liking by follow-up towards young people who were physically aggressive or who had an adverse impact on other children in the household, which may relate in part to the carers' need to protect their own or other fostered children. Furthermore, if carers began or continued to dislike the young person over the course of the placement, the likelihood of place-ment breakdown increased. This is an area that needs to be monitored by social workers who could provide appropriate intervention or guidance.

The amount or type of education that the young person received was not significantly related to the likelihood of placement disruption, nor was school attendance. However, as we have seen, young people who had little or no con-fidence in their school work were more likely to experience a placement dis-ruption, and young people who lacked confidence in their social relationships at school were less likely to experience good quality placements. This high-lights the importance of foster carers' involvement in helping the young person to become more confident at school, both in terms of academic achievement and in building and maintaining social relationships. As men-tioned earlier, young people who had some special skills or interests of their own were more likely to have good quality placements than those who did not. It is possible that developing a hobby or skill may have an impact upon a child's confidence in their school work and friendships, so it is important for the foster carers to view the young person's education and leisure activities as part of their remit.

Parenting changes during the placement

In the main, the foster carers' parenting skills and approaches did not change greatly during the course of the study. However, where a change did occur, it was likely to be a reduction rather than an increase in the carers' parenting capacity (Table 9.1). For example, a third of the carers had less control over the young person's behaviour by follow-up, a fifth of the carers supervised the young people less closely within the placement and the same proportion decreased their supervision of the adolescents outside the placement. A quarter of the foster carers showed less commitment or increased aggression towards the young person. Conversely, a quarter of the carers increased the amount of warmth they demonstrated towards the young person and almost a fifth became more engaged or liked the young person more.

Some of the changes in parenting capacity were related to poorer outcomes for the fostered adolescents. For example, lowered levels of supervision outside the placement were significantly related to poor outcomes in terms of placement disruption and the quality of the placement for the young person.

Table 9.1 Changes in parenting behaviours during the one year follow-up

Parenting behaviour	Percentage of carers showing a change in each behaviour		
	No change	Increase	Decrease
Preparation for leaving care	98	1	<1
Disciplinary consistency	98	<1	<1
Supervision within placement	78	3	19
Supervision outside placement	75	5	20
Indulgence	68	14	18
Control	65	3	32
Engagement	64	17	19
Aggression	63	25	12
Sensitive responding	63	15	22
Commitment	61	14	25
Warmth	58	25	17
Liking	53	22	25

Similarly, lessened commitment, warmth and control over the young people, increased displays of disciplinary aggression, more inconsistent discipline and not liking the young people were all related to an increased risk of placement disruption and poorer quality placements. It is likely that the foster carers became discouraged by their apparent inability to affect the young people's conduct if they continued, or began, to demonstrate difficult behaviour.

Overall, 34% of the fostered young people's relationships with their carers improved during the placement; 25% of the relationships were maintained at the same level; but 41% of the relationships worsened during the placement. Not surprisingly, a deterioration in the young person's relationship with their carers was closely related to poorer outcomes on both of our measures.

Changes in parenting skills associated with child-related factors

Changes in parenting approaches were related in some cases to specific child or carer characteristics. Most were the kinds of change that could be expected when poor behaviour did not improve or when new difficulties emerged. For example, carers showed more disciplinary aggression at follow-up to young people who were violent towards others or who scored highly on a childish attachment measure. The latter were teenagers who, for example, sought a lot of attention from the carers and often showed affection like a younger child. Lower levels of warmth were also shown to young people who lacked attachment to any adult. A number of identifiable behaviours and characteristics were consistently related to considerable changes in parenting and these will now be discussed.

New difficult behaviours

Twenty-five per cent (17) of the young people demonstrated a new type of difficult behaviour during the placement, for example becoming involved in drug use or demonstrating aggressive or destructive behaviour. Generally, placements in which the young person began to show a new type of difficult behaviour tended to be characterised by a lack of control by the carers and poor supervision outside the placement. Carers were also more likely to show average, rather than low, levels of aggression but also increased disciplinary indulgence in these situations. For example, Sam began to show destructive behaviour that he had not shown at the beginning of the placement, damaging walls, carpets and furniture within the house. The foster carer became more aggressive and angry with him, but also more indulgent. She started to give in to some of Sam's demands, such as having his own bedroom and being given money rather than a packed lunch, requests that she had previously denied Sam and continued to deny the other fostered boys. Whilst the foster carer managed to maintain an average level of supervision outside the placement, the level of supervision and control within the placement deteriorated.

Inappropriate sexual behaviour

As noted above, some young people demonstrated inappropriate sexual behaviour during the placement which either put them at risk or was damaging to others. The carers' management of this behaviour changed during the course of the placement, with parenting capacity decreasing when adolescents put themselves at risk sexually but, conversely, increasing when the young person posed a risk to others.

SEXUAL RISK TO THE YOUNG PERSON

Thirteen (19%) of the young people were at risk due to their sexual behaviour during the placement and this was significantly related to the likelihood of placement disruption. Decreased supervision both within and outside the placement was especially common for those who were at risk, and the carers were less involved in facilitating the activities of these young people. Both of these factors may of course contribute towards an explanation of why the young people continued to be at risk due to their sexual behaviour during the placement. However, these young people are very hard to supervise, particularly as they may be heavily influenced by people outside the placement, such as older men. Carers may become frustrated if they feel that they are being ineffective in protecting such young people and begin to withdraw from them. Furthermore, the risk of allegations against a carer by a young person who is behaving inappropriately may lead carers to distance themselves from them.

SEXUAL RISK TO OTHERS

Five (7%) of the young people had put others at risk due to their sexual behaviour during the placement. The carers of these young people were characterised by showing an increase in sensitive responding and engagement with the young people (see also Farmer and Pollock 1998). For example, Adrian had been overheard talking in a sexually inappropriate way with another boy, and had also exposed himself to a girl at school. His foster carers showed increasing sensitivity to Adrian during the placement and became more engaged with him. There are a number of explanations for why carers become more involved with young people who pose a sexual risk to others. For example, young people who put others at risk may be less likely to be placed with other children, or will be placed with older children, and so might receive more attention from the carers who have fewer demands on their time. Children who spend more time with their carers, and who are more highly supervised may be more rewarding for the carers. Although it was not possible to show it within this study, it is feasible that children who present a sexual risk to others have a different behavioural profile than other children and may demonstrate fewer other difficult behaviours within the placement.

The impact of the young person on other children within the household

From the analysis of changes in the young people's behaviour over time and the corresponding changes in parenting strategies, it was apparent that the key behavioural issue which foster carers found difficult to manage and that tended to lead to placement breakdown and / or to poor quality placements, was when young people had a negative impact on the other children in the household (see also Triseliotis 1989).

Young people who had a negative effect on other children in the household were likely to experience a deterioration in parenting by the foster carers, particularly a decrease in warmth and commitment, as well as the carers' showing less control and more aggression. For example, Lucy was verbally abusive towards the other children in the household and set a bad example by becoming involved in substance abuse and possibly prostitution. By the second interview the foster carer expressed considerably less warmth towards Lucy and was much less committed to her. The foster carer had almost no control over Lucy's behaviour, although in this instance she did not show an increase in aggression.

As previously mentioned, carers generally increased their supervision of the young people within the foster home when they were concerned about their use of drugs or alcohol. The fact that the level of supervision outside the placement did not increase suggests either that the carers were principally concerned about the impact of the young person's substance use on other children within the family and did not want to condone drug use within their house or found it particularly difficult to influence the young people's activities outside the home.

There were more placement disruptions when a young person had by follow-up had a negative impact on other children in the household. It seems clear that carers are less likely to tolerate young people who have had a negative impact on either their own children (as in the example given above) or on other foster children. The carers' commitment to and protection of their own children or other foster children overrides their commitment to the young person. Social workers therefore need to be aware of wider issues within the family and to view the family holistically, rather than just being concerned with the fostered child, to determine whether other children in the household are being adversely affected by the fostered young person.

Changes in parenting skills related to carer-related factors

As noted earlier, carers who had experienced significant stress prior to the start of the placement parented the young people less well. Furthermore, carers who were under serious strain on the GHQ at the second stage showed a decrease in liking for the young person and increased disciplinary indulgence, that is, they were less effective at providing consistent appropriate limits. These carers were also likely to show a changed level of aggression towards the young person. This could be either an increase in aggression, for example if the carers were frustrated by their inability to alter the young people's behaviour or a decrease in aggression if the carers began to withdraw from them.

Carers reported high levels of strain when they were looking after young people who they considered to have behaviour problems ($p = 0.05$) or who were violent to other children ($p = 0.05$). Thus it can be seen that strain depleted the resources of the carers. As previously noted, strained carers were less committed and engaged with the young people and less sensitive to them. They also felt more dissatisfied and less well supported. As a result, the needs of the young people in these placements were not well met.

Conclusions

This chapter has discussed the changes in the parenting strategies and approaches used by the foster carers, and how those changes related to the changes in the young people's behaviour. We found that where young people had a negative impact on other children within the family it was associated with deterioration in parenting and an increased likelihood of disruption. Clearly, worsening behaviour that is not influenced by carers' parenting strategies is linked with deteriorating interactions between young people, other children in the family and the carers, and also to poor outcomes. The child and carer characteristics linked to these worsening situations may suggest opportunities for assistance and intervention.

These findings clearly have a number of implications for policy and practice, relating to both the general omissions in parenting approaches and those which were predictive of placement outcomes. Greater consideration of the extent of stressful or difficult events that the carers have experienced prior to the placement is necessary since placing a young person with carers who have experienced high levels of prior stress may put the young person at a considerable disadvantage early in the placement. Additional support to the carers or the placement of a less demanding child might limit these detrimental effects.

There are a number of areas where there is a general need for more involvement in specific aspects of parenting by foster carers, including assistance with the development of life skills, managing the young people's sexual relationships, discussing their sexual health and contraception and more active engagement with schools and with leisure activities. Routine reviews of the foster carers' parenting approaches during placements would enable any 'risk' areas to be identified (for example, a decline in the level of control the carer has over the young person, an increasingly indulgent attitude or the carer appearing not to like the young person) and would allow appropriate intervention. Foster carers also need additional training on managing adolescent sexual behaviour, particularly inappropriate sexual behaviour that could place either the young person or others at risk. As noted above, this was an especially difficult area for some carers to deal with and many had not had relevant training. In addition, there needs to be an increased awareness of the needs of girls, since these are sometimes overlooked.

Good supervision outside the home is linked to improved placement outcomes and is important in keeping the young people safe in terms of offending behaviour, prostitution, drug use and sexual risk. Carers should therefore be encouraged to extend their view of the fostering task to include supervision outside the placement as well as within it. Training could also address strategies for such monitoring of young people's activities outside the home.

There were fewer placement disruptions when young people were able to talk about difficult events in their past and when foster carers were able to respond to the young person's emotional age. Such responsiveness indicates sensitivity and understanding that many looked-after young people function emotionally at an immature level well below their chronological age, and need regular opportunities for play and nurture appropriate to a much younger child, in order to meet these earlier unmet needs. More extensive training on child development might therefore be useful, particularly to raise awareness of the potential disparity between a young person's chronological age and their emotional age. Once any such disparities are recognised, foster carers need a range of skills and strategies to enable them to address the gaps in these young people's developmental experiences.

Now that the parenting approaches of the foster carers have been described we turn to examine the young people's contact with family members and its impact on the foster families.

Chapter Ten

The Young People's Contact with Family Members

As we saw in Chapter 2, contact levels have greatly increased since the implementation of the Children Act 1989. However, little is known about how contact is working for adolescents or about the impact of contact on foster carers. In this chapter we examine the contact experienced by the young people in the study, how far it changed over time and its impact on the foster families, the young people and on the placements themselves.

Family backgrounds

Three-fifths of the placements had been made as a result of relationship breakdowns between the young people and their parents or previous carers and, as we have seen, many had experienced a variety of adversities, including neglect, abuse and rejection before being looked after. The difficulties of the young people's parents included psychiatric disorder, offending, domestic violence and misuse of drugs and alcohol. This then was the background against which contact would take place.

The extent of contact at the first interview stage
Birth mothers

Before moving to the study placement, only 10% of the young people had been living with their fathers (Table 10.1). It was therefore not surprising that the young people much more often had contact with their mothers than their fathers.

Table 10.1 Parents with whom the young person had lived before being looked after

	Number	Percentage
Lived with mother and stepfather	26	38
Lived with lone birth mother	19	28
Lived with both birth parents	9	13
Lived with father and stepmother	4	6
Lived with lone birth father	3	4

Note: In addition, 3 young people moved from an adoptive family and some young people lived with other relatives and friends before being admitted to care.

Nearly three-quarters (71%) of the young people had some contact with their mothers, but of these, one in five saw their mothers less than once a month. However, 20 young people (29%) had no contact at all with their mothers at the first interview: three mothers had died and in one case, a court order prevented contact. There was no contact for the other 16, either because the young people, their mothers or both did not want to see each other. Most of these situations where there was no contact with the mother involved girls (14 girls and 2 boys).

Birth fathers

Far fewer of the young people saw their fathers and only one in five (19%) saw them regularly. Seven of the fathers had died but more than half (56%) of the young people, whose fathers were alive (20 girls and 14 boys), had no contact with them at all. Many fathers had played no part in the lives of the young people for some time.

Siblings

Four of the young people were only children but the remainder had complex family structures, which often included half and step as well as full siblings. Only two were initially placed with a sibling, but another 31% of the young people (21) had siblings in other foster or residential placements and the remainder had brothers and sisters who still lived with one or both of their parents.

Over half of the young people (58%) maintained regular contact with their siblings. There were a number of reasons for the absence of contact with siblings for the others. Lack of sibling contact occurred significantly more often when young people had been scapegoated by their families before admission ($p = 0.003$) and in some cases sibling contact was blocked by parents. For others, all family contact had ended before a previous closed adoption and, in a few cases, contact with siblings was considered to pose risks of sexual abuse and had been terminated by social services, at least temporarily.

Grandparents and others in the family network

Since fathers were often absent from the lives of the young people, contact with maternal grandparents was more common than with paternal grandparents. More than a quarter of the young people (26%) had contact with their maternal grandparents, compared with one in six (15%) who had contact with one or both paternal grandparents. One in five (19%) had lived with grandparents at some time during their childhood and when other extended family members are included this rose to 37%. A similar proportion (38%) had contact with aunts, uncles and cousins and, in two cases, ex-step fathers who continued to provide support.

Young people with no contact

Nine young people (6 girls and 3 boys) had no contact with anyone from their family network. Three had been adopted as young children with severance of all ties with birth family members. When their adoptive placements broke down in adolescence, they had no contact with anyone in their adoptive families either. For others, one or both parents had died and other family members had lost contact with the child. For the remainder, contact was prohibited because adolescents had made allegations of sexual abuse or the alleged abusers blocked contact.

Adam (aged 13), for example, was five years old when first admitted to care with his older brother and sister as a result of physical abuse and the fact that a Schedule I offender had moved into the household. A previous foster family eventually adopted him. Subsequently, the adoption failed and Adam returned to residential care before being placed in the study foster placement. He had three sisters and two brothers with whom he had had no contact for many years and had no information about their whereabouts. Most of them had been adopted early and their adoptions had also been closed. After the breakdown of the adoptive placement Adam wanted to have contact with his adoptive mother whom he regarded as his proper mother but she refused to see him.

Kristin, who had alleged sexual abuse by her father, had had supervised contact with him. He subsequently withdrew from this arrangement and her mother also refused to resume contact. Another girl, Leonie, was not permitted to have contact with her father whilst investigations into allegations of sexual abuse continued. She was also unable to see her maternal grandmother, as there were concerns about her grandmother's partner.

In spite of the fact that nine young people had no contact with any family member, only one social worker was considering the appointment of an Independent Visitor for the young person, as specified by the Children Act 1989 for such children.

Contact difficulties at the first interview

When all the contact in each case was considered in detail, drawing on all of the interviews, only five young people had contact that was without any difficulty. Susie, for example, arranged her own contact with her younger sisters and saw them whenever she could. Will was bailed to foster care and continued to have regular contact with his mother and siblings. Pete controlled the contact he had with his family and saw them fairly regularly with no problems and Clive's family contact was also reasonable at the time of the first interview. Martin (aged 15) had only recently been admitted to the care system after living with his grandparents from a young age. They were becoming too elderly to care for him and it was also felt that he needed contact with other young people. After moving into his foster placement he continued to have good and regular contact with his grandparents and was learning, with the help of the foster carers, to begin to consider their needs before his own.

Since entry to care had often been occasioned by longstanding relationship difficulties with parents and/or their partners, the contact problems experienced by the majority of the young people were not surprising. What was more surprising was the lack of help offered to the teenagers to enable them to negotiate these family relationships or to keep themselves safe.

Difficulties in contact

A third (34%) of the foster carers felt at the first interviews that the current contact arrangements were not in the best interests of the young people and almost half (49%) considered that the young person placed with them had difficulties in their contact with family members. These difficulties fell into five distinct groups.

UNRELIABLE CONTACT

Unreliable contact affected 37% of the adolescents. Young people were greatly affected when a parent did not turn up for a visit or was consistently late and many reverted to the behaviour of much younger children in their distress. For example the foster carer for one 17-year-old boy said:

> [Darren gets] upset when arranged meetings fail. He does not control himself. He will punch walls, jump up and down like a two-year-old displaying tantrums and become very withdrawn.

Another carer described how a mother's unreliability affected the girl she was fostering:

> [She] gets very upset when Mum is late or arrangements are changed. [She] gets upset after promises are not kept.

Similarly, another foster carer commented that the young woman she looked after:

> feels let down by father who regularly fails to keep contact meetings. [She gets] upset but half expects the contact to fail.

The foster families were also affected as they waited in vain for relatives who were late or did not arrive at all and their own children and others in the placement missed their activities.

INAPPROPRIATE AMOUNTS OF CONTACT

Over half the young people were considered by the foster carers to have contact that was of an inappropriate frequency or duration. Whilst some children suffered because a parent did not want as much contact as they did, others had too much. Catherine, for example, spent all her time planning her weekly visits and frequently phoned her younger brothers in another placement to discuss plans for contact with their mother. This preoccupation prevented her from engaging more fully with the foster family and unsettled her brothers. As we shall see later, the social worker in this case was able to improve this situation by altering the frequency and length of the contact.

SAFETY DURING CONTACT

Safety during contact had been identified as an issue for some young people, given that in nine cases contact was supervised, either by the social worker (5), foster carer (3) or both (1). Of the nine young people whose contact was supervised, five were on care orders and four were accommodated. In another seven cases contact with a named individual was forbidden (1 birth mother, 1 adoptive mother, 1 father, 3 stepfathers, 1 paternal grandfather).

The remainder of the young people were left to make their own contact arrangements and a number were at risk of physical or sexual abuse during contact. For example, Ben, who was 12, had begun to settle into his placement and was taking pride in his appearance and schoolwork and making friends. However, contact with his mother and stepfather was very difficult. His foster mother said:

> He comes home [after contact] with an attitude problem; he is difficult to manage and very upset. He ends up crying in bed.

Things were even worse after he spent two weeks with his mother and stepfather at Christmas:

> [He was] real stroppy. A real bolshie kid – real nasty kid. He stopped bothering about his clothes, shoes and hygiene again and his schoolwork deteriorated. Everything went downhill.

After this visit, the progress he had made deteriorated dramatically and over the next few months, Ben began to make disclosures to the foster mother about sexual abuse by his stepfather.

Legal arrangements did not always protect young people who were determined to keep in contact with family members. For example, the court had banned Danny's stepfather from any contact with him but Danny (aged 15) desperately wanted to see his mother and made many visits to her at home. He suffered numerous beatings from his stepfather as a consequence and his foster mother said:

> [He] found difficulty in understanding why his birth mother continually rejected him. [Her] partner continually threatened and physically abused him [and he] found it difficult to express his feelings. Little professional help was offered to assist him in coming to terms with this.

Some children suffered emotionally from their parents' negative attitude to them. For example, Ashley's foster carer commented:

Occasionally he is ostracised by parents when he does something they disapprove of…on occasion, even whilst home for the weekend, parents have not spoken to him.

REPLAY OF NEGATIVE RELATIONSHIPS

Many of the teenagers appeared to have entrenched, unresolved attachment difficulties that were regularly re-enacted during contact. They persistently sought out parents who were highly rejecting, neglectful or abusive to them but few received any help in dealing with these very hurtful experiences. The original difficulties that had led to the placement were replayed during contact, leaving the adolescents with painful experiences that they seemed unable to process.

It was clear from Danny's behaviour, described above, that there were unresolved issues about attachment to his mother. His foster carer was concerned that he had received no help with these issues, yet Danny had been in the care system since before the age of five.

CONTACT DIMINISHED THE INFLUENCE OF THE FOSTER CARERS

Another source of concern was when the carers' influence was directly undermined by the actions of family members who encouraged anti-social or risk-taking behaviour. For example, a mother and grandmother sent cigarettes and cannabis in the post to a 12-year-old girl and encouraged her 30-a-day habit when the carers were trying to get her to cut down.

The impact of contact difficulties on the foster carers and on other children at the first interview stage

Contact had a significant effect on the fostered adolescents but its impact also spread more widely to affect others in their placements with 41% of the foster carers (28) saying that the young person's contact had a negative effect on them. This was usually because of the concern they felt about the impact of contact difficulties on the young person. The carers were aware that the parents with whom the young people had contact were frequently rejecting, unreliable or unpredictable in their attitudes towards them. They were also aware of the situations encountered by the young people during contact. Shelley's foster carers for instance, were concerned about the effect that contact visits had on her because weekend visits with her mother resulted either in her being used as a babysitter whilst her mother went out to a night-club or in Shelley (aged 15) going out with her mother and drinking heavily herself. Shelley frequently telephoned her carers to ask them to collect her early from weekend visits.

The foster carers also reported that in one in five cases the young person's contact had negative repercussions for the other children in the foster family who were affected by the teenagers' distress and who missed out on their activities. Time taken to transport young people to contact visits could mean that foster carers were not available to watch other children play sport, take them on outings or transport them to the various activities that they enjoyed.

Contact visits that took place within the carers' house sometimes put additional stress on the carers and others in the foster family. For example, Ruth's mother, who was a homeless drug-user, would sometimes turn up at the foster family home 'stoned' or wanting to use Ruth's room to take drugs in. Obviously the carers were concerned for Ruth but did not want to stop her mother visiting the house because otherwise, if Ruth wanted to see her mother, she wandered around the streets and subways until she found her. Her mother had used Ruth and her younger sister to beg for money to fund her drug habit and she was often in the company of other drug-users who exerted a negative influence on Ruth. The carers found this situation difficult to manage because, whilst there were advantages for Ruth in having contact with her mother at their home, they did not want to be seen to be condoning drug-use by allowing Ruth's mother to take drugs in their house.

It was clear from the first interviews that contact difficulties had a profound effect on the young people and on their foster families. We were interested to examine how contact developed over time, its effect on the placements and on the outcomes for the young people. These issues will be considered next.

Changes over the one year follow-up

Changes in birth family households since the first interviews

According to the young people's social workers, changes had occurred in nearly half the birth families whilst the young people had been in the study foster placement (46%). These changes had included parents and siblings moving house, separations between parents or between a parent and a former partner. Sometimes one or both parents had remarried or found a new partner. In some families, new siblings or half-siblings had been born or new step-siblings had moved into the family home, while in others, siblings had moved into care or had returned to the family home from care.

For example, Audrey (aged 14) had no contact with her parents at the first interview. Her mother was schizophrenic but dependent on a man who had sexually abused Audrey and he blocked contact between Audrey and her sisters, who remained at home with their mother and her partner. Audrey's father was a drug addict and very unreliable. By the second interview, her mother had moved home twice without telling Audrey, which had been very distressing for her. Subsequently Audrey's social worker had arranged for her to meet a solicitor to arrange a contact order to enable Audrey to see her sisters. This did not work out, however, and at the second interview nearly a year later, Audrey was still not sure what was happening about contact with her sisters.

Changes in the frequency of contact

When the young people were followed up one year after their placements had begun, the frequency of contact had remained the same for nearly half (48%) of them, whilst 30% had more contact and 22% had less than at the beginning.

Changes in the quality of contact

Using all the available data, the researchers made overall ratings of contact for each adolescent that indicated changes in the quality of contact over the one-year follow-up. As can be seen in Table 10.2, in over one in five cases, poor contact improved but for by far the largest group (57%) contact remained problematic.

Table 10.2 Changes in the quality of contact over the one year follow-up		
	Number	*Percentage*
Good and stayed good	11	16
Poor and became good	15	22
Poor and stayed poor	39	57
Good and became poor	3	5

Given these findings we were interested to see what action social workers or others took to bring about positive changes.

Improvements in contact

Improvements in contact were brought about in some cases by proactive social work. It was notable that this happened only when contact was supervised and as a result the extent of difficulties was known to the social worker. A good example of this was a social worker who improved contact by arranging longer visits that were less frequent.

Catherine was the young woman described earlier who was preoccupied with contact to the exclusion of everything else. During supervised contact with her mother, Catherine watched TV for an hour while her mother sat in silence, her brothers played in the bedroom with their toys and the family rarely spoke to each other except to say 'Hello' and 'Goodbye'. The social worker changed contact from one hour a week to two hours a fortnight, which meant that Catherine and her family could do things together. In addition, her brothers moved placement and their foster carer was a friend of the foster carer who was looking after Catherine so that contact with them was easier. The foster carer described the situation as being 'like an extended family'. After these changes, Catherine became more relaxed about the arrangements and was able to engage positively with the foster family, as were her brothers with theirs. This was a good example of contact arrangements being taken seriously and the individual circumstances monitored and adapted in ways that catered for the needs of the various people involved and ultimately ensured that the contact was a good experience for everyone.

Another social worker suggested spending contact time visiting another relative to improve the quality of the time a young woman spent with her family. Stacy was having supervised contact once a month at home with her mother and stepfather. When she arrived, her mother and stepfather were always in the middle of an activity, like doing the laundry or decorating, and during the visits they too sat in the lounge with nothing to say to each other. When the social worker discovered that Stacy had been very close to her grandmother and had not seen her for a long time, she made plans for Stacy and her mother to make regular visits to her grandmother. This gave them a more relaxed time together on the bus journey without the stepfather or the need for supervision.

For some young people, although there was no change in the quality of contact with their parents, more contact with another family member helped them. For example, Clive was admitted to care at the age of 11 because of long-term neglect, lack of food and poor living conditions. He had regular supervised contact with his parents with whom his relationship was poor. By the second interview, Clive's social worker and foster carer had established contact between Clive and an aunt with whom he was staying every other weekend. The attention he received from his aunt and his foster carer meant that Clive was beginning to thrive in his placement and become more confident.

In a few cases the young person's relationship with a parent improved without any outside help. Frank, who was aged 15, for example, was having more contact with his mother and was staying one night a week with her by follow-up. His relationship with her and with his siblings had improved and they were getting on better than previously.

Deterioration in contact

There were a few cases where the contact situation worsened over the one year follow-up, sometimes despite serious attempts by social workers to find a viable solution to the difficulties. For example, Roger's mother had previously provided shared care with the foster family. After a row in which Roger threatened to smash a bottle in his mother's face, she reduced contact to half an hour a week. Roger was 12 years old when we first interviewed him and had ADHD (Attention Deficit Hyperactivity Disorder) and traits of Asperger's Syndrome and autism. His behaviour was extremely difficult and his potential for seriously harming someone was increasing as he became older and larger. In the absence of suitable respite carers, weekend residential care was arranged, but this made the situation worse because Roger felt doubly rejected by his mother and his foster carer. Despite the carer's commitment to Roger, the placement was under great strain and at breaking point at the second interview.

Occasionally contact worsened because of a change in arrangements and this shows the need for regular re-assessment of contact and its effects on young people. For example, in spite of severe sexual abuse in the past, Maxine's contact with her parents was very positive when it had clear boundaries and was supervised by the foster carers in their home. Maxine looked forward to seeing them. They were always reliable, were happy to see her and always brought gifts for her. Because the arrangements were so positive, contact was changed from one hour per fortnight to two hours a month unsupervised contact away from the foster home. Maxine immediately began to show signs of very disturbed behaviour before and after contact and the original arrangement was quickly reinstated.

Continuing difficulties in contact

Whilst there were changes in the quality of contact for some young people, as we have seen, for the majority (57%) contact continued to be poor (Table 10.2). This meant that many of the teenagers regularly saw relatives who were rejecting, unreliable and neglectful towards them and it was clear that the young people were unable to cope with or understand these experiences. On the contrary, they frequently demonstrated a need to repeat them compulsively. In addition, by follow-up foster carers felt under increased strain when there were considerable difficulties in the young people's contact with family members.

Victor (14), for example, was the victim of a longstanding pattern of confusing and rejecting messages from his mother and had been yo-yoing between her and local authority care since he was eight years old. A pattern had been established whereby his mother requested that he be accommodated, after which she moved house and often local authority area, telling him that she needed to get away from him. Once he was settled in a placement, she then contacted him and wanted him to return home. As a result, he had had 28 different placements and had attended 15 different schools in the previous 6 years. The foster carer in the study said that Victor was very angry with his mother when he returned from contact visits and would vent his frustration through violence and vandalism in their home. At such times, his carers found it hard to cope with him and his behaviour continued to be difficult for some time after contact. The fact that no boundaries had been placed around this situation had led to chronic instability for Victor.

Testing the reality of return to parents

Amongst the young people with unresolved attachments to parents who could not offer them consistent care, a few needed to return home to test reality against their fantasy of everything turning out right. Where returns of this sort were extremely likely to fail, it was important for placements to be kept open so that the young people could go back to their original carers if the reunification was unsuccessful. Keith, for example, returned home to his mother shortly before his sixteenth birthday but three weeks after his case was closed his mother threw him out, saying she had to choose between him and his stepfather. In the meantime his place had been filled in the foster family and at the age of 16 he had missed his school exams and was homeless and living on the streets.

Two other young people returned home to parents who could not care for them. Shelley's first placement with her foster carers broke down and she returned home to a turbulent relationship with her mother. The return home did not survive long and she was fortunately able to go back to the foster carers with whom she had become close. Hugh (aged 15), on the other hand, had been in care since he was two years old and had not seen his mother in the past 13 years. She then got in touch with him and encouraged him to go and stay with her, saying that social services could not do anything to stop him. All four of her children had been admitted to care when young and were looked after on care orders. There were real concerns, however, that Hugh's mother would let him down, as she had done previously with his 16-year-old brother.

The impact of contact on placement outcomes

The presence of contact difficulties as described by the foster carers at the first interview stage predicted later placement disruption ($p = 0.02$). Over half (56%) the placements broke down when there were contact problems, compared with less than a quarter (24%) when there were no contact difficulties. In five cases, contact with parents undermined foster placements so much that they broke down as a direct result. In many more cases contact difficulties or difficulties in relationships between the young people and their parents were one of a number of factors that influenced placement disruption. Whilst contact problems were related to conduct disorders on the SDQ, the relationship between contact difficulties and placement breakdown was independent of any conduct problems.

At the beginning of his placement, for example, Ben (aged 12) had supervised visits only with his mother. He had no contact with his father who was a drug-user and violent. He had brothers and sisters in other foster placements but had little contact with any of them. Ben's mother moved near to the placement and this created so many problems within the placement that it broke down after eleven months. The foster carer said:

> Once Ben's mother moved close to us, it made the placement impossible to handle and my boundaries could not be implemented.

The foster carer felt that Ben's mother deliberately set out to destroy the placement. She felt that Ben's mother destroyed the trust between herself and Ben by telling him lies about her and openly criticising her to Ben. He stopped responding to the foster carer and would storm off to his mother's house despite the fact that only supervised contact was allowed. She was unable physically to prevent him going there because he became violent and aggressive. After one argument he went to his mother's house, saying that he was never going back to the placement. At this point, social services moved him to temporary foster carers and then into a therapeutic unit. The foster carer continued to have contact with Ben who visited for tea once a week. At follow-up he said that he felt that his mother had spoiled things for him and he only wanted to see her once a month.

In addition, sometimes family members influenced young people and their placements even in the absence of direct contact. In spite of the fact that Sandra had no contact with her family, her mother continued to wield influence over her and over her placement. The local authority accommodated Sandra and her younger brother because their mother's partner physically abused them. Sandra had a very difficult relationship with her mother who did not want to see her but when she heard that Sandra was referring to the foster placement as 'home' she said that Sandra was no longer part of their family. This outright rejection led to a deterioration in Sandra's behaviour and the placement broke down before the second interviews were due to take place.

Assistance in the maintenance of placements by supportive relatives

On the other hand, we found that supportive relatives sometimes helped to maintain foster placements at the same time as supporting the young people.

Beverly (aged 15), for instance, had no contact with her mother at the first interviews but said that this was her choice. Before coming into care she had lived with her 'Nan' for a long time but, as Beverly got older and her grandparents began to have health problems, they were no longer able to care for her. At the time of the first interview, her grandfather was dying of cancer and had been in and out of hospital for treatment. Beverly had telephone contact with her grandmother every day and saw her two sisters and her cousins regularly. At the beginning of the placement Beverly missed her grandparents very much and was always very happy when she saw them. Beverly's contact with her extended family continued and she and her foster carer visited her cousins regularly. At the time of the second interviews, her sister had gone to university and they were seeing less of each other but were still in regular contact. The placement itself had not been easy and Beverly had had a lot of difficulties. Her foster carer said that she would not have been able to cope, and it was unlikely that the placement would have survived, had it not been for the help and support of Beverly's grandmother. Beverly had a tendency to be very insecure and at the beginning of the placement her mood swings were dramatic. At times she would become very upset and in these circumstances would get everything out of proportion and would then want to move out. In tears, she would telephone her grandmother who would let her talk and was able to calm her down and help her to see things differently. Her grandmother provided a constant person for Beverly who truly cared about her and her presence and influence enabled the placement to succeed very well for Beverly.

The contact situation by follow-up and its relationship with outcomes

Detrimental contact

At the one year follow-up, we found that almost two-thirds (63%) of the young people had contact with someone that was rated by the researchers as detrimental to them. These young people found it more difficult than others to express emotion ($p = 0.006$). Unsurprisingly, young people who experienced such detrimental contact also had the most difficult past histories. They were, for example, more likely than others to have high numbers of past adversities ($p<0.05$); to have been on the Child Protection Register ($p<0.05$) and had more often than others been admitted to care from a reconstituted family ($p<0.05$). This suggests the importance of disruption, abuse and, in particular, conflict between step-parents and children in precipitating an adolescent's entry to care and in subsequent contact difficulties. The young people in the study who were under the age of 14½ were more likely to have contact that was detrimental to their safety, well-being or both than the older children. This might be because the older young people were more able to opt out of seeing people who had a negative impact on them.

Deidre (aged 17) for instance, by the time of the second interview had decided that, despite her efforts, her contact with her parents and siblings was deeply hurtful and she had chosen not to see them any more. By that time she had established a very good relationship with her foster carer who continued to act as a support when she moved into her own flat. In addition she also continued to have a good relationship with her maternal grandparents. At the second interview she said of her foster placement:

> I found it [the placement] very supportive and very stable. She [the foster carer] was understanding and there when I needed her. She would help if she could. I never had that support in my family. I enjoyed having that support.

Although there were no significant relationships between the young people who had detrimental contact and whether their placement disrupted or survived, they were significantly less likely than others to have a placement that was considered by the researchers to be beneficial to them ($p = 0.022$).

Beneficial contact

By the one year follow-up over two-thirds (69%) of the young people had contact with someone in their family that was rated by the researchers as beneficial to them, but it was of some concern to find that almost a third (31%) had no beneficial contact with anyone. Boys (85%) were more likely to have beneficial contact than girls (54%) ($p = 0.009$). We found that those with beneficial contact were also more likely than others to have been able to talk with foster carers from the beginning of the placement about their past experiences ($p = 0.02$), a factor that was related to improved outcomes in this study and in a sample of looked-after sexually abused and abusing adolescents (Farmer and Pollock 1998). They were also more likely to show improvement in their well-being at the one year follow-up ($p = 0.038$). Furthermore, this factor was itself associated with successful placements ($p < 0.00$). Thus, beneficial contact with a family member was linked in a number of ways with better outcomes for the young people.

Lack of contact with significant adults

Nearly a quarter of the young people (22%) were upset by lack of contact with someone important to them, generally their mothers ($p = 0.003$), their siblings ($p = 0.07$) or their fathers ($p = 0.027$). An example was Nina (aged 14) who was initially placed with her older sister in a foster placement that broke down for Nina after five years. Her sister remained in the placement and contact between them was difficult after Nina left, because she felt that the foster carers had scapegoated her and that they liked her sister but disliked her. The lack of contact with her former foster carers reinforced her feelings of rejection by them. Sometimes contact was blocked by a parent so that, for example, Lucy's father refused all contact and would not allow her to see her brother, sister or grandmother. She was extremely hurt by this and missed them. In other cases, contact was prohibited while abuse allegations were investigated or preparations for a court hearing were undertaken.

All of the boys who were distressed by lack of contact with a significant adult had been physically abused by their main carer before coming into the care system ($p<0.05$). However, the majority of those who had no contact with significant people were girls who had been sexually abused before admission ($p = 0.029$) and many of these young people were unable to talk about their past with their foster carers ($p = 0.042$). Interestingly, whilst contact difficulties were directly related to placement outcome, absence of contact with significant adults was not.

Young people who had no contact

As we saw earlier, nine young people had no contact at all and this did not relate to how long they had been in the care system. It was interesting to find that there was no relationship between having no contact and either placement breakdown or placement success. Yet it was in these situations that social workers were most dissatisfied about the young people's contact situation.

Over the period of the placement, there had been no change in contact for most of these young people. Tara, however, had had one meeting with her brother and sister and another was planned. Alison (who had been adopted at the age of 2½ and whose adoptive placement broke down when she was 16) had made tentative enquiries about contacting her birth family. The most dramatic change, however, was for Sharon. Her mother had been ill and Sharon started visiting to help her out and their relationship improved as a result. By the time of the second interview Sharon was having contact with her mother at least once a week. In addition, she had developed a relationship with a previous foster carer with whom she had briefly stayed. The carer no longer worked as a foster carer but Sharon visited her regularly and felt that she was able to confide in her.

Our other findings suggest that contact can have quite negative consequences for some young people. These young people with no contact were shielded from that situation and may also have been freer to invest themselves in their placements.

The link between contact with grandparents and outcomes

Contact with maternal grandparents was particularly associated with good quality or 'successful' placements at follow-up ($p = 0.024$) and with improved relationships between young people and their foster carers during the placement ($p<0.05$). Moreover, when the young people were able to identify someone to whom they could turn in times of need, this linked with placement success ($p = 0.031$) and those providing this support were most often maternal grandparents ($p = 0.004$). The grandparents probably acted as an 'anchor' in the lives of these young people – providing a constant figure and support throughout difficult times.

Whilst adolescents with grandparent contact were also often the younger adolescents (under 14½) and those with the fewest behaviour difficulties before placement, it was clear from the interviews that grandparents frequently played an important role in supporting their grandchildren and their placements and orchestrated contact with other family members, particularly mothers and siblings.

Conclusions

Our findings show that the majority of the fostered young people in the study experienced considerable problems in their contact with their families and over the one year follow-up many of these difficulties persisted. In view of the repeated rejection and neglect experienced by the young people, it is clear that contact needs to be managed more proactively for adolescents than it is at present. This could help to increase placement stability, since contact difficulties at the start of placement predicted later disruption. It became apparent that there was a need for social workers to consider what the purpose of contact was for each individual. Was it a step towards reunification and/or to maintain the young person's sense of identity and their place within their family network? Was it to improve relationships between young people and their parents and resolve attachment issues or to reassure young people that they had not been rejected? Or was it for a combination of some or all of these reasons? The purposes of contact need to be considered carefully so that the way in which it is managed matches those aims.

The difficulties encountered by young people whose contact was not supervised were often not apparent to their social workers. As many of our examples show, foster carers were in a good position to observe the effects of contact on the young people they looked after and regular discussion between the social worker and foster carers would assist in the regular review of contact arrangements.

In those cases where social workers took action, changes usually resulted in definite improvements for the young people and their placements. The changes were often quite small adjustments to the frequency and duration of contact or the involvement of other relatives. Young people with no family contact were identified by the Children Act 1989 as likely to benefit from an Independent Visitor and more use of this service could usefully be considered.

There was little evidence from our research of work with parents to effect positive changes in their relationships with their teenage children. It appeared that in practice the 'solution' to difficulties with adolescents was separation from parents and the problems that led to the placement were not addressed. Whilst there may be limits on how far long-standing relationship patterns can be changed, negotiation of meaningful contact with children is an important task.

The study showed the important part that positive contact with relatives such as grandparents, aunts, uncles and cousins can play. Such relatives may be a key source of stability and continuity and counteract troubled relationships with parents (see also Cleaver 2000; Marsh and Peel 1999). They may also act as a link with other branches of the family that function well. Findings from this study and from current research investigating children living with relatives and friends (Farmer and Moyers forthcoming) show that, at times, members of the extended family are unaware of the child's situation. This is especially true if these relatives live in a different area or if they have been excluded from the family by a controlling parent. These findings suggest that consideration needs to be given to family members apart from parents who might provide sustaining relationships with looked-after young people.

The research showed that when young people were able to talk about their past experiences and troubled family relationships with their carers or with others, there were fewer disruptions. Similarly, when the adolescents had access to at least one confidante fewer placements broke down. Our examination of contact, coupled with these findings, strongly suggests that more work with young people is needed to help them to understand and manage their relationships with family members more effectively. When negative relationship patterns persist young people need help in integrating the reality of their parents' actions and dealing with their own experiences of rejection and loss in ways that allow them to move on, build up a sense of self-worth in spite of these experiences and make use of other more sustaining relationships. Their ability to form and maintain healthy adult relationships is likely to be seriously jeopardised if they are not given help to deal with these issues.

Whilst social workers do a lot of work in relation to contact arrangements for younger children, it was apparent from this study that adolescents were often left to manage it themselves. This needs to change. Contact arrangements for each adolescent need careful planning that matches the young person's changing needs, the capacity of family members and takes full account of the purpose of contact. In addition, contact arrangements need to be subject to vigorous review so that harmful or unhelpful arrangements are altered and boundaries placed around contact that is detrimental to the safety or well being of young people. Over and above this is the need to help young people to understand and move on from parental rejection and ambivalence.

Now that the situation of the young people and their carers in the placements has been examined, we look next at the factors that related to placement outcome.

Chapter Eleven

Predicting Placement Outcome

This chapter draws out the factors that were significantly related on statistical tests to our two outcome measures: first, placement disruption within our one year follow-up and second, placement quality (that is that the placement went well or resulted in a planned and appropriate move as opposed to disrupting or continuing unhappily). This second measure we refer to as placement 'success' (see Chapter 3). The words statistically significant have been used sparingly in this chapter, but should generally be assumed unless stated otherwise.

The second interviews were conducted 9 months after the first interviews, so the continuing placements had lasted for 12 months. The length of the 27 disrupted placements before they broke down ranged from 2 months to 12 months, with an average length of 8.8 months. The placements that ended in a planned, positive way lasted from between 4 and 10 months, with an average length of 6.57 months.

On the basis of all the evidence from the follow-up interviews the researchers noted the principal reason for placement breakdown. The reasons for the disruption of the placement are shown in Table 11.1.

Our research focuses on adolescents between the ages of 11 and 17 and our findings about the factors that predict outcome relate to these older children, their foster carers and to the professional help provided for them. The chapter falls into two sections. The first focuses on pre-placement issues and the second on the placement itself.

Considering the difficulties the young people brought with them to their placements, the outcomes achieved in this study are testimony to the hard work and commitment of foster carers, the young people themselves and those who assisted them. For example, the aims had been met for over half of the adolescents' placements (a similar figure to that for teenagers in specialist fostering in the study by Rowe and her colleagues (1989)) and the needs of three-fifths of the young people had been well met in the placement.

Table 11.1 Principal reasons for placement disruptions		
Reason	*Number of placements*	*Percentage of disrupted placements*
Young person's behaviour	13	48
Parent/s undermined the placement	5	19
Young person wanted to live elsewhere	3	11
Another child moved into the placement	2	7
Breakdown in the relationship between the young person and carer	2	7
Initiated by carer	1	4
Allegation against a foster carer	1	4
Total	27	100

Pre-placement issues

The young people's previous experiences

Within this sample there were no differences in placement outcome according to broad definitions of neglect, physical or sexual abuse before placement. High levels of past adversity (eight or more adversities), on the other hand, were significantly related to our second outcome measure of poorer quality or 'unsuccessful' placements.

Far more telling was the young person's previous behaviour. Previous difficult behaviour at home or outside the home (whether immediately prior to placement or at some time in the past) and aggressive behaviour before the placement were all significantly related to placement breakdown, principally because previous disruptive behaviour tended to be repeated in the placement.

There were also more unsuccessful placements among young people who had been living with their birth or reconstituted families immediately before the study placement as compared to those who had been living in substitute care or with relatives. This may have been because some of these young people wanted to return home, were in conflict with step-parents, were concerned about their siblings or because there were difficulties with contact. In addition, the young people who had little or no attachment to an adult at the start of the placement frequently experienced disruption and had more unsuccessful placements.

Age

Age at placement did prove influential, as has been shown in previous research. The younger teenagers (aged under 14½ at placement) had more successful placements than those who were older. This needs to be borne in mind when placements are made.

Foster carer strain prior to the placement

Placements with foster carers who had experienced a high number of stressful life events (six or more experiences such as bereavements, relationship difficulties, illness, financial worries and changes in the family) in the six months before the study placement had an increased risk of disruption. The link between an accumulation of stress and higher levels of placement breakdown may in part relate to the lowered levels of sensitive parenting shown by these stressed carers and to their reduced capacity to like the young people placed with them. In addition, carers with high levels of previous strain were less active than others in ensuring that the young people's needs were met in placement (for example for appropriate education or counselling) and less able than others to accommodate to the young people to help them to fit into the family. In short, their capacity for parenting was reduced. This will be discussed in more detail later since strain during the placement was also related to poor outcomes.

Foster carers' previous work experience and training

Interestingly, the length of time carers had previously spent fostering did not affect outcomes, but those who had other relevant work experience such as nursing, teaching or social work had significantly more successful placements. This is likely to be because they were able to transfer their skills and knowledge and (sometimes ongoing) training from work to the foster carer role.

Two types of training also related to greater success with placements: training in dealing with birth parents and in 'letting children go'. These may have been chance findings or having attended such training might relate to a greater depth of fostering experience. Research by Sinclair and his colleagues (2000) found that almost a quarter of their sample of foster carers had experienced severe difficulties with their foster child's birth parents, such as aggressive or violent behaviour or the disruptive influence of the birth parents on the foster child. In this study, two-fifths of the foster carers said that the young person's contact had had a negative effect on them, and together these findings suggest that dealing with birth parents and understanding transitions for children are important areas for training.

Preparation for placement

It is often argued that since so many placements are made in an emergency, adequate preparation is almost impossible. We found that only just over a third of the placements were actually made in an emergency (that is, at less than two days' notice) so that in two-thirds of cases there was an opportunity (albeit sometimes limited) for preparation and initial visits. Placements were, however, less successful when there had initially been problems in finding a placement, whether the reasons for the difficulties resulted from the young person's behaviour or from issues within social services, such as placement shortages. In addition, emergency placements were significantly more likely to disrupt than other placements. Emergency placements were no more often made for young people with disturbed scores on the SDQ than were planned placements. Moreover, the explanation does not seem to be that worse placement choices were made, since planned placements were no more likely than emergency ones to be considered suitable by social workers. This suggests that the reason for this finding about emergency placements is connected with issues about preparation for placement.

The practice and research literature lays considerable emphasis on the importance of preparation of children for placement and of giving adequate information to carers. Our research suggests that adequate preparation can make a real difference to outcomes. In this study, however, as we have seen involvement of all the relevant parties (that is the young people, their parents and the foster carers) in discussions about the placement occurred in only two out of five cases and a third of the young people said that they had not been consulted about the move. The young people told us in clear terms that they did not feel adequately involved in the process. A third of them had not had an opportunity to meet their carers before moving to the placement. Whilst acknowledging the difficulty of tight timescales, these findings suggest that there is some way to go in ensuring adequate involvement by the key parties.

Placements in which the young person felt that they had been given adequate information about the foster carers and their family before the move had better outcomes on both of our measures, but this may have been partly because these were also the placements that young people wanted to be in and in some cases they already knew the carers. When young people had been extensively consulted about the move there were also more successful placements. Young people emphasised that they considered it important to have advance information about the details of the people who lived in the family and about the family rules that they could expect.

Two-fifths of the carers in the study said that there was information about the young person that they had needed and did not have and almost a quarter had been given information that was neither accurate nor up to date. These deficiencies were not related simply to emergency moves – they affected the range of placements. There were significantly more disruptions when foster carers were not given adequate information about the young person's school attendance and progress, the plans for their education or employment or about the plans for their long-term care. The same deficiencies in information were significantly related to less successful placements with one addition: information about the young person's health. Whilst there was a tendency for social workers to give less information about the children with the more disturbed behaviour, this alone did not explain these outcomes. It therefore seems that there are aspects of preparation that are extremely important. Indeed, we found that the more experienced carers had developed the habit of telephoning other carers to seek information about young people before accepting a new placement, as they had found that social workers could not be trusted to give them full information. The lack of information given to carers led in some cases to high risk adolescents being placed in situations where they posed considerable sexual risks to other children in the family. Without prior knowledge about this, carers had been unable to take steps to keep their own (or visiting) children safe (see also Farmer and Pollock 1999b).

As we have seen, in over two-thirds of cases the carers' understanding of the plans for the young person did not match that of the social workers, partly because a number of social workers had presented the young people as a short-term prospect, whilst planning that they would stay long-term and partly because one in five carers did not know the plans for the young person. When foster carers and social workers had the same view of the placement plans there were fewer disruptions and fewer carers felt under strain. A particularly pertinent finding was that there were significantly fewer placement breakdowns when the young people had been no more difficult to manage than the carers had expected. This suggests that within certain parameters foster carers may be able to manage difficult adolescents as long as they take them with full knowledge of their difficulties.

Matching young people and foster families

GENDER PREFERENCES

Placements were also more likely to break down if the foster carers had a definite preference about the gender of the children they looked after and in this placement it was ignored. Foster carers usually had very good reasons for these preferences, such as concerns about fostering teenage girls in a family of boys and had thought carefully about what worked best in their family. Overriding foster carers' preferences in such situations should be avoided whenever possible.

PLACEMENT WITH OTHER CHILDREN

Previous research (see for example Berridge and Cleaver 1987; Parker 1966; Trasler 1960) has identified placing young people with others of a similar age as a factor in placement breakdown. For this adolescent group a rather different picture emerged.

We found that when the foster carers had a birth child between two and five years younger than the placed young person, placements were at increased risk of disruption. It may be that children two to five years younger than the placed adolescent were in the age group that was vulnerable to the difficult and on occasion violent behaviour of some placed adolescents and were not well equipped to defend themselves. Similarly, young people who were highly sexualised or misusing drugs or alcohol might be thought likely to exercise an influence on other children close in age but younger than them. In contrast, although the numbers are small, it appeared that closeness in age (that is, less than two years younger or older) could act as a protective factor for fostered adolescents, no doubt partly because of the friendships that sometimes sprang up between the young people and the fact that the carers' teenage children were in a position to assist the young person to get involved in positive peer relationships and deal with school. Of course, notwithstanding these findings, there were also instances of difficulty between the young people and carers' children of a similar age. Nonetheless, adolescents who have grown up as 'fostering children' may develop a range of strategies to deal with the children their parents foster, whether they make friends with them or lead parallel lives and indeed, as we show later, they are an important part of the support system of their parents.

The placement during the one year follow-up
Early expressions of dissatisfaction
The initial reactions of the foster carers towards the young people (for example, whether or not they liked them) often continued and affected the course of the placement and young people, too, were often clear from very early on about which placements were right for them. When carers or young people were dissatisfied with the placement at the first interview, this predicted unsuccessful placements by follow-up. For these reasons both the carers and the adolescents suggested that trial periods at the start of placements would be helpful. Then if the placement was clearly not going to work out, a move would have much less emotional salience than at present.

Young people's behaviours
YOUNG PEOPLE'S BEHAVIOURS AT THE START OF THE PLACEMENT
At the start of the placements the young people (in common with other looked-after children) showed fairly high levels of behaviour difficulties. The foster carers' SDQ ratings showed that more than two-thirds of our adolescents had conduct difficulties, three-fifths had difficulties with peers, half were hyperactive and two-fifths had emotional problems. Two-thirds of the young people experienced periods of depression during the placement on foster carer ratings. Eleven young people admitted to recent incidents of self-harm and nine to suicide attempts, although foster carers were not always aware of these. In addition, three-quarters of the young people had few skills and interests.

As previous research has shown, the behaviours that particularly predicted poor outcomes on both of our measures were hyperactivity (see also Quinton *et al.* 1998) and conduct problems in the placement itself. More boys than girls were hyperactive but similar proportions of boys and girls had conduct difficulties. In contrast, those young people who had shown psychological or emotional distress in the past had a much greater chance of *not* experiencing placement breakdown, probably because they turned their difficulties inwards rather than acting them out.

In addition, young people who stole from the foster carers or other family members early in the placement were significantly more likely to have a placement disruption than those who did not. Adolescents who were violent to others also had fewer successful placements.

The young people who, in the foster carers' view, had little or no attachment to an adult at the start of the placement (a third of the sample) frequently experienced disruption and unsuccessful placements. These were young people with a variety of disadvantages, including long periods in care and sometimes a failed adoption. Whilst in the beginning foster carers often thought that such adolescents were getting close to them, these young people had ambivalent and rejecting relationships with at least one parent, characterised by violent outbursts and extreme interactions. For example, Shelley (aged 14) was accommodated at her mother's request as a result of severe relationship difficulties and conflict between Shelley and her mother. Their relationship swung between them going out together to nightclubs like friends, and having violent rows which culminated in either the mother throwing Shelley out or in Shelley absconding. There were various attempts at returning Shelley home, none of which lasted for very long.

However, as the placements of these young people with poor attachments progressed, additional needs often became apparent and there was increasing conflict between them and their carers. Many of these placements eventually broke down. It was noticeable, in some cases, that after young people had apparently settled into the foster family well, when they began to get close to the carers they appeared to set about undermining the placement themselves. There may have been an element of testing the commitment of the carers by increasingly challenging behaviour. Alternatively, after settling a little and beginning to trust carers enough to start to disclose events in the past, the young people might well have felt exposed and started to retreat in order to feel safer.

Even though it appeared that these young people became scared at the prospect of closeness, they did not do well when placed with foster families where closeness was not encouraged either. There were more disruptions when a young person with little or no attachment to an adult was placed in a foster family with a disengaged or separated family style, that is families where members did not generally act as a family unit but led somewhat separate lives.

BEHAVIOUR CHANGES ONE YEAR ON

Not surprisingly, young people whose behaviour had worsened by follow-up had an increased risk of poor outcome on both of our outcome measures. Deterioration in behaviour however was much less common among those young people who had high levels of emotional problems on the SDQ. (This sub-scale includes questions about whether the child has somatic symptoms, many worries, is often unhappy or fearful, shows anxiety or lack of confidence).

A quarter of the young people showed a new type of difficult behaviour during the placement and the emergence of new behavioural difficulties was significantly related to poor outcomes, in part because of the impact this behaviour had on other children in the placement. Young people who demonstrated new behavioural difficulties often had a history prior to this move of truanting and non-attendance at school and had become involved in more negative peer relationships by the second interview.

Over the course of the placements there was an increase in high risk sexual behaviour and in the numbers of young people considered to be violent. Increases in the former were related to a heightened risk of disruption – again principally because of the impact on other children in the household – and increases in the latter to unsuccessful placements. Placements also often broke down when foster carers were concerned about the young people's substance misuse, as occurred in a quarter of cases.

Relationships with other children in the household

We were interested in examining the young people's relationships not only with the foster carers but also with other children in the family. The findings of the study show the close link between placement outcome and the impact of the fostered adolescents on the carers' own children (see also for example Quinton *et al.* 1998; Triseliotis 1989) and other fostered young people.

YOUNG PEOPLE WHO HAD A NEGATIVE IMPACT ON OTHER CHILDREN IN THE FOSTER FAMILY

Those young people who by follow-up had emerged as having a negative impact on the other children in the placement had poorer outcomes on both of our measures.

Not surprisingly, young people who had medium to high levels of behaviour difficulties often had an adverse effect on other children in the family. Moreover, the emergence of new difficult behaviours and demonstration of high risk sexual behaviour (adolescents who put themselves sexually at risk) were related to a greater risk of placement disruption, primarily because of the negative impact these behaviours had on other children in the household.

Researcher ratings at follow-up identified two other behavioural changes that were related independently to both placement disruption and to an adverse effect on other children in the household. These were deteriorating peer relationships (that is young people who became involved in negative peer groups or who had noticeably fewer friends by follow-up) and behaviour that worsened during the course of the placement. When either of these occurred in combination with the adolescent having a negative impact on other children in the family there was an increased risk of placement disruption. However, when young people had a positive impact on the other children in the fostering household, worsening peer relationships or behaviour did not significantly relate to disruption. Thus, it appears that foster carers may be able to cope with a certain range of difficult behaviours as long as their own (or other fostered) children are not badly affected.

When foster carers were looking after a young person who had an adverse effect on the other children in the foster family their parenting approaches changed for the worse. By follow-up it was apparent that the carers liked these adolescents less, they showed them more aggression in their attempts to discipline them, together with lower levels of warmth and commitment, and had less control over their behaviour. Carers had also made less effort to assist with the friendships of these young people. It was therefore not surprising that by follow-up the quality of these placements was poor.

YOUNG PEOPLE WHO HAD LITTLE IMPACT ON OTHER CHILDREN IN THE FOSTER FAMILY

At the first interviews we also identified a group of young people whose placements were less likely than others to disrupt. These were young people who excluded themselves from the activities and relationships within the foster family. They had usually experienced high levels of adversity before admission and were often depressed and bullied by others. In the foster family they were compliant, behaved well and had little impact on the other children in the family. Their behaviour suggested a survival strategy of blending into the wallpaper that, whilst apparently working in the placement, could lead to their needs being overlooked and would have consequences for their subsequent development. Indeed, in some of these cases children's unhappiness in the placement went unnoticed. For example, Hannah was depressed and rather than being part of a family, she felt 'like just a kid in a house'. The researcher commented:

> Hannah said there were no arguments because she would bite her tongue rather than say anything if she was upset or angry. The foster carer did not notice if she was upset or unhappy or helped around the house.

The fostered children in this household were treated very differently to the carers' own children and the researcher commented that Hannah was one of those who 'get their heads down and get on with it'.

The integration of the young person in the foster family

Young people who the foster carers thought were not very settled in the foster family at the beginning of the placement were significantly more likely to experience a placement disruption than those who were seen by the carers as being quite or very well settled in the placement. Similarly, those young people who did not share many enjoyable activities with the foster carers early in the placement had an increased risk of disruption compared with those who shared many activities with them.

Confiding

As we will see in a moment, there were also fewer disruptions when young people had been able to talk to others about the past, and disruption occurred less frequently when young people had access to people (foster carers or others) in whom they could confide (see also Farmer and Pollock 1998; Macaskill 1991). In addition, young people who said that they had an adult, other than their parents or foster carers, to whom they could turn in a crisis, had more successful placements. Whilst the latter finding may reflect the difficulties of those young people who had lost ties to important adults, these findings show the importance of ensuring that young people have at least one person with whom they can discuss important personal issues.

Peer relationships

PEER GROUP INVOLVEMENT BY FOLLOW-UP

The influence of the young people's peer group was rated at the first and second interviews. Those young people who by follow-up had become involved in a more negative peer group had poorer outcomes on both of our outcome measures.

GENERAL DIFFICULTIES WITH PEERS

It was interesting to find that young people who, at the outset, had difficulties in making and maintaining adequate relationships with peers (as measured on the SDQ) had significantly *fewer* disruptions and *more successful* placements. Conversely, young people whose peer relationships were normal had more disrupted placements. Other findings supported the idea that difficulty in sustaining peer relationships aided the maintenance of the placement. Those with such difficulties with peers, for example, were less likely to get into trouble than other teenagers in the sample, more likely to have beneficial relationships with their foster carers, to have their major needs met by them and they had an increased chance of behavioural improvement. In the light of their difficulties in relating appropriately with peer age children, it was not surprising to find that they were not usually involved with a negative peer group and that other adolescents in the placements often excluded them from their activities.

We know that establishing and maintaining good peer relationships is an important aspect of adolescent development and aids successful transitions into adulthood. These teenagers either had no friends or, whilst good at making initial contact with other children, could not sustain the relationship. Some sought the company of younger or much older children and many were shunned by young people of their own age. Some of the older adolescents established exclusive relationships with the opposite sex, which excluded them from 'normal' peer relationships. In order to survive their earlier dysfunctional relationships these young people had learned different strategies, which included techniques to keep people at a distance (silly stories, anger, conduct difficulties), emotionally manipulative strategies or an ability to fade into the background and become invisible. Whilst these characteristics did not endear them to their peers, it did not appear to impede the development of relationships with their carers.

It could be argued that at the stage of the placement the pre-eminent need for these young people was to be able to develop positive and functional relationships with caring adults, since their previous relationships with adults had often been neglectful, abusive or rejecting. Their foster carers would need to assist them to develop peer relationships but this might only be possible once they felt safer in their relationships with the carers.

The foster carers' parenting skills and changes over the year

PARENTING SKILLS AT THE START OF THE PLACEMENT

Foster carers who did not like the young people at the outset, significantly less often showed them warmth, were less engaged with them and were less aware of their needs. Interestingly, carers significantly less often liked those young people who had been scapegoated by their own families or who had had multiple separations from their own caregivers. This may link to findings from other studies that show that younger rejected children present particular behavioural difficulties for adoptive parents (see Quinton *et al.* 1998).

At the time of the first interviews three months into the placements only a small number of parenting approaches were found to be significantly related to placement outcomes and therefore of potential use as predictors. However, those that emerged are important. We found that there were fewer disruptions when the foster carers had been able to respond to the young person's 'emotional age' when it was considerably younger than their chronological age. Such responsiveness indicates sensitivity to the need of many of these young people to rework some of their earlier missed developmental experiences, for example for children's play activities and nurture, and a willingness to supply some of these in the placement. It implies tolerance and understanding that looked-after adolescents who may appear superficially street-wise and 'mature' may need a regular opportunity to regress in their behaviour, alongside the more general routine of age-appropriate activities and relationships.

We also found that there were fewer disruptions when young people had been able to talk about their past histories with their carers or with others. Such sharing of sensitive information implies receptivity by the carers, time made or allowed for the teenagers to share difficult issues and probably the capacity on the part of carers to bear to hear painful past events (see also Farmer and Pollock 1998; Macaskill 1991). It may be that the link with reduced disruption lies in the greater closeness such sharing can bring between the carer and young person or that close relationships enabled confidences to be shared and also in the teenagers' increased capacity to integrate past painful events. It may also be that such sharing extended to discussion of current difficulties, such as those that arose during contact with their parents. As already noted, there were also fewer disruptions when young people had access to people (foster carers or others) in whom they could confide.

In addition, there were more placement disruptions and fewer successful placements when carers became highly involved in attempting to manage the contact between the young person and family members. Carers became involved in contact issues in this way when young people had particularly difficult histories, problematic contact and showed the kinds of disruptive behaviour that related to placement breakdown. Their ability to assist in resolving contact issues, however, was circumscribed unless the child's social worker took action to intervene.

Two other parenting approaches were related to our other outcome variable – the success of the placement. Carers who were rated as average in encouraging young people to learn life skills and undertake age-appropriate independent activities provided more successful placements than those who offered little or a lot of encouragement. It may be that high expectations of independence were made with the more vulnerable adolescents (and sometimes this singled them out from other children in the placement). On the other hand, little encouragement to learn life skills was related to carer strain and suggested a lack of awareness of the needs shared by all young people to develop age-appropriate skills. The provision of average levels of help, on the other hand, suggested an appropriate concern in preparing young people for the future and some attunement to their needs. This fits with the finding that a considerable minority of the carers did not take action to help young people increase their skills in managing their lives.

Placements were also more successful when foster carers exercised high levels of supervision when young people were outside the house. Of course, young people whose activities were hard to monitor were sometimes involved in activities such as high risk sexual activity that were connected with poor placement outcomes. At the same time, supervising or monitoring young people when they are not actually with the family is clearly a difficult but not impossible task (see Farmer and Pollock 1998 for a discussion of this issue). It requires considerable skill and commitment and an extended view of the foster carer role. Nonetheless it is important, especially for those young people who are unable to keep themselves safe or out of trouble when away from the family. This is not to deny that some adolescents make it extremely hard for even the most capable carer to supervise them.

PARENTING CHANGES OVER THE YEAR

A number of changes in the parenting of these young people occurred over the one year follow-up and some were related to poorer outcomes. Most were the kinds of change that could be expected when poor behaviour did not improve or when new difficulties emerged.

Low levels of supervision outside the placement by follow-up were significantly related to poor outcomes on both of our measures. Decreased supervision on both fronts was especially common when young people were at risk due to their sexual behaviour (and therefore no doubt very hard to supervise). In contrast, carers generally increased their supervision of the young people within the foster home when they were concerned about their use of drugs or alcohol.

Lessened commitment, warmth and control over the young people, displays of disciplinary aggression, more inconsistent discipline and not liking the young people were all related to poorer outcomes on both measures. Again, a lack of response to the child's emotional age was related to placement disruption.

Changes in such parenting approaches were related in some cases to specific child or carer characteristics. For example, carers showed more disciplinary aggression at follow-up to young people who were violent towards others or who scored highly on a childish attachment measure. The latter were teenagers who, for example, sought a lot of attention from the carers and often showed affection like a younger child. Lower levels of warmth were also shown to young people who lacked attachment to any adult. At the same time increased disciplinary indulgence and a decrease in liking for the young person were a feature of carers who were under serious strain on the GHQ at the second stage. Interestingly, when young people were considered to be at risk of showing sexually abusing behaviour carers showed an increase in sensitive responding and in their engagement with them.

A quarter of the carers liked the young people less by follow-up and not liking was significantly related to poorer outcomes on both of our placement measures. Again lowered levels of liking for the young people occurred significantly more frequently when the young people had an adverse effect on other children in the family and when the young people were violent.

Clearly, worsening behaviour that is not influenced by carers' parenting strategies is linked to deteriorating interactions between young people, other children in the family and the carers, and also to poor outcomes. The child and carer characteristics linked to these worsening situations may suggest opportunities for assistance and intervention.

Using researcher ratings, we noted that overall, the teenagers' relationships with their carers either improved (34%) or were maintained (25%) in three out of five cases and worsened in the remainder (41%). Not surprisingly, the quality of the relationship with carers was closely related to both of our outcome measures.

Education

It will be recalled that lack of information to carers about the educational histories and needs of the young people prior to placement was related to poor outcomes on both our outcome measures. At the time of placement almost two-thirds of the adolescents were in mainstream school. However, six were in some form of special educational provision and twelve had been excluded from school. The local authorities in the study varied considerably as to how they dealt with young people who were looked after and not attending school. In some, a minimum of home tuition (a few hours a week) was provided, leaving foster carers with the young person at home all day. In others, imaginative packages of activities were developed. The independent fostering agencies in our study took a particularly active role in providing appropriate educational facilities for the children in their schemes and ensured that the foster carers remained very actively involved in liaising with the schools.

A third of the young people had changed school when they moved to the placement and it is important to note that for almost all of them this was seen as positive, for example in giving them a fresh start or in removing them from negative peer influences. Problems in relation to schooling continued in placement, with a third showing attendance problems and nearly half demonstrating conduct difficulties in school. Given these levels of difficulty, it was encouraging to find that, at the outset, half of the foster carers were actively involved with schools on the young person's behalf, but the other half were much less involved – including twenty who reported having no contact with the young people's school teachers.

Once placed, school attendance improved for just under one-third of the young people but worsened for a quarter. Just under half showed no change in attendance. Worsening school attendance was related to both a decrease in the number of friends the young people had by follow-up and to involvement in a negative peer group. But interestingly, school attendance itself did not relate to outcomes. Two factors that were evident at the first interviews, however, did. Low confidence in schoolwork was related to disruption and lack of confidence in social relationships at school was significantly related to low success rates in placements. In addition, young people with particular skills and interests (which may have been developed at school or at home) had an increased chance of having a successful placement.

Strain

We saw, at the start of this chapter, that an accumulation of stressful life events for the carers *before* placement was related to reduced parenting skills with the young people. By the time of the first interviews, two-fifths of the carers reported feeling under strain in coping with the placed young person and more than a quarter showed serious levels of strain on the General Health Questionnaire.

Strain tended to occur in situations when the carers had only accepted the placed child with reluctance, or under some pressure, and with taking an adolescent with considerable behaviour problems. This may connect to the finding that placements were generally of poorer quality if there had initially been problems in placing the young person, whether because of issues within social services or with the adolescent's behaviour. Feelings of strain were again related to poorer parenting and to lack of support in certain areas. Carers under strain at the first interviews three months into the placement responded less sensitively to the young people, were less able to respond to their emotional age, were less committed and engaged with them and disliked them more. They also gave little attention to preparing the young people for independence. Importantly also, these carers significantly more often than others found the children's social workers difficult to contact and more often felt that their views were not taken seriously by the professionals involved with the young person. They also received fewer visits from the children's social workers than did the carers under less strain.

By the time of the follow-up interviews, the foster carers with higher strain levels on the GHQ had significantly often had at least one change of social worker, been looking after young people who were hyperactive or who had contact difficulties. (We noted that half the adolescents had had one or more changes of social worker by follow-up or by then had no social worker at all.)

By the time of the follow-up interviews there was a significant increase in the number of foster carers who were experiencing difficulties in their social functioning on the GHQ. Almost all the main carers, who returned both questionnaires, had reduced capacity for coping with their everyday lives by this time. Further analyses showed that worsening day-to-day functioning was significantly related not to the numbers of serious stressors in foster carers' lives prior to placement but to experiencing these stressors as having an intense *impact*. It is important to note that these stressed carers had also expressed dissatisfaction with the index placement at the outset and subsequently most of their placements had disrupted by the second interview.

Better day-to-day functioning by carers was significantly related to two aspects of intermediate outcomes: improvements in the young people's well-being and to the adolescents' main needs being met. This suggests, not surprisingly, that carers whose day-to-day functioning was good were able to be attentive and effective in meeting the various needs of the young people in their care.

Placement support services and their impact

MENTAL HEALTH SERVICES FOR YOUNG PEOPLE

It was clear that for the carers appropriate help for the young people was a crucial strand in their overall support systems. Over a third of the young people were seeing a specialist for counselling and carers tended to feel better supported when this was the case. Conversely, when foster carers considered that a young person needed specialist help and it was not provided, this did much to make them feel unsupported. Over and above this, there were fewer disruptions when appropriate therapeutic help was provided for young people (or was not needed) and more successful placements when young people reported that they were receiving such assistance. There were more disruptions when carers had felt the need to seek mental health help for the young people they looked after and been unable to locate such assistance.

REQUESTS FOR HELP DURING THE PLACEMENT AND ASSISTANCE AFTER ABRUPT DISRUPTIONS

It is clear from our findings that the foster carers who were looking after young people with either conduct problems or hyperactivity had difficulty in coping with these young people on their own. A significant proportion of foster carers were clearly dissatisfied with the placements at the time of the first interviews and asked for help, primarily for the young people but also for themselves. Occasionally excellent help was provided, but most carers received either no assistance at all or a service that was inadequate or insufficiently tailored to the needs of the young people and their carers.

Foster carers rarely asked for help for themselves when a placement ended in an abrupt or painful manner. Nonetheless, they told us that they would have greatly appreciated an opportunity to talk through what had happened. Social services departments too would benefit from an analysis of why placements end in order to refine subsequent placement decisions, whether through disruption meetings or by some other means.

The relationship between support and placement outcome

A number of areas of support from the first interviews were significantly related to placement outcome and could therefore help to reduce placement instability. The carers who had a lot of support from their own children (including adult children) had fewer disruptions (see also Ames 1993 in relation to placements of children with severe learning disabilities). More recognition is needed of the important role played by the carers' children in supporting placements. These children wanted their views to be listened to and their difficulties acknowledged, including the stresses of bedroom sharing, feelings of jealousy and lack of attention. We should also note that some of these children are potential recruits to the next generation of foster carers.

In addition, there were significantly more successful placements when the carers were receiving substantial support from family members (principally their parents, partners and children), from their social networks and from local professionals, such as doctors and teachers. As previously mentioned, there were also fewer placement breakdowns when young people had appropriate therapeutic help and more successful placements (using our other outcome measure) when the young people reported that they were receiving counselling. Clearly, the provision of mental health help for young people when required is vital. In addition, when social workers had arranged some services for the young people, placements were more often successful. Finally – and this finding links to a number of others – support from the young person's social worker was significantly related to the success of the placement.

CHANGES IN SUPPORT LEVELS

The proportion of carers who were rated as being poorly supported rose during the follow-up period (from 19% to 34%) but this did not in itself predict placement outcome on either of our two main measures. The carers who felt poorly supported one year after the start of the placement were those where, at the outset, both the initial information and preparation for the placement had been deficient and insufficient provision to support the placement had been made. The other factors that related to carers feeling poorly supported by follow-up were that, at the start of the placement, the mental health needs of the young people had not been adequately addressed, other specialist interventions for young people that were needed had not been provided, they had searched for help unsuccessfully, the carers had found the social worker difficult to contact or the worker had not been willing to take their views seriously. Significantly more of the carers who looked after the younger teenagers felt very well supported at follow-up as compared with those looking after the older adolescents. The carers who felt well supported by follow-up had often received help from a psychologist, counsellor or psychiatrist, had access to professional help if needed, had not been under strain at the start of the placement and were satisfied with the out of hours service at the first interview.

The foster carers with substantial social networks and local professional support at follow-up had an increased chance of being satisfied with the placements by that stage. They also offered more warmth to the young people than more poorly supported carers and the young people they looked after had a significantly increased likelihood of having their major needs met and showing improved well-being.

Contact

In spite of the fact that social workers were concerned when young people lacked contact with their families, we found that such lack of contact was not related to outcome. However, as we have seen, for those who saw family members, some aspect of contact was problematic for the great majority (see also Sinclair *et al*. 2000). Difficulties with contact were significantly related to higher disruption rates.

Young people who had contact with their maternal grandparents had more successful placements. This may have been in part because the younger teenagers had more successful placements than the older ones and the young people who maintained contact with their grandparents were generally the younger adolescents with the fewest behaviour difficulties. It was probably also because the grandparents ensured that contact with other family members occurred and because they themselves provided enriching relationships for the young people.

Conclusion

The study aimed to investigate the contribution of foster carer parenting skills, supports and other factors to outcomes for fostered adolescents. A summary of the main factors from the first interviews that were significantly related to our two outcome measures one year later is given in Appendices 11.1 and 11.2. It should be borne in mind that these factors are not causal, but nonetheless practitioners and foster families need to be aware of the best evidence on predictors. These in turn need to be understood in the context of the specific sample in this study, paying attention to such issues as the length of the follow-up.

Whilst the discussion has in part focused on individual factors that relate to placement outcomes, in practice placement progress depends on the interaction between these factors and also on the relationships built between the key participants. When we considered the issue of support we hypothesised that placement outcomes would depend on the combination of positives and negatives in four areas. These are the formal services to the foster carers (such as family placement workers, social workers, GPs and teachers); the formal services provided for the young people (such as counselling); the informal supports of the carers (for example from their own children, partners or friends) and those of the young people (such as relationships with peers and other children in the foster family as well as with members of their birth families). Factors in all four areas emerged as important to outcome, either as sources of support or as obstacles to the progress of the placement. Moreover, these influences were not static. Over the course of a placement, a useful source of support may be withdrawn, key professionals change jobs, a family member who was supportive of a placement may later become distant or antagonistic or a new relative may emerge as helpful to the young person and thus to the placement as a whole.

It is important to highlight the way in which many issues that are important in placements may function either to hinder or help. Two such findings that were of interest were first the important role of foster carers' own children as potent sources of support to the foster carers and the young people but also as a reason for placement difficulties if they were adversely affected by the actions and attitudes of the placed adolescent. Second, contact with some family members could function as a source of support to placements (such as shared care with a mother or a supportive grandmother), but with other relatives contact could undermine placements and some young people were subject to both supportive and adverse contact within their network of relatives.

Some of these research findings have implications for the selection, training, preparation and support of foster carers and their children whilst others are relevant to other aspects of child care policy and practice. In the final chapter, therefore, we turn to consider the implications for policy and practice from the findings of the study.

Appendix 11.1 Factors from the first interviews that were significantly associated with placement disruption

Factors relating to the young people

Placements were more likely to disrupt when the young people:

- exhibited difficult behaviour before the placement and in the past
- had low confidence in their schoolwork
- displayed hyperactive behaviour or conduct difficulties in the placement
- stole from their foster carers
- exhibited additional needs during the course of the placement
- had no attachment to an adult
- were in frequent conflict with foster carers.

Protective factors

Placements were less likely to disrupt when the young people:

- had experienced emotional or psychological distress in the past
- had poor peer relationships during the placement
- excluded themselves from activities with other children in the placement
- shared activities with foster carers
- had access to at least one confidante.

Placement preparation

Placements were more likely to disrupt when:

- young people were placed in an emergency
- foster carers had expressed dissatisfaction at the outset of the placement.

Placements were less likely to disrupt when:

- young people received adequate information
- adequate information was given to foster carers about the young people's current school attendance and progress, plans for their education and employment and plans for their long-term care
- young people were no more difficult to manage than foster carers had expected
- the placement matched foster carers' gender preferences.

Support

Placements were less likely to disrupt when young people:

- received appropriate mental health or therapeutic help.

Placements were more likely to disrupt when foster carers:

- sought mental health or therapeutic help for young people.

Other children in the household

Placements were less likely to disrupt when foster carers:

- received a lot of support from their own children
- had children of their own who were close in age to the young people (within two years).

Parenting

Placements were less likely to disrupt when:

- foster carers responded to the emotional age needs of the young people as well as their chronological age needs
- young people said that they were able to talk to foster carers (or to others) about their backgrounds.

Strain

Placements were more likely to disrupt when foster carers:

- had experienced high levels of general stress pre-placement
- were under considerable strain in the placement.

Contact

Placements were more likely to disrupt when:

- there were difficulties in contact between young people and their families.

Appendix 11.2 Factors from the first interviews that were significantly associated with the quality (success) of the placement

Factors relating to the young people

There were fewer successful placements when young people:

- were aged over 14½ at the start of the placement
- exhibited difficult behaviour within the home and community pre-placement
- had a history of behavioural problems outside the home
- had a high number of adversities in their past
- entered the study placement from their parental home rather than from care
- had medium to high levels of behavioural difficulties in the placement
- showed symptoms of hyperactive behaviour
- demonstrated conduct difficulties
- had high total scores on the Goodman Strengths and Difficulties questionnaire
- had 'normal' peer relationships
- presented a physical risk to other children
- had little confidence in social relationships at school
- had no attachment to any adult.

Protective factors

Placements were more likely to be successful when the young people:

- had placements that were planned
- had poor peer relationships
- had special skills and interests
- had an adult apart from the foster carer or a parent who they could turn to for help.

Placement preparation

Placements were more likely to be successful when:

- young people felt they were consulted about the placement
- young people had received adequate information

- adequate information had been given to foster carers about the young people's health and education, plans for their education and employment and plans for their long-term care
- foster carers had received training in 'letting children go' and in dealing with birth parents
- young people were no more difficult than foster carers had expected them to be.

Placements were less likely to be successful when:

- there were initial problems in finding a placement for the young people
- when the foster carer or the young person expressed dissatisfaction with the placement at the outset.

Support

Placements were more likely to be successful when:

- young people were receiving counselling
- foster carers received support from immediate family members
- foster carers received useful support from their own children
- foster carers received support from their social network and community professionals
- foster carers received useful support from the young people's social workers
- social workers arranged services for the young people
- single foster carers had very useful support from family members.

Placements were less likely to be successful when young people:

- needed mental health help and were not receiving any.

Parenting

Placements were more likely to be successful when foster carers:

- had other relevant work experience
- helped young people to learn age-appropriate independence skills
- provided high levels of supervision and monitoring outside the placement.

Contact

Placements were more likely to be successful when young people:

- had contact with their maternal grandparents.

Chapter Twelve

Implications for Practice and Policy

In this chapter we draw attention to some of the implications of our findings for policy and practice. Since our study focuses on adolescents between the ages of 11 and 17 the findings relate to these older children, their foster carers and to the professional help that they use.

Matching

Two issues emerged as key in matching young people to placements. The first was the importance of placing young people of the gender requested by the foster carers. The second finding showed an increased rate of placement disruptions when there are children from two to five years younger than the placed adolescent. This finding will need to be verified in other studies but it does suggest that, when this cannot be avoided, there is a need for some discussion with carers about how they can protect younger children close in age to the placed young person from the impact of problems such as violence and highly sexualised behaviour. On the positive side, placement with other adolescents close in age (less than 2 years younger or older) appeared to help to sustain placements.

It is also important that social workers are not tempted to persuade or pressurise reluctant foster carers to take a young person. Where this had occurred carers often became strained and parented less effectively, leading to poor outcomes.

Increased support for high risk young people

Foster carers who were looking after young people who were hyperactive, had conduct problems or had little or no attachment to an adult had great difficulty in containing these young people on their own and these placements were vulnerable to poor outcomes on both of our measures. To enable these placements to have a chance of success, it is clear that comprehensive plans for placement support, including contingency plans, need to be in place before the young people arrive.

We wondered whether setting up integrated packages of support geared to the needs of these particular children and their foster families might be more feasible if different organisational arrangements were considered. For each social worker to start this afresh with a case may not be the best use of resources. The employment of a skilled practitioner who could act as service coordinator and direct worker for groups of high risk young people might be helpful. Packages of support might include specialist assessment, identification and coordination of appropriate specialist and community agency services and regular review. Alternative approaches might be considered, such as shared care between two foster families, dedicated respite care, buying in the services of specialist helpers for these young people for periods of time weekly and purchasing therapeutic counselling. Certainly, in the United States there have been very encouraging results from Treatment Foster Care programmes which provide a comprehensive carer preparation and parenting skills programme and high service levels during placements (see for example Chamberlain and Reid 1998; Chamberlain 2000).

Preparation for placement

Whilst most practitioners subscribe to the idea that preparation for placement is important, practice remains extremely variable. It has become agreed wisdom that preparation and clear information before a major event, such as admission to hospital for major surgery or relocation, is needed and can affect how well that event is managed. This is also true in relation to preparation for placements. This research showed that inadequate preparation for foster carers was directly related to increased disruption levels and poorer quality placements. The study showed that there were gaps in the information given to carers in many areas and a lack of up to date accurate information. In particular, there is a need for fuller information to be provided to carers about young people's school attendance, progress and health, the plans for their education or employment and the plans for their long-term care. In addition, social workers need to ensure that they and the foster carers have a shared understanding of the placement plan. Over and above this, it is important that social workers share fully and honestly the information they have about young people. Social workers have some way to go before foster carers can trust them to have shared everything they know about the children they seek to place. Our findings suggest that within certain parameters, foster carers can manage difficult adolescents as long as they take them with full knowledge of their problems.

Young people, too, need advance information about the foster families to which they will go. If family placement workers supplied regularly updated profiles with photographs (perhaps written by the families themselves) young people would have some basic data. Visits beforehand are immensely helpful and if not possible a preparatory telephone call would provide reassurance. Since only a third of placements were genuine emergencies made at less than two days' notice, there was generally some time for such preparation.

Early expressions of dissatisfaction or dislike

Early expressions of dissatisfaction turned out to be early warning signs of placement difficulties that, if not dealt with, often led to placement breakdown. Foster carers who were under strain, even before the young people arrived, expressed dissatisfaction with the placements at the first interviews, and subsequently most of their placements disrupted. In a similar way, the initial reactions of the foster carers towards the young people (for example, whether or not they liked them) often continued and affected the course of the placement. Young people who were not liked experienced much less adequate parenting and care. Clearly, family placement workers and children's social workers need to ask how things are going early on and be alert to dissatisfaction and dislike so that ways to improve the situation can be found.

Particular care is needed when placing young people who have been singled out for rejection and scapegoated in their birth families or who have had multiple separations from their parents, as they were particularly often disliked by their foster carers. Foster carers for young people with these backgrounds may require additional preparation, support and training to prevent negative interactions with such adolescents developing and becoming entrenched from the start of the placement. These adolescents may require increased attention and interventions from other professionals if their needs are to be adequately met.

Dealing with foster carer strain

Given the increased risk of placement breakdown and the poorer quality of placements when foster carers were under considerable strain before the start of the placement, family placement workers need to review the personal situation of the carers before a new placement is made. They need to ask about the impact on them of stressful life events, such as caring for a sick relative, recent bereavements, relationship and work difficulties and painful placement endings. Foster carers who are already under a great deal of strain need to be offered a less demanding adolescent, enhanced levels of support or both. Indeed, the practice of paying a retainer to allow foster carers a little time without a child in placement might be particularly appropriate in some instances.

A careful watch on carers' strain levels during placement could also avert placement breakdowns. We have already mentioned the importance of not pressurising carers to take young people when they are doubtful. In addition, improvements in four aspects of service could help to lessen carer strain.

The first is the vital issue of social workers responding rapidly to contact by the foster carers. The difficulties that carers had in contacting the children's social workers was a recurring theme in our interviews and requires serious attention by managers. Again and again it emerged that such difficulties in making contact with social workers were related to carers feeling poorly supported and increasingly strained. As many as 70% of the foster carers had these difficulties.

Social workers in child care teams with mixed caseloads are unlikely to give foster carers priority, when they have to respond to the demands of child protection, court or intake work. Siting children's social workers in long-term looked-after teams would appear to be a much more suitable arrangement. In addition, the allocation of responsibilities between young people's social workers and foster carers needs to be revisited. It is encouraging that the practice of social workers giving permission for overnight stays for young people has now changed. These and other tasks need to be devolved to the foster carers so that they are not awaiting replies on such minor yet important issues.

Whilst there may be a range of reasons for the communication deficits found in the study, we also wondered if it would not be possible for long-term looked-after teams to be served by a skilled secretary who would take telephone messages, attend to many of the routine tasks currently undertaken by qualified social workers (for example, sorting out payments) and ensure that foster carers receive a rapid response to their requests. It is also vital for field social workers to understand the central importance of their role to foster carers, the frustration that mounts up when they do not return telephone calls and the benefits of keeping in regular contact with foster carers and children. Some of that contact could be by telephone. Much of it might help forestall crises.

The second issue related to carer strain is low visiting levels by the children's social workers. Again, specialist teams and an emphasis on the importance of the role of the young people's social workers in supporting placements is needed. The finding of the 1994–5 Inspection of Local Authority Fostering (Department of Health 1995) that few social workers had received training specifically in relation to fostering remains relevant. The new social work degree should place fostering and substitute care firmly on the agenda so that the services of children's social workers are no longer the weak link in the local authority support chain.

The third issue is ensuring that the views of foster carers are taken much more seriously by practitioners, since not being taken seriously was linked to carer strain. This also means that requests for help should if at all possible be acted on.

Finally, delivering the services that the fostered young people need is likely to improve outcomes and reduce strain, an issue that will be taken up later.

Partnership with foster carers

Given the current emphasis on partnership with service users it was disappointing to find that partnership with foster carers was often honoured in the breach. More than half the carers did not reliably feel that they were an important member of the professional team and just under half did not usually find that their views were taken seriously. Some foster carers spoke bitterly about practitioners who, on a brief contact with a young person, thought that they knew best and overruled decisions that carers and other professionals had made. As we have seen, there was a significant relationship between foster carers feeling that their views were not taken seriously and being under strain. Whilst foster carers were enthusiastic in their praise for social workers who involved them and valued their views, these findings again suggest that more training and support is needed for practitioners who have responsibility for looked-after children. The task of the children's social worker is a far from easy one, but this material suggests that more could be done to build and maintain good relationships with foster carers, without which the child's best interests are unlikely to be served.

Therapeutic help for the young people

Appropriate therapeutic counselling or mental health support was linked to more successful placement outcomes. This finding surprised us. Because young people with the most severe problems generally get such help, it is rare for there to be a link between such help and better outcomes. Assessment of the need for mental health services or counselling is needed before each placement or soon after. When foster carers asked for such help it was important that their requests were taken very seriously. Such requests showed that the carers felt unable to manage without outside assistance. Poor outcomes were associated with situations in which foster carers were left trying to find such help without success. Unfortunately in the study, when foster carers found that they could not cope, it was rare for their requests for assistance to be adequately met. Usually, carers received no help, a service that was inadequately tailored to the needs of the young people or one that arrived too late. Yet adequate mental health help for young people proved to be a vital aspect of support for foster placements.

Essential services for foster care placements

From our analyses we concluded that foster carers experience formal support systems very much like nets – they are only as strong as the weakest link. We found that all four of the key formal support services that we examined in detail needed to be in place if foster carers were to report that they had adequate support. When there was a weakness in any one service, foster carers reported that they felt generally unsupported. These formal direct services (direct in the sense of delivered directly to the carers) are those of the family placement worker, the child's social worker, foster carer groups and the out of hours service. Satisfaction with the out of hours arrangements was greatest when carers had access to a specialist out of hours service, usually run by the family placement service. In addition, as we have seen, a key indirect service (that is a service to the young person that functioned to support the carers) was therapeutic help for adolescents. Moves to strengthen one part of the service (for example the out of hours service) at the expense of another (for example family placement workers) are likely to lead to considerable dissatisfaction. Indeed, in one of our authorities during the study, enhanced levels of pay were introduced, linked to the loss of family placement workers, to the consternation of the foster carers.

There may well be other services that have the potential to play a vital part in support services, such as confidential staff counselling services (used by half of the few carers with access to this service), 24-hour telephone help lines staffed by experienced carers (introduced by one authority at the end of the study period) and respite care for young people. However, these could not be explored further, as they were so scarce in the authorities in which we worked.

The relationship between services and need

We examined how far professional support was tailored to meet the needs of different foster carers. As might be expected, the young people's social workers made more frequent visits to the children who had the more severe behaviour problems. However, in contrast, social workers visited to see the carers and the young people least often when the carers were most under strain. This could mean that attentive social work reduces strain or that strain increases when there is too little visiting or both. However, it did mean that where there were more difficulties in the placement for the carers the young people's social workers actually visited less.

In addition, the young people's social workers and the family placement workers saw the foster carers with good social and local professional support more frequently than they saw those with more fragile support systems. It may be that the carers with good social and professional support knew how to get a better service from local authority professionals or that fewer social work visits led to fewer referrals to other professionals. However, it also emerged that the more experienced carers had the better social and community professional support. This could be either because they were more skilled at eliciting such support or because they had had longer to establish good support systems in the context of their work as foster carers. Single carers also received lower levels of support from the local authority than couple carers even though they also had weaker social support systems, as we discuss later.

These findings suggest that rather than services being tailored to meet the needs of foster carers, those with fairly good support systems get more help than those who may be more vulnerable. It appears that social workers and family placement workers need to find out more about the carers' overall support systems to ensure that services better match individual needs.

The supports that related to placement outcome

The supports that had a direct relationship to placement outcome were those in both the formal and informal systems of the foster carers. This suggests that family placement workers need to discuss how extensive carers' informal support systems are and the extent of their access to local professionals when deciding on an appropriate level of service. Key supports in the informal system came from the carers' own children, both those in the family and adult children living nearby, and also from the carers' partner or parents. Given the strength of the finding about the link between support from the carers' children and reduced disruption levels, it is important that the carers' children are included in placement preparation (including adult children who live nearby) and in support during the placement, so that difficulties may be rapidly picked up and assistance given.

The formal supports that made a difference to outcomes were the young people's social workers, therapeutic help for the adolescents and help from local professionals such as doctors and teachers. Social services departments are already in the position to work towards improving the service offered by children's social workers. If local provision of mental health help is inadequate, departments can also opt to supplement local services, for example, by purchasing the help of local therapists, as independent fostering agencies have done for some time.

Organisational structures

It will come as no surprise that foster carers who worked for specialist schemes were more satisfied with their income from fostering and with the placement itself than mainstream carers and more often felt well supported. It was important though to find that fewer specialist carers felt under strain during the placement, since the absence of strain is linked to better outcomes. As would be expected, they had access to better support services, such as personal counselling schemes and specialist out of hours services and were also more able to find professional advice to help them when they needed it.

The findings about the benefits of specialist foster care schemes and specialist out of hours services suggest that organisational structures that are well-resourced and staffed and where the focus is on the needs of foster carers and young people are related to improved satisfaction and reduced levels of strain for carers. Key weaknesses in the formal support services to foster carers and young people were the variability in both the service provided by the young people's social workers and in the access to counselling for the adolescents. Some consideration is needed about how these services can be improved since they are organisationally separate from specialist schemes and the benefits of such schemes do not accrue to them. A strong focus on planned direct assistance to children (including therapeutic work and suitable educational provision) and to foster carers appears to characterise the service provided by some independent fostering agencies. If local authorities provided these focused services themselves, as some are beginning to do, it might be cost-effective since the alternative may be a much more expensive type of placement.

Warning signs during the placement

Our findings suggest a number of specific issues that predicted poor outcomes. Catching these at an early stage might avert placement breakdown. They should be checked during visits and particularly at reviews. We were struck by how knowledgeable and perceptive foster carers were about issues such as contact and the impact of the young person on the other children in the family, yet this information was often not known to practitioners. Social workers need to spend time asking foster carers specifically about these issues as the placement progresses. Mention has already been made of the importance of watching out for signs that carers are under strain or do not like the fostered young person.

Young people with a negative impact on other children in the foster family

As we have seen, young people who by follow-up had emerged as having a negative impact on the other children in the placement had poorer outcomes on both of our outcome measures. They also received poorer parenting while the placement lasted. However, these problems had not been evident at the start of the placement. Ultimately, foster carers will move to end a placement that threatens the well-being of other children in the family. This issue should therefore figure high on the agenda of social workers during visits and at reviews, so that action can be taken to try to improve relationships and lessen the impact of the young person on others. Adolescents who put themselves sexually at risk were one group who had an adverse impact on other children, so intervention in these cases is important.

Involvement with a negative peer group

Involvement with a negative peer group was linked to poorer outcomes as placements progressed. This is a difficult area for intervention although it does connect with truanting and non-attendance at school that may be more amenable to help. It is also linked with the issue of supervision outside the placement, that we raise later.

Young people who excluded themselves from relationships in the foster family

As we have seen, young people who avoided relationships with other children and activities in the foster family were those whose needs were often over-looked even though their placements tended to continue. Signs of this behaviour should alert social workers that this may be the case and they need to take special care to talk to these vulnerable young people alone and find out how happy they are in the placement.

Similarly, young people who have difficulty in making and keeping friends with their own age group may need above all to consolidate their relationships with their carers. The carers may also need help in assisting the young people to get involved in activities and in giving them gentle encouragement to develop and sustain peer relationships.

Contact

Contact difficulties predicted poor outcomes and required much more scrutiny and intervention during the placement than they receive at present, as we discuss later.

Education

The findings of the study show that attention to the young people's education varied greatly in terms of the involvement of the local education authority, the foster carers and the young people's social workers. There is a risk that the education of looked-after adolescents will take low priority, particularly as they approach school-leaving age. Yet low confidence in their schoolwork or in social relationships at school were related to poor placement outcomes for young people. In addition, worsening school attendance was related to involvement in a negative peer group, which was itself linked to poor outcomes.

We were impressed by the enormous efforts made by some practitioners to arrange suitable education or other activities to enable young people to have some relevant work experience and occupation. We were, however, disappointed by the lack of priority given by many education departments to these vulnerable young people. The situation was further compounded at times by a lack of clarity about whether arranging a suitable educational placement for a looked-after young person was the responsibility of the birth parent, the young person's social worker or the foster carer, and by the difficulty experienced in achieving the leverage necessary to make changes.

Clearly, foster carers need to be fully informed before placement about the educational background and plans for the young person and supported in helping the young people reach their potential and increase their confidence in their ability to cope at school. Many of the carers had excellent links with the local schools and some made imaginative moves to help the young people into the workforce. However, the carers who are less involved may need training and support to help them to become more actively involved in the young people's education. Local authority expectations of foster carers in this area may also need to be more explicit.

Contact

Nine of the adolescents had no contact at all with family members. Much more could have been done to meet the requirement in the Children Act to give consideration to the provision of independent visitors for such children. However, we found that having no contact at all with family members was not related to outcome.

As early as the first interviews it was clear that, for those who saw family members, some aspect of contact was problematic for the great majority (see also Sinclair et al. 2000). The foster carers considered that half of the young people had difficulties in their contact with family members. The main problems were that relatives were often unreliable about visiting; that over-frequent contact with parents left some young people preoccupied with trying to get their needs met at the cost of not investing in the foster family; and that some young people were exposed to considerable risk or to abuse during contact. Most of the young people were in the care system because of rejecting, neglectful or ambivalent parents and parent figures with whom they had very troubled relationships. Contact provided frequent opportunities for these difficulties to be re-enacted, but there was rarely a sign of improvement in these relationships, which was not surprising as no interventions had been provided that were aimed at changing them. As a result, the young people often returned from contact extremely upset and hurt and acted out their distress in regressive or disturbed behaviour and sometimes in violent outbursts.

Two-fifths of the carers said that the young person's contact was having a negative effect on them, principally because of their concerns for the young people's welfare. In addition, the carers' influence was sometimes actively undermined by parents who were not working with but against the placement.

By follow-up, the researchers rated two-thirds of the young people as having beneficial contact with someone but a worrying one-third had no beneficial contact with anyone. When young people had such beneficial contact there was a significant link with improvements in their well-being. On the other hand, almost two-thirds of the young people were rated as having some contact that had a detrimental effect on them. This occurred significantly more often for adolescents admitted to care from a step-family and for those who had many adversities in their backgrounds. These young people with detrimental contact were significantly less likely than others to have a placement that was assessed as being beneficial for them overall.

We rated almost a quarter of the young people as being considerably affected by lack of contact with someone whom they valued. This occurred especially often for young people with backgrounds of sexual abuse, probably because the allegation had led to exclusion from the family. Perhaps not surprisingly, these young people also had particular difficulties in talking about the past with their carers.

We found that the young people who had contact with their maternal grandparents had more successful placements. This was partly because the adolescents with this contact were younger and had less troubled backgrounds. It was probably also because the grandparents made sure that other family members maintained contact and because they themselves provided sustaining relationships with the young people.

For most adolescents there was remarkably little change in the quality of their contact with family members over the course of the placement. For the majority (57%) poor quality contact was still poor one year after placement. In a few cases proactive social workers had taken commendable action to improve contact, usually by arranging for less frequent contact but of a higher quality or by involving another family member in contact, like a grandparent or aunt, who could provide attention and nurture. We are aware that a missing voice in our analysis of contact is that of parents and other close family members. Had we interviewed them, this would have given us more understanding of the difficulties in their lives that related to these troubled contacts.

As we have seen, difficulties with contact were significantly related to higher disruption rates. This is an area where changes in practice are urgently needed. The purposes of contact need to be considered more carefully so that the way in which it is managed matches those aims. More work with parents might be useful to help them to negotiate meaningful contact with their children. There is also a real need for work with young people to help them to integrate the reality of their parents' actions in ways which allow them to move on and make use of other more sustaining relationships. In addition, more attention needs to be given to contact with family members, such as grandparents, who might be able to offer stability and caring to these young people (see also Cleaver 2000; Marsh and Peel 1999). Finally, contact arrangements need to be subject to vigorous review so that harmful or unhelpful arrangements are altered and boundaries placed around contact that is detrimental to the safety or well-being of young people.

Leaving care

Fourteen of the young people had officially left school by follow-up but reaching the age of sixteen at the time of the research was often also considered by the local authorities as the age at which looked-after children should leave care. Their lack of education and preparation for employment, coupled for many with few independence skills, did not bode well for their futures.

Leaving their placements was particularly problematic for one small group of adolescents whose parents could neither manage the adolescent at home nor allow them to settle elsewhere. In turn, the young people often needed to return home to test out the reality of living with a parent against the idealised fantasy. These often precipitate returns home were correctly seen by social workers as highly likely to fail. There was a real need for these adolescents' placements to be kept open for them for a period of time so that, should the return prove unsuccessful, they had the chance of returning to their former carers more able to take up the opportunities on offer in the placement (see also Triseliotis *et al.* 1995). However, if the placement was not kept open, then a return home which rapidly broke down could lead to a downward spiral of unsuccessful placements and, in one case in the study, to a young man being homeless and living on the streets.

Fostering teenage girls

More thought needs to be given to gender differences in fostering, since it emerged that carers were significantly less sensitive to the needs and anxieties of girls than boys and because, in a small number of cases, the real unhappiness of girls in their placements had not been apparent to their foster carers or social workers. Moreover, foster carers reported uncertainty about how to look after and help young people (predominantly girls) who were suicidal or self-harmed during placement. It was also apparent that carers were at a loss as to how to manage young people (again predominantly girls) who put themselves at risk as a result of their sexual behaviour, for example through indiscriminate sexual contact, forming relationships with men who were much older or likely to exploit them or involvement in prostitution (see also Farmer and Pollock 1998). At present, foster carers tend to withdraw from such young people, pay less attention to their needs, involve them less in activities and exercise decreasing levels of supervision over them. As a result, their placements are at increased risk of disruption. This was in contrast to the management of young people (usually boys) who showed sexually abusing behaviour, where carers became more engaged and showed increased sensitivity to their needs.

Other research has shown that staff in residential care and in secure units have a more negative attitude to working with girls than boys and that male staff tend to withdraw and become more punitive because of their fears that an allegation of sexual abuse might be made against them (Farmer and Pollock 1998; O'Neill 2001). This study showed that girls who place themselves at risk sexually often have backgrounds of sexual abuse. It may be, therefore, that these young people need more counselling about the abuse in their backgrounds so that they do not need to act out their distress in these ways. More research is needed on developments in practice that can provide ideas about how to work effectively with adolescent girls, particularly those who show inappropriate sexual behaviour. This is especially important as young people who put themselves at risk sexually had significantly increased risks of placement disruption.

Training

Placement outcomes are likely to be improved if training includes the parenting skills found in this study to predict better placement outcomes. This means emphasis on helping foster carers to respond to young people's emotional and developmental age; assisting carers in dealing with birth parents and with contact issues; encouraging carers to talk to young people about the past and about difficulties in their relationships with their families (including in relation to contact) and monitoring adolescents' activities outside the home. The latter issue is not an easy one but carers are likely to benefit from the ideas of more experienced carers who have had some success in this area and from discussion and sharing of ideas on how this can be done. Helping young people deal with transitions also emerged as an important area of training. Training for foster carers and social workers needs to emphasise the importance to young people of having someone in whom they can confide: a role that foster carers, social workers or others can take.

In addition, since better outcomes were associated with young people who had particular skills and interests, training should encourage carers to see this as an important area for development. Training could also alert foster carers to the need to be sensitive to the needs and anxieties of girls and to look out for depression and unhappiness in girls, since these sometimes went unrecognised.

Among the training gaps identified by the carers was: working with withdrawn, depressed and suicidal young people; the management of deliberate self-harm; dealing with young people who sexually abuse others and managing violent behaviour.

Clarification of expectations of foster carers

There were gaps in the practice of these experienced foster carers that were likely to have an impact on the young people's future life chances. Training and greater clarification of who is responsible for these tasks is important.

As we have seen, two-fifths of the carers did not discuss sexual health or sexuality with the young people, even though many looked-after young people are poorly informed about normal sexual development, sexual health and contraception. This is an area in which local authorities need clear policies encouraging foster carers to discuss these issues with young people or, where this does not seem suitable, nominating a specific professional to take on this responsibility.

In addition, two-fifths of the carers showed little encouragement for the young people to develop age-appropriate life skills that would prepare them for leaving care and later life, such as budgeting, helping with cooking meals and completing forms. Since this may not have been an expectation in the past, this needs to be built into preparation and training for foster carers.

We were surprised that half of the foster carers had little involvement with schools, including 20 who reported having no contact with the young people's school teachers. As mentioned in the section on Education, there is clearly a need for greater clarity about the importance of this area for young people.

There is also scope for carers to be more active in encouraging young people to get involved in activities and sports and in giving active assistance, when it is needed, to assist young people in making and keeping friends.

The particular difficulties of single carers

We found that single carers were more disadvantaged than couple carers in a variety of ways. The single carers in this sample had had less experience of fostering than the couple carers, although this difference was not significant. This might in part explain some of our findings. Other findings about the single carers appeared to be linked to their particular circumstances, in particular family formation, higher levels of paid work and their greater difficulty in accessing services when child care was not provided.

The single carers in this sample had received less training than the couples who fostered and they also received lower levels of local authority services overall. In addition, significantly fewer of the single carers attended the foster carer groups. This was for a variety of reasons, principally the lack of child minding, pressure on their time if they worked, and a feeling that the groups were not serving their needs.

The single carers also received less support than couples from local professionals, and they had weaker social support networks. Single carers also got less useful support from family members. When single carers *were* receiving useful support from other family members they were significantly more likely to have successful placements than when this was not the case. This connection did not appear for couple carers. This would suggest that lack of family support for single carers might indicate a need for higher levels of support from social services. On the plus side, more single than couple carers received useful support from their friends. We also found that single carers significantly less often than couples took active steps to facilitate the young people's education. This might have been because of their higher levels of workforce participation and pressure on their time.

These findings that single carers are at increased risk of lacking social, local authority and other professional support and that they make less use of training and foster carer groups deserve further exploration. Increased attention to the needs of single carers and greater provision of child care might well benefit lone foster carers and help local authorities to retain their services.

Conclusion

Foster carers do not ask for a great deal. They want information about the young people who are coming to live in their families, that their requests for help receive a positive and timely response, good out of hours services and counselling for the most troubled adolescents. In addition, they want to be accorded respect by other professionals and consulted about key decisions. The standard of care provided by foster carers of adolescents is generally very high and this research suggests areas of training and key areas where clarification of expectations of foster carers would bring the standard even higher.

Whilst the services of family placement workers were highly rated, those of the young people's social workers act as the weak link in the chain of local authority support. This is very unlikely to change unless children's social workers are allowed to specialise in working with looked-after children and relieved of the conflicting demands of child protection work, as is the case in independent fostering agencies. Social workers need to have access to the services that placed young people require, to realise the crucial importance of their work to foster placement success and to treat foster carers as partners.

Specific qualifying training for children's social workers needs to be developed that builds on the findings of research. Such training would emphasise the importance of preparation for placement and responsiveness to requests for help. It would also highlight the issues that need to be vigorously reviewed if placement stability is to increase, in particular the strain levels of foster carers, the impact of the placed young person on the other children in the family and the effects of contact with family members. More generally, practitioners need to find out more about foster carers' overall support systems to ensure that services better match individual needs. At the same time some young people, for example those who have conduct disorders or are hyperactive require intensive packages of support, if their placements are to survive.

These are real challenges for local authorities but there is evidence to suggest that a well-resourced and staffed service could reduce placement disruption.

Foster carers for adolescents are a key community resource for looked-after children and most are very skilled at what they do. Many provide a good service despite poor support but our evidence shows that improved support is related to less strain and to better parenting skills and so to better placement outcomes. Thus, the introduction of improved services for foster carers and young people is likely to lead to greater placement stability. Providers of foster care can make the choice to improve the support offered to foster care and this, together with the skill and commitment of adolescent foster carers, is likely to lead to better placement outcomes and to be of lasting benefit to looked-after young people.

References

Abidin, R. (1992) 'The determinants of parenting behaviour.' *Journal of Clinical Child Psychology 21*, 4, 407–412.

Aldgate, J. (1977) 'The identification of factors influencing children's length of stay in care.' PhD thesis, University of Edinburgh.

Aldgate, J. (1993) 'Respite care for children – an old remedy in a new package.' In P. Marsh and J. Triseliotis (eds) *Prevention and Reunification in Child Care.* London: British Agencies for Adoption and Fostering/Batsford.

Aldgate, J. and Hawley, D. (1986a) *Foster Home Breakdown.* London: British Agencies for Adoption and Fostering.

Aldgate, J. and Hawley, D. (1986b) 'Helping foster families through disruption.' *Adoption and Fostering 10*, 2, 44–49.

Aldgate, J., Maluccio, A. and Reeves, C. (1989) 'Adolescents in foster families – an overview.' In J. Aldgate, A. Maluccio and C. Reeves (eds) *Adolescents in Foster Families.* London: Batsford.

Almeida, M.C., Hawkins, R.P., Meadowcroft, P. and Luster, W.C. (1989) 'Evaluation of foster-family based treatment in comparison with other programs: A preliminary analysis.' In J. Hudson and B. Galaway (eds) *The State as Parent.* Dordrecht: Kluwer.

Ames, J. (1993) *'We Have Learned a Lot from Them': Foster Care for Young People with Disabilities.* Barkingside: Barnardo's/National Children's Bureau.

Asher, S.R., Hymel, S. and Renshaw, P.D. (1984) 'Loneliness in children.' *Child Development 55*, 1456–1464.

Association of Directors of Social Services (1997) *The Foster Care Market: A National Perspective.* Ipswich: Suffolk Social Services.

Barn, R. (1993) *Black Children in the Public Care System.* London: Batsford.

Baumrind, D. (1971) 'Current patterns of parental authority.' *Developmental Psychology Monographs 4*, (1, Part 2), 1–103.

Baxter, S. (1989) *Fostering Breakdown: An Internal Study.* Belfast: Department of Health and Social Security.

Beautrais, A.L. (2000) 'Risk factors for suicide and attempted suicide among young people.' *Australian and New Zealand Journal of Psychiatry 34*, 3, 420–436.

Bebbington, A. and Miles, J. (1989) 'The background of children who enter local authority care.' *British Journal of Social Work 19*, 5, 349–368.

Bebbington, A. and Miles, J. (1990) 'The supply of foster families for children in care.' *British Journal of Social Work 20*, 4, 283–307.

Belsky, J. (1984) 'The determinants of parenting: a process model.' *Child Development 55*, 83–96.

Berridge, D. (1994) 'Foster and residential care reassessed: a research perspective.' *Children and Society 8*, 2, 132–150.

Berridge, D. (1997) *Foster Care: A Research Review.* London: The Stationery Office.

Berridge, D. and Cleaver, H. (1987) *Foster Home Breakdown.* Oxford: Basil Blackwell.

Biehal, N., Clayden, J., Stein, M. and Wade, J. (1992) *Prepared for Living? A Survey of Young People Leaving the Care of Three Local Authorities.* London: National Children's Bureau.

Biehal, N., Clayden, J., Stein, M. and Wade, J. (1995) *Moving On. Young People and Leaving Care Schemes.* London: HMSO.

Blyth, E. and Milner, J. (1993) 'Exclusion from school: a first step in exclusion from society?' *Children and Society 7*, 3, 255–268.

Bogart, N. (1988) *A Comparative Study of Behavioral Adjustment between Therapeutic and Regular Foster Care in the Treatment of Child Abuse and Neglect.* Doctoral dissertation, Memphis State University.

Bradley, M. and Aldgate, J. (1999) 'Short-term family based care for children in need.' In M. Hill (ed) *Signposts in Fostering: Policy, Practice and Research Issues.* London: British Agencies for Adoption and Fostering.

Brown, G. (1983) 'Account, meaning and causality.' In G. Gilbert and P. Abell (eds) *Accounts and Action.* Aldershot: Gower.

Bullock, R., Little, M. and Millham, S. (1998) *Secure Treatment Outcomes: The Care Careers of Very Difficult Adolescents.* Aldershot: Ashgate.

Butler, S. and Charles, M. (1999) 'The past, the present, but never the future: Thematic representations of fostering disruption.' *Child and Family Social Work 4*, 1, 9–20.

Butler, I. and Payne, H. (1999) 'The health of children looked after by the local authority.' In M. Hill (ed) *Signposts in Fostering. Policy, Practice and Research Issues.* London: British Agencies for Adoption and Fostering.

Caesar, G., Parchment, M. and Berridge, D. (1994) *Black Perspectives on Services for Children in Need.* Barkingside: Barnardo's/National Children's Bureau.

Campbell, C. and Whitelaw-Downs, S. (1987) 'The impact of economic incentives on foster parents.' *Social Service Review 61*, 5, 599–609.

Cautley, P.W. (1980) *New Foster Parents: The First Experience.* New York: Human Services Press.

Chamberlain, P. (1990) 'Comparative evaluation of a specialized foster care for seriously delinquent youths: A first step.' *Community Alternatives 2*, 2, 21–36.

Chamberlain, P. (2000) 'What works in treatment foster care?' In M.P. Kenger, G. Alexander and P.A. Curtis (eds) *What Works in Child Welfare?* Washington: Child Welfare League of America Press.

Chamberlain, P., Moreland, S. and Reid, K. (1992) 'Enhanced services and stipends for foster parents: Effects on retention rates and outcomes for children.' *Child Welfare 71*, 5, 387–401.

Chamberlain, P. and Reid, J. B. (1998) 'Comparison of two community alternatives to incarceration for chronic juvenile offenders.' *Journal of Consulting and Clinical Psychology 66*, 624–633.

Cleaver, H. (2000) *Fostering Family Contact.* Norwich: The Stationery Office.

Cliffe, D. with Berridge, D. (1991) *Closing Children's Homes: An End To Residential Childcare?* London: National Children's Bureau.

Coffin, G. (1993) *Changing Child Care: The Children Act 1989 and the Management of Change.* London: National Children's Bureau.

Colten, M.E. and Gore, S. (1984) *Adolescent Stress: Causes and Consequences.* New York: Aldine de Gruyter.

Dance, C. and Rushton, A. (1999) 'Sibling separation and contact in permanent placement.' In A. Mullender (ed) *We Are Family. Sibling Relationships in Placement and Beyond.* London: British Agencies for Adoption and Fostering.

Denby, R., Rindfleisch, N. and Bean, G. (1999) 'Predictors of foster parents' satisfaction and intent to continue to foster.' *Child Abuse and Neglect 23*, 3, 287–303.

Department of Health (1988) *The Boarding-Out of Children (Foster Placement) Regulations 1988.* LAC(89)4. London: Department of Health.

Department of Health (1991a) *The Children Act 1989. Guidance and Regulations, Volume 2: Family Support, Day Care and Educational Provision for Young Children.* London: HMSO.

Department of Health (1991b) *The Children Act Guidance and Regulations, Volume 3: Family Placements.* London: HMSO.

Department of Health (1991c) *Children in Care of Local Authorities, 31 March 1989, England.* London: Department of Health.

Department of Health (1995) *Inspection of Local Authority Fostering 1994–5. National Summary Report, Social Services Inspectorate.* London: HMSO.

Department of Health (1996) *Inspection of Local Authority Fostering 1995–6. National Summary Report, Social Services Inspectorate.* London: HMSO.

Department of Health (1998b) *Quality Protects.* London: Department of Health.

Department of Health (2001) *Children Looked After by Local Authorities, Year Ending 31 March 2000, England.* London: Department of Health.

Department of Health (2003) *Children Looked After by Local Authorities, Year Ending 31 March 2002, England.* London: Department of Health.

Department of Health, Social Services Inspectorate (1994) *Contact Orders Study.* London: Department of Health, Social Services Inspectorate.

Department of Health, Social Services Inspectorate and Office for Standards in Education (1995) *The Education of Children Who Are Looked After by Local Authorities.* London: Department of Health, Social Services Inspectorate and Office for Standards in Education.

Devine, C. and Tate, I. (1991) 'An introductory training course for foster carers.' In D. Batty (ed) *Sexually Abused Children: Making Their Placements Work.* London: British Agencies for Adoption and Fostering.

Downes, C. (1982) 'Assessing adolescents for time-limited foster care.' *Adoption and Fostering 6*, 4, 26–30.

Downes, C. (1988) 'Foster families for adolescents: the healing potential of time-limited placements.' *British Journal of Social Work 18*, 5, 473–487.

Elgar, M. and Head, A. (1997) *From Court Process to Care Plan: An Empirical Study of the Placement of Sexually Abused Children.* The Centre for Socio-legal Studies, Wolfson College, Oxford University.

Farmer, E. and Moyers, S. (forthcoming 2004) *Placements with Relatives and Friends: Placement Patterns and Outcomes.* Report to the Department of Health. School for Policy Studies, University of Bristol.

Farmer, E. and Parker, R. (1991) *Trials and Tribulations: Returning Children from Local Authority Care to their Families.* London: HMSO.

Farmer, E. and Pollock S. (1998) *Sexually Abused and Abusing Children in Substitute Care.* Chichester: Wiley.

Farmer, E. and Pollock, S. (1999a) 'Sexually abused and abusing children: their impact on "foster siblings" and other looked after children.' In A. Mullender (ed) *We Are Family: Sibling Relationships in Placement and Beyond.* London: British Agencies for Adoption and Fostering.

Farmer, E. and Pollock, S. (1999b) 'Mix and match: planning to keep looked after children safe.' Special Issue on Children in the Public Care, *Child Abuse Review 8*, 6, 377–391.

Farrington, D.P. (1996) *Understanding and Preventing Youth Crime.* York: Joseph Rowntree Foundation.

Fenyo, A., Knapp, M. and Baines, B. (1989) *Foster Care Breakdown: A Study of a Special Teenager Fostering Scheme.* Personal Social Services Research Unit, University of Kent.

Fergusson, D.M. and Lynskey, L.T. (1997) 'Physical punishment/maltreatment during childhood and adjustment in young adulthood.' *Child Abuse and Neglect 21*, 7, 617–630.

Fletcher Campbell, F. and Hall, C. (1991) *Changing Schools? Changing People? A Study of the Education of Children in Care.* Windsor: National Foundation for Educational Research/Nelson.

Fratter, J., Rowe, J., Sapsford, D. and Thoburn, J. (1991) *Permanent Family Placement: A Decade of Experience.* London: British Agencies for Adoption and Fostering.

Fry, E. (1992) *After Care: Making the Most of Foster Care.* London: National Foster Care Association.

Garnett, L. (1992) *Leaving Care and After.* London: National Children's Bureau.

Garnett, L. (1994) 'The educational attainments and destination of young people looked after by Humberside.' Report of Directors of Social Services and Education Services, unpublished paper.

George, V. (1970) *Foster Care: Theory and Practice.* London: Routledge and Kegan Paul.

Gibbons, J., Gallagher, B., Bell, C. and Gordon, D. (1995) *Development After Physical Abuse in Early Childhood.* London: HMSO.

Gilligan, R. (2000) 'Promoting resilience in foster care.' In G. Kelly and R. Gilligan (eds) *Issues in Foster Care. Policy, Practice and Research.* London: Jessica Kingsley Publishers.

Goldberg, D. P. and Hillier, V. F. (1979) 'A scaled version of the General Health Questionnaire.' *Psychological Medicine 9*, 139–145.

Goodman, R. (1994) 'A modified version of the Rutter Parent Questionnaire including extra items on children's strengths – A research note.' *Journal of Child Psychology and Psychiatry 35*, 8, 1483–1494.

Goodman, R. (1997) 'The Strength and Difficulties Questionnaire: A research note.' *Journal of Child Psychology and Psychiatry 38*, 581–586.

Greef, R. (ed) (1999) *Fostering Kinship: An International Perspective on Kinship Foster Care.* Aldershot: Ashgate.

Haimes, E. and Timms, N. (1985) *Adoption, Identity and Social Policy: The Search for Distant Relatives.* Aldershot: Gower.

Harrington, V. (2000) 'Underage drinking: Findings from the 1998–99 Youth Lifestyles Survey.' *Research Findings 125.* London: Research, Development and Statistics Directorate.

Harrison, C. (1999) 'Children being looked after and their sibling relationships: the experience of children in the working in partnership with "lost" parents research project.' In A. Mullender (ed) *We Are Family. Sibling Relationships in Placement and Beyond.* London: British Agencies for Adoption and Fostering.

Hazel, N. (1981) *A Bridge to Independence.* Oxford: Basil Blackwell.

Hazel, N. (1990) 'The development of specialist foster care for adolescents: Policy and practice.' In B. Galaway, D. Maglajlic, J. Husdon, P. Harmon and J. McLagan (eds) *International Perspectives on Specialist Foster Care.* St Paul, MN: Human Services Associates.

Hazel, N. and Fenyo, A. (1993) *Free To Be Myself: The Development of Teenage Fostering.* St Paul, MN: Human Services Associates.

Heath, A., Colton, M. and Aldgate, J. (1989) 'The educational progress of children in and out of care.' *British Journal of Social Work 19*, 6, 447–460.

Heath, A., Colton, M. and Aldgate, J. (1994) 'Failure to escape: a longitudinal study of foster children's educational attainment.' *British Journal of Social Work 24*, 3, 241–260.

Hester, M. and Radford, L. (1992) 'Domestic violence and access arrangements for children in Denmark and Britain.' *The Journal of Social Welfare and Family Law 1*, 57–70.

Hester, M., Humphries, J., Pearson, C., Radford, L. and Woodfield, K. (1994) 'Separation, divorce, child contact and domestic violence.' In A. Mullender and R. Morley (eds) *Children Living with Domestic Violence.* London: Whiting and Birch.

Hicks, C. and Nixon, S. (1989) 'Allegations of child abuse: foster carers as victims.' *Foster Care 58*, 14–15.

Hill, M., Lambert, L. and Triseliotis, J. (1989) *Achieving Adoption with Love and Money.* London: National Children's Bureau.

Hill, M., Nutter, R., Giltinan, D., Hudson, J. and Galsway, B. (1993) 'A comparative survey of specialist fostering schemes in the UK and North America.' *Adoption and Fostering 17*, 2, 17–22.

Hodges, J. and Tizard, B. (1989a) 'Social and family relationships of ex-institutional adolescents.' *Journal of Child Psychology and Psychiatry 30*, 77–97.

Hodges, J. and Tizard, B. (1989b) 'IQ and behavioural adjustment of ex-institutional adolescents.' *Journal of Child Psychology and Psychiatry 30*, 53–75.

Holman, R. (1975) 'The place of fostering in social work.' *British Journal of Social Work 5*, 1, 3–29.

House of Commons Health Committee (1998) *Children Looked After by Local Authorities Volume 1.* London: HMSO.

Howe, D. (1996) 'Adopters' relationships with their adopted children from adolescence to early adulthood.' *Adoption and Fostering 20*, 35–43.

Howe, D. (1997) 'Parent reported problems in 211 adopted children: some risk and protective factors.' *Journal of Child Psychology and Psychiatry 38*, 401–411.

Howe, D. and Hinings, D. (1989) *The Post-Adoption Centre, First Three Years: Adopted People.* University of East Anglia.

Howe, D., Brandon, M., Hinings, D. and Schofield, G. (1999) *Attachment Theory, Child Maltreatment and Family Support.* Basingstoke: Macmillan.

Hunt, J., Macleod, A. and Thomas, C. (1999) *The Last Resort: Child Protection, the Courts and the 1989 Children Act.* London: The Stationery Office.

Jackson, S. (1987) *The Education of Children in Care.* Bristol: University of Bristol, School of Applied Social Studies.

John, K. (1997) 'Adaptive social functioning of children and adolescents: a cross-national study.' Unpublished doctoral thesis, Institute of Psychiatry, London.

Jones, E. and Parkinson, P. (1995) 'Child sexual abuse, access and the wishes of children.' *International Journal of Law and the Family 9*, 1, 54–85.

Kelly, G. (2000) 'The survival of long-term foster care.' In G. Kelly and R. Gilligan (eds) *Issues in Foster Care: Policy, Practice and Research.* London: Jessica Kingsley Publishers.

Kent Social Services (1986) *Kent Family Placement Service – 10 Years On: 1975–1985.* Canterbury: Kent County Council.

King, J. (1991) 'The tip of the iceberg.' *Community Care*, 21 November 1991, 20–22.

Kirton, D. (2001) 'Love and money: payment, motivation and the fostering task.' *Child and Family Social Work 6*, 3, 199–208.

Kovacs, M. and Beck, A. T. (1977) 'An empirical clinical approach towards a definition of childhood depression.' In J.G. Schulterbrandt and A. Raskin (eds) *Depression in Children: Diagnosis, Treatment and Conceptual Models.* New York: Raven.

Lerner, R. M. (1985) 'Adolescent maturational changes and psychosocial development: A dynamic interactional perspective.' *Journal of Youth and Adolescence 14*, 4, 355–372.

Lipscombe, J. (2003a) 'Another side of life: foster care for young people on remand.' *Youth Justice 3*, 1, 34–48.

Lipscombe, J. (2003b) 'Children's participation in decision-making in the criminal justice process.' *Representing Children 16*, 2, 122–136.

Lowe, K. (1990) *Teenagers in Foster Care: A Survey by The National Foster Care Association.* London: National Foster Care Association.

Lowe, M. (1989) *The Challenge of Partnership: A National Foster Care Charter.* London: National Foster Care Association.

Lowe, M. (1990) 'Will foster care survive the 1990s?' In National Foster Care Association's *Foster Care for a New Decade*, three papers presented to NFCA's biennial conference. London: National Foster Care Association.

Lowe, M.I. and Verity, P. (1989) 'The right to dignity, fairness and compassion.' *Foster Care 57*, 14–15.

Macaskill, C. (1991) *Adopting or Fostering a Sexually Abused Child.* London: Batsford.

Macaskill, C. (2002) *Safe Contact? Children in Permanent Placement and Contact with their Birth Relatives.* Lyme Regis: Russell House Publishing.

Maccoby, E. and Martin, J. (1983) 'Socialisation in the context of the family: parent-child interaction.' In M. Hetherington (ed) *Handbook of Child Psychology.* Chichester: Wiley.

Maclean K. (1989) 'Towards a fee-paid fostering service.' *Adoption and Fostering 13*, 3, 25–28.

Marsh, P. and Peel, M. (1999) *Leaving Care in Partnership: Family Involvement with Care Leavers.* London: The Stationery Office.

Martin, G. (1993) 'Foster care: the protection and training of carers' children.' *Child Abuse Review 2*, 1, 15–22.

McAuley, C. (1996) *Children in Long-Term Foster Care.* Aldershot: Avebury.

McAuley, C. and Trew, K. (2000) 'Children's adjustment over time in foster care: cross-informant agreement, stability and placement disruption.' *British Journal of Social Work 30*, 91–107.

McFadden, E.J. (1998) 'Kinship care in the United States.' *Adoption and Fostering 22*, 3, 7–15.

Millham, S., Bullock, R., Hosie, K. and Little, M. (1986) *Lost in Care: The Problems of Maintaining Links Between Children in Care and their Families.* Aldershot: Gower.

National Children's Home (1992) *The Report of the Committee of Enquiry into Children and Young People Who Sexually Abuse Other Children.* London: National Children's Home.

National Foster Care Association (1988) *Policy and Practice Guidelines No. 1: Agency Procedures for Handling Complaints Against Foster Carers.* London: National Foster Care Association.

National Foster Care Association (1994) *Foster Care Service: Making it Work: Support to Foster Carers.* London: National Foster Care Association.

National Foster Care Association (1997) *Foster Care in Crisis.* London: National Foster Care Association.

National Foster Care Association (1998) *Focus on Teenage Fostering.* London: National Foster Care Association.

National Foster Care Association (1999) *UK National Standards for Foster Care.* NFCA UK Joint Working Party on Foster Care. London: National Foster Care Association.

Nelson, K.A. (1985) *On the Frontier of Adoption: A Study of Special Needs Adoptive Families.* Washington: Child Welfare League of America.

Nixon, S. and Hicks, C. (1989) 'Unsubstantiated accusations of abuse: A survey of foster carers' experiences', unpublished report.

O'Brien, D. (1990) 'Factors affecting outcomes and admission of children into care.' *Practice 4,* 3, 199–210.

O'Neill, T. (2001) *Children in Secure Accommodation: A Gendered Exploration of Locked Institutional Care for Children in Trouble.* London: Jessica Kingsley Publishers.

Packman, J. and Hall, C. (1998) *From Care to Accommodation. Support, Protection and Control in Child Care Services.* London: The Stationery Office.

Packman, J., Randall, J. and Jacques, N. (1986) *Who Needs Care?* Oxford: Blackwell.

Parker, G., Tupling, H. and Brown, L.B. (1979) 'A parental bonding instrument.' *British Journal of Medical Psychology 52,* 1–10.

Parker, R. (1966) *Decision in Child Care.* London: Allen and Unwin.

Parker, R., Ward, H., Jackson, S., Aldgate, J. and Wedge, P. (1991) *Looking After Children. Assessing Outcomes in Child Care.* London: HMSO.

Part, D. (1993) 'Fostering as seen by the carers' children.' *Adoption and Fostering 17,* 1, 26–31.

Patterson, G.R. (1982) *Coercive Family Process.* Eugene, OR: Castalia Press.

Pithouse, A. and Parry, O. (1999) 'Local authority fostering in Wales: The All Wales Review.' In M. Hill (ed) *Signposts in Fostering: Policy, Practice and Research Issues.* London: British Agencies for Adoption and Fostering.

Prosser, H. (1978) *Perspectives on Foster Care.* London: National Children's Bureau and National Foundation For Educational Research.

Quinton, D., Messer, J. and Ehrich, K. (1996) 'Intergenerational transmission revisited: continuities and discontinuities in parenting difficulties.' Paper presented at the ISSBD Conference, Montreal, unpublished.

Quinton, D., Rushton, A., Dance, C. and Mayes, D. (1997) 'Contact between children placed away from home and their birth parents: research issues and evidence.' *Clinical Child Psychology and Psychiatry 2,* 3, 393–413.

Quinton, D., Rushton, A., Dance, C. and Mayes, D. (1998) *Joining New Families: A Study of Adoption and Fostering in Middle Childhood.* Chichester: Wiley.

Quinton, D. and Rutter, M. (1984) 'Parents with children in care: current circumstances and parenting skills.' *Journal of Child Psychology and Psychiatry 25,* 211–230.

Quinton, D. and Rutter, M. (1988) *Parenting Breakdown: The Making and Breaking of Intergenerational Links.* Aldershot: Avebury.

Ramsay, D. (1996) 'Recruiting and retaining foster carers.' *Adoption and Fostering 20,* 1, 42–46.

Rowe, J., Cain, H., Hundleby, M. and Keane, A. (1984) *Long Term Foster Care.* London: Batsford/British Agencies for Adoption and Fostering.

Rowe, J., Hundleby, M. and Garnett, L. (1989) *Child Care Now. A Survey of Placement Patterns.* London: British Agencies for Adoption and Fostering.

Rushton, A., Treseder, J. and Quinton, D. (1988) *New Parents for Older Children.* London: British Agencies for Adoption and Fostering.

Rushton, A., Treseder, J. and Quinton, D. (1993) 'New parents for older children: support services during eight years of placement.' *Adoption and Fostering 17*, 4, 39–45.

Rushton, A., Treseder, J. and Quinton, D. (1995) 'An eight year prospective study of older boys placed in permanent substitute families.' *Journal of Child Psychology and Psychiatry 36*, 687–695.

Rutter, M., Giller, H. and Hagell, A. (1998) *Anti-Social Behaviour by Young People.* Cambridge: Cambridge University Press.

Rutter, M., Quinton, D. and Liddle, C. (1983) 'Parenting in two generations: looking backwards and looking forwards.' In N. Madge (ed) *Families at Risk.* DHSS/SSRC Studies in Separation and Disadvantage. London: Heinemann Educational.

Rutter, M., Tizard, J. and Whitmore, K. (eds) (1970) *Education, Health and Behaviour.* London: Longman.

Schofield, G., Beek, M. and Sargent, K. with Thoburn, J. (2000) *Growing Up in Foster Care.* London: British Agencies for Adoption and Fostering.

Scottish Office (1988) *Fostering and Adoption Disruption Research Project: The Temporary Placements.* Edinburgh: Scottish Office.

Scottish Office (1991) *Adoption and Fostering: The Outcome of Permanent Family Placements in Two Scottish Local Authorities.* Edinburgh: Scottish Office.

Sellick, C. (1992) *Supporting Short-Term Foster Carers.* Aldershot: Avebury.

Shaw, M. and Hipgrave, T. (1983) *Specialist Fostering.* London: Batsford.

Shaw, M. and Hipgrave, T. (1989a) 'Specialist fostering 1988 – A research study.' *Adoption and Fostering 13*, 3, 17–21.

Shaw, M. and Hipgrave, T. (1989b) 'Young people and their carers in specialist fostering.' *Adoption and Fostering 13*, 4, 11–17.

Sinanoglu, P.A. and Maluccio, A.N. (1981) *Parents of Children in Placement: Perspectives and Programs.* New York: Child Welfare League of America.

Sinclair, I., Baker, C., Wilson, K. and Gibbs, I. (2003) *What Happens to Foster Children?* Report Three of the 'Supporting Foster Placement' Project to the Department of Health, Social Work Research and Development Unit, University of York. Forthcoming (2005) as *Foster Children: Where they Go and How They Get On.* London: Jessica Kingsley Publishers.

Sinclair, I. and Gibbs, I. (1998) *Children's Homes: A Study in Diversity.* Chichester: Wiley.

Sinclair, I., Gibbs, I. and Wilson, K. (2000) *Supporting Foster Placements.* Reports One and Two to the Department of Health, Social Work Research and Development Unit, University of York. Now Sinclair, I., Wilson, K. and Gibbs, I. (2004) *Foster Placements: Why They Succeed and Why They Fail.* London: Jessica Kingsley Publishers, and Sinclair, I, Gibbs, I. and Wilson, K. (2004) *Foster Carers: Why They Stay and Why They Leave.* London: Jessica Kingsley Publishers.

Sinclair, R., Garnett, L. and Berridge, D. (1995) *Social Work and Assessment with Adolescents.* London: National Children's Bureau.

Skuse, D., Bentovim, A., Hodges, J., Stevenson, J., Andreou, C., Lanyado, M., Williams, B., New, M. and McMillan, D. (1996) 'The influence of early experience of sexual abuse on the formation of sexual preferences during adolescence.' Report to the Department of Health. London: Behavioural Sciences Unit, Institute of Child Health.

Smith, G. (1995) 'Do children have the right to leave their pasts behind them? Contact with children who have been abused.' In H. Argent (ed) *See You Soon: Contact with Looked After Children.* London: British Agencies for Adoption and Fostering.

Smith, P.M. (1986) 'Evaluation of Kent placements.' *Adoption and Fostering 10*, 1, 29–33.

Speak, S. (1995) The difficulties of setting up home for young single mothers. Findings Series, *Social Policy Research, 72.* York: Joseph Rowntree Foundation.

Stein, M. and Carey, K. (1986) *Leaving Care.* Oxford: Basil Blackwell.

Strover, A. (1999) 'How foster parents experience social work with particular reference to placement endings.' In M. Hill (ed) *Signposts in Fostering: Policy, Practice and Research Issues.* London: British Agencies for Adoption and Fostering.

Thoburn, J. (1990) *Success and Failure in Permanent Family Placement.* Aldershot: Avebury/Gower.

Thoburn, J., Murdoch, A. and O'Brien, A. (1986) *Permanence in Child Care.* Oxford: Blackwell.

Thomas, N. and Beckett, C. (1994) 'Are children still waiting? New developments and the impact of the Children Act 1989.' *Adoption and Fostering 18,* 1, 8–16.

Thorpe, R. (1974) 'The social and psychological situation of the long-term foster child with regard to his natural parents.' PhD thesis, University of Nottingham.

Tizard, B. (1977) *Adoption: A Second Chance.* London: Open Books.

Tizard, B., Blatchford, P., Burke, J., Farquar, C. and Lewis, I. (1988) *Young Children at School in the Inner City.* Hove: Lawrence Erlbaum Associates.

Tizard, J., Schofield, W. and Hewison, J. (1982) 'Collaboration between teachers and parents in assisting children's reading.' *British Journal of Educational Psychology 52,* 1–15.

Trasler, G. (1960) *In Place of Parents.* London: Routledge and Kegan Paul.

Triseliotis, J. (1989) 'Foster care outcomes: a review of key research findings.' *Adoption and Fostering 13,* 3, 5–17.

Triseliotis, J. (1990) 'Foster care – its strengths and weaknesses.' In National Foster Care Association's *Foster Care for a New Decade,* three papers presented to NFCA's biennial conference. London: National Foster Care Association.

Triseliotis, J., Borland, M., Hill, M. and Lambert, L. (1995) *Teenagers and the Social Work Services.* London: HMSO.

Triseliotis, J., Borland, M. and Hill, M. (1999) 'Foster carers who cease to foster.' In M. Hill (ed) *Signposts in Fostering: Policy, Practice and Research Issues.* London: British Agencies for Adoption and Fostering.

Triseliotis, J., Borland, M. and Hill, M. (2000) *Delivering Foster Care.* London: British Agencies for Adoption and Fostering.

Utting, Sir William (1991) *Children in the Public Care. A Review of Residential Child Care.* Social Services Inspectorate. London: HMSO.

Utting, Sir William (1997) *People Like Us: The Report of the Review of the Safeguards for Children Living Away from Home.* Department of Health and the Welsh Office. London: The Stationery Office.

Verity, P. and Nixon, S. (1995) 'Allegations against foster families.' *Foster Care 13.*

Vernon, J. and Fruin, D. (1986) *In Care: A Study of Social Work Decision Making.* London: National Children's Bureau.

Wade, J., Biehal, N., Clayden, J. and Stein, M. (1998) *Going Missing: Young People Absent from Care.* Chichester: Wiley.

Walker, M., Hill, M. and Triseliotis J. (2002) *Testing the Limits of Foster Care: Fostering as an Alternative to Secure Accommodation.* London: British Association for Adoption and Fostering.

Ward, H. (ed) (1995) *Looking After Children: Research into Practice.* The Second Report to the Department of Health on Assessing Outcomes in Child Care. London: HMSO.

Waterhouse, S. (1992) 'How foster carers view contact.' *Adoption and Fostering 16,* 2, 42–46.

Waterhouse, S. (1997) *The Organisation of Fostering Services: A Study of the Arrangements for Delivery of Fostering Services in England.* London: National Foster Care Association.

Webb, S. and Aldgate, J. (1999) 'Using respite care to prevent long-term family breakdown.' In M. Hill (ed) *Signposts in Fostering: Policy, Practice and Research Issues.* London: British Agencies for Adoption and Fostering.

Wheal, A. (1995) *The Foster Carers' Handbook.* London: National Foster Care Association.

Wilson, H. (1974) 'Parenting in poverty.' *British Journal of Social Work 4,* 3.

Wilson, K., Sinclair, I. and Gibbs, I. (2000) 'The trouble with foster care: the impact of stressful "events" on foster carers." *British Journal of Social Work 30,* 193–209.

Yelloly, M. (1979) *Independent Evaluation of Twenty-five Placements in the Kent Family Project.* Maidstone: Kent County Council.

Youniss, J. and Smollar, J. (1985) *Adolescent Relations with Mother, Fathers and Friends.* Chicago: University of Chicago Press.

Subject Index

Author Index